A Public
Missiology

A Public Missiology

HOW LOCAL CHURCHES
WITNESS TO A COMPLEX WORLD

Gregg Okesson

Baker Academic
a division of Baker Publishing Group
Grand Rapids, Michigan

© 2020 by Gregg Okesson

Published by Baker Academic
a division of Baker Publishing Group
PO Box 6287, Grand Rapids, MI 49516-6287
www.bakeracademic.com

Printed in the United States of America

Library of Congress Cataloging-in-Publication Data
Names: Okesson, Gregg A., author.
Title: A public missiology : how local churches witness to a complex world / Gregg Okesson.
Description: Grand Rapids : Baker Academic, a division of Baker Publishing Group, 2020. | Includes index.
Identifiers: LCCN 2019028747 | ISBN 9780801098079 (paperback)
Subjects: LCSH: Evangelistic work. | Missions. | Church work.
Classification: LCC BV3753 .O34 2020 | DDC 266—dc23
LC record available at https://lccn.loc.gov/2019028747

ISBN 978-1-5409-6270-6 (casebound)

The appendix to this book is used with permission from the Public Missiology Working Group.

20 21 22 23 24 25 26   7 6 5 4 3 2 1

To the villages of Selare and Pahi in north-central Tanzania,
and to my students at Scott Theological College in Machakos, Kenya:

You have led me on a journey deeper into the public nature
of witness, and for that I am deeply grateful.

Contents

Preface

The seeds of this book germinated in 1998 within a couple of remote villages in north-central Tanzania. Until my family moved there, I had never really considered the nature of public witness. Like most Westerners, I thought of witness primarily as a personal enterprise, something one does with individuals. Of course, as a missiologist I had studied contextual theology and knew, at least conceptually, that the gospel moves into public spaces, but nothing in my education prepared me for what I would face. In the villages, I encountered a "thickness" to the public realm that defied any simplistic answers. In a classroom we could discuss the different realms of public life, such as ethnicity, clan, economics, and politics, but in the villages each of these intermingled with the others like the dust devils that skip and dance across the arid Maasai Steppe.

We moved to Tanzania to plant churches, but I quickly realized one could not do evangelism, nor discipleship, nor ecclesiology of any kind, without taking seriously the public realities surrounding the people. And the publics we encountered in the villages were not just a matter of academic deliberation but were something we experienced with our bodies, such as with malnutrition or disease. My family struggled with malaria, worms, tuberculosis, and other sicknesses along with daily challenges of nutrition. Early on I sought simple solutions to what I thought were relatively simple problems, only to realize that one of the reasons the publics were so virulent was due to the ways they interpenetrated one another, or to their thickness. I eventually began asking myself, How does church planting relate to poverty, or evangelism to health, or religion to development? I did not have good answers to those queries, but the questions lingered with me and resulted in this book.

After living in the village two years, my family moved to Kenya, where I taught theology and mission at Scott Theological College in Machakos for a decade. My students deepened this public trajectory through their questions in the classroom, along with sharing with me their lives and ministries outside in public spaces. During that time I also began studying local congregations. In the beginning I did it as part of my PhD studies. But I then realized something equally as dramatic as what I had learned in the villages: the thickness of the public realm was countered by a different kind of thickness found in congregations. At first I only saw the slightest glimmers of thickness within churches, but the more I studied them, I came to realize that all local congregations are filled with movements. I liken the thickness of local congregations to the delicate movements of diverse threads that weave in and out within the liturgy and sacraments of the church, and then outside into public spaces, and back inside again, in a never-ending knitting of dense fabric.

Of course, not all local congregations are thick. And not all churches are thick in the same way. However, instead of spending an entire book bemoaning the introversion or thinness of a local congregation, I have chosen to take a different course: to show how missiology helps us witness through movement, which I have likened to the threads of a dense fabric, and how local congregations do so within and for their surrounding publics.

As I have reflected on those years in Africa, I have come to see that many Western Christians, and especially those from my "tribe" (called evangelicals), love to approach complex, thick problems with simplistic, thin solutions. Some of this arises from our socioreligious background emanating from the Enlightenment, where our knee-jerk reaction is to retreat from the public realm altogether or attempt to solve complex social challenges with simplistic, individual answers (e.g., "if only poor people would work harder"). Hence, we eagerly rally around political leaders who reinforce our ideological positions (and may even attend our churches). Our reticence to talk about public witness also proceeds from our theological heritage of using Christology and soteriology to solve only individual, spiritual issues (such as sin management or where one will spend eternity) but not the redemption of public life. As Christians we do not possess a robust heritage of embracing complexity, or what I am calling "thickness." Our understandings of salvation tend to go no further than the individual. Thus it is not surprising that the thinness of our faith does little to interpenetrate the thickness of the public realm, and that is as true for the context of large cities in North America as it was for my villages in Tanzania.

In this book I seek to accomplish three related goals. First, I want us to see complexity, or thickness, not as the enemy of the church but as our greatest ally. Second, I hope to demonstrate how thickness arises from different movements, and why missiology is so critical in highlighting various movements within the *missio Dei* to redeem the fullness of God's world. Finally, I desire to show how congregations possess their own thickness, arising from different movements of thread, and how they use that weave of movement to witness to the public realm around the church.

Let me acknowledge a group of key dialogue partners who helped shape my early ruminations on this book. They are members of a working group on public missiology within the American Society of Missiology (ASM): George Hunsberger, Gregory Leffel, Charles Fensham, Robert Hunt, Hendrik Pieterse, and Bill Kenney. Hunsberger initially championed these discussions on public missiology with his presidential address at the ASM annual meeting in 2005. The subject was then picked up by Leffel during the 2016 ASM meetings. Since that time, our working group, led by Leffel, has been presenting papers, dialoguing, and attempting to parse what we mean by public missiology. This book is my attempt to do so and should in no manner reflect the consensus opinion of the working group. But I would be remiss to neglect their valuable influence.

Let me also identify some key individuals who have contributed to this book. I want to thank bishops Timothy Ndambuki of the Africa Brotherhood Church and Rice Broocks of the Bethel churches. The latter read chapter 9 and gave me helpful feedback. I am also grateful for the ethnographic papers written by my DMin students, Delvin Pikes, David Houston, and Steve Murrell, for their insights into Bethel World Outreach Church. I am also appreciative of Graham Singh, who read iterations of chapter 8, along with Michael Rynkiewich and Steve Ybarrola, who offered helpful feedback on chapters 2 and 6, respectively. Finally, I am grateful for George Hunsberger who read an early version of this manuscript and provided insightful comments. I accept full responsibility for any gaps or wayward thinking, but each of these individuals made the book better than it would have been without their valuable input.

I am also grateful for the administration at Asbury Theological Seminary for a sabbatical in which to write and for allowing me to travel internationally. This book was written not only in Wilmore, Kentucky, where I currently live, but also in São Paulo, Brazil; Montreal, Canada; Manchester, England; Nairobi, Kenya; Kampala, Uganda; Hyderabad, India; Antalya, Turkey; Panama City, Panama; and Tallinn, Estonia, along with many other locations in the United States. Each of these cities afforded not only a desk and chair in which to write but a context in which to further reflect on public missiology and the local congregation. I trust this book is "thicker" as a result of the locations in which I have enjoyed time learning.

Finally, I am grateful for Jim Kinney's patience with my early thoughts as well as his wisdom in guiding this book to completion. I am equally appreciative to the entire team at Baker Academic, including Brian Bolger and his excellent editorial group for the ways they strengthened the manuscript.

Let me provide one final word about the scope of this study before we begin. Public missiology (much like public theology) reveals many different characteristics. I am offering a public missiology *of the local congregation*. This study does not present all the different types of public missiology but focuses on the movement taking place in and around the church and how these movements provide churches with a form of witness within and for the publics surrounding the local congregation.

Introduction

> The basic unit of [a] new society is the local congregation.
>
> —Lesslie Newbigin, *Truth to Tell*[1]

> I have come to feel that the primary reality of which we have to
> take account in seeking for a Christian impact on public life is the
> Christian congregation. . . . I am suggesting that the only answer,
> the only hermeneutic of the gospel, is a congregation of men and
> women who believe it and live by it.
>
> —Lesslie Newbigin, *The Gospel in a Pluralist Society*[2]

The city of Buffalo, New York, faces a thick array of difficulties. It lies
in a part of the United States called the rust belt. Decades of economic
decline, labor outsourcing, population decline, environmental decay, and deep
racial tensions have left the city with a complex assortment of interrelated
problems. This is particularly the case in east Buffalo, where the majority of
blacks live. Few businesses exist in that part of the city. Schools receive scant
resources to face the demands facing their communities. Meanwhile, political
leaders devote most of their energies to other parts of Buffalo, where wealthy
voters live. Crime is high. Unscrupulous people swoop down on east Buffalo
to sell drugs and set up pawn shops, preying on people's vulnerabilities. The
challenges are compounded by mythic perceptions throughout the city. People

---

1. Lesslie Newbigin, *Truth to Tell: The Gospel as Public Truth* (Grand Rapids: Eerdmans,
1991), 85.
2. Lesslie Newbigin, *The Gospel in a Pluralist Society* (Grand Rapids: Eerdmans, 1989), 227.

avoid going anywhere near east Buffalo, saying, "That's where all the drug dealers live." Hence, the challenges facing the city are not just empirical, such as with the high percentage of people living below the poverty level, but also imaginary, influencing everyday perceptions of people living in the region.

First Baptist Church exists within and for east Buffalo.[3] Most of the parishioners have resided in that part of the city for generations. The church has worship services several times a week. Parishioners carry their public challenges with them, bringing things such as poverty, violence, and political neglect into the liturgy and doxology of the community. Once there, such thorny, public aspects of life are woven into sermons, songs, and prayer. Public realities come into contact with God's kingship and the persons of the Trinity, causing parishioners to think of them in new ways. Congregants scatter throughout the neighborhood as collective agents of the kingdom of God, in and for east Buffalo. One family begins a business in the worst part of town. The church opens up an after-school mentoring program in one of its Sunday school rooms. Several families start a neighborhood watch program to alert people to the presence of crime or drug problems. They walk throughout the neighborhoods developing relationships with young men in the area, providing them positive role models and proclaiming Christ's rule over their difficulties. The church assists several young people in getting their GED. First Baptist also partners with a Hispanic church in the area, and together the two churches develop a program to meet the needs of new refugees who are moving into the neighborhood from Syria, Democratic Republic of the Congo, and Honduras—opening up "space" in the community for diverse ethnicities to live together. Slowly, the character of east Buffalo begins to change, eventually influencing the perceptions of people in the city.

The public realm, as we experience it in the twenty-first century, is complex and thick, formed by the interpenetration of many elements. People everywhere in the world experience the public realm thickly. There are no simple publics. And this, I contend, is one of the major reasons Christians hesitate to witness to the public realm.[4] The size of our gospel limits the scope of our witness. Christians recoil from witnessing to the public realm because we too often possess thin forms of faith. The thinness of our faith struggles to

3. While the complex predicament facing east Buffalo is faithful to the facts, First Baptist Church is a fabricated example of a public missiology of a local congregation. I do borrow some of the inspiration for the example from Jonathan Blackburn's excellent PhD dissertation, "The Role of Black Churches in Response to African-American Well-Being in the Rust Belt Region: A Single Location Case Study of East Side Churches of Buffalo, NY" (Asbury Theological Seminary, 2015).

4. Throughout this book I will speak of witnessing to the public realm and witnessing in and through our publics. This will become clearer after chapter 2.

interpenetrate the thickness of the public realm, and so we don't witness to these valuable aspects of life.

This book is about public witness. It attempts to unpack what Lesslie Newbigin means when he says, "The basic unit of [a] new society is the local congregation," or when he refers to the church as the "hermeneutic of the gospel." This book is a call for Christians to thicken their witness, and to do so in and through local congregations.

Why Witness through Local Congregations?

We don't often think of local congregations as "the basic unit of [a] new society," even as we hesitate to consider the church as the "hermeneutic of the gospel." Meanwhile, the word *public* has become all the rage these days.[5] After years of lurking in some shadowy existence, Christianity in the West has begun to step out boldly into the public realm. At the same time, local congregations have retreated from view. We love all things "public" and almost nothing that smacks of the church. Hence, we run wildly into social entrepreneurship, political advocacy, and marketplace ministries, and away from anything suggestive of the church.[6] It is almost as if our uneasy history with the Enlightenment has preconditioned us to think of the church as a "private" entity, and thus at odds with anything "public."

Does our current infatuation with everything public come at the expense of any inward distinction? Indeed, we risk losing what Martin Marty calls "special interiority" in an effort to be utterly open.[7] This same reaction can be seen elsewhere. We have become anti-buildings as a result of the focus on buildings in a previous era. We have also become anti-institutions because of the oppressive nature of institutions under Christendom. It's almost as if we have become so anti-anything-we-were-in-the-past that I am not sure anymore what we are in favor of. Perhaps I am hyperbolizing for effect—and, indeed, things are not always this extreme—but unless we vilify the church in its gathering, it's as if we cannot talk about public engagement. That is precisely my concern. As we move out into the public realm, we have exchanged ecclesiology for public

5. I will explain the public realm in some depth in chapter 2. At this point, it might be best to think of it as comprising a shared sense of togetherness, drawing on different aspects of what it means to be human.

6. Some try to connect "social entrepreneurship" or "marketplace ministries" with church planting; however, I am concerned that in doing so we inadvertently elevate economics as the greatest good and lose sight of what it means to be the church in and for the world.

7. Marty borrows the phrase from Pope John Paul II. See Martin E. Marty, *The Public Church: Mainline, Evangelical, Catholic* (1981; repr., Eugene, OR: Wipf & Stock, 2012), 4.

change (especially elevating key domains, such as economics or politics), and we have jettisoned any commitment to "witness" or "evangelism" (out of fear for any cultural baggage associated with those terms) for more sanitized terminology of "engagement." Hence, our turn toward public has included a shift away from ecclesiology as well as the accompanying loss of any witness to public realities through the local congregation.

At the heart of this book is an attempt to rethink the apostolic nature of the church, especially in regard to the public realm. I will explain how we need to cultivate back-and-forth movement between gathering and scattering to effectively witness to the surrounding publics. This book is therefore predicated on movement and, with this movement, the desire to nurture a thickness of identity within and for the publics of this world.

Let me say up front that I don't think the church provides us with everything we need to witness to the public realm. We need to be careful not to limit God's mission to what happens in and through local congregations. David Bosch rightly reminds us, "The church should continually be aware of its provisional character."[8] Or, as Johannes Hoekendijk helps us to appreciate, we should take seriously the secular realm as the location of the coming kingdom of God and not view everything exclusively through the church.[9] By talking about churches, I am not saying they are identical with God's mission. God's mission is always much larger than the church.

However, I still believe that local congregations are the primary engine of a new society. And I want us to appreciate the public nature of the church. To integrate these, I need to hold three things together: congregations, publics, and witness. There are scholars who incorporate different configurations of these elements, such as Martin Marty and Emmanuel Katongole, who focus on churches and publics;[10] Jürgen Moltmann, Miroslav Volf, and Vinoth Ramachandra, who speak about publics and witness;[11] and Darrell Guder, who writes about congregations and witness.[12] A few scholars combine all

8. David Bosch, *Transforming Mission: Paradigm Shifts in Theology of Mission* (Maryknoll, NY: Orbis, 1991), 377.

9. Johannes Hoekendijk, *The Church Inside Out* (London: SCM, 1967).

10. Marty, *Public Church*; Emmanuel Katongole, *The Sacrifice of Africa: A Political Theology for Africa* (Grand Rapids: Eerdmans, 2010).

11. Jürgen Moltmann, *God for a Secular Age: The Public Relevance of Theology* (Minneapolis: Fortress, 1999); Miroslav Volf, *A Public Faith: How Followers of Christ Should Serve the Common Good* (Grand Rapids: Brazos, 2011), esp. 106–9 for witness; Vinoth Ramachandra, *Subverting Global Myths: Theology and the Public Issues Shaping Our World* (Downers Grove, IL: IVP Academic, 2008).

12. Darrell L. Guder, *Called to Witness: Doing Missional Theology* (Grand Rapids: Eerdmans, 2015).

three, such as Lesslie Newbigin, Stanley Hauerwas,[13] and George Hunsberger.[14] However, I will go further. Not only will I integrate these three elements, but I will describe what public witness looks like in three actual case studies. This book moves from theoretical foundations (outlining a public missiology of the local congregation) to descriptive analysis (showing what it looks like in living color).

My central thesis is this: congregations participate in different movements, lending them a witness capable of interpenetrating the thickness of the public realm to witness to it from within.

Why Thickness?

One should not be surprised to see a missiologist talking about movement. Sending and receiving remain central to our discipline. However, I will talk about movement in different kinds of ways. Geographical movement is one example of movement. Never before in history have we seen such incredible flows of migration occurring across the globe. But we are seeing other forms of movement in the world as well, and some of the most significant varieties occur within and around the local congregation. To make this point, I need to connect movement with thickness.

The Relationship between Movement and Thickness

Let me use the analogy of weaving. In order to weave, you must possess two critical components. First, you need to have various threads—or string, twine, hair, or anything that is long and supple and can be maneuvered to fit around other entities. Second, you must have movement, whereby the different pieces of thread can be wrapped around the other elements. The more threads being used, along with the greater movement of the pieces back and forth across each other, the thicker the resultant weave.

All congregations possess this back-and-forth movement. It is actually possible to diagram what it looks like. Take, for example, a map of your city and draw lines that connect the location of your church building with parishioners' neighborhoods, workplaces, schools, and places of leisure. I suspect that if you did this for just twenty families in your church, the map would display an ornate crisscrossing fabric of lines extending from your

13. Stanley Hauerwas and William H. Willimon, *Resident Aliens: Life in the Christian Colony* (Nashville: Abingdon, 1989).

14. George Hunsberger, *The Story That Chooses Us: A Tapestry of Missional Vision* (Grand Rapids: Eerdmans, 2015).

congregation throughout the city. However, each of these lines is not a one-way movement outward from the congregation but a two-lane highway with traffic streaming back and forth. The threads thicken through movement. Parishioners enter the church with their publics (carrying with them their notions of public life), where together with other believers they are exposed to Christ in the form of liturgy, sacrament, preaching, and worship. As congregants depart the church, they witness to their neighborhoods, work, and "third places" (locations where people spend time outside of work and home) in and through the liturgy, sacrament, preaching, and worship that have influenced their understanding of public life.

In this book I will draw on a wide range of metaphors for speaking of movement, from ecology to metallurgy, from weaving to communal characteristics. Theologians likewise use different analogies, especially to describe the Trinity. These include dance, drama, and dialogue. I will draw on all these resources to show how movement results in a thickening of our witness in and for the world.

What Kind of Thickness?

Since the relationship between movement and thickness plays such a critical role in my argument, let me propose a few analogies to help us visualize what thickness looks like.

First, consider the seashore. As waves move back and forth—crashing against the beach, then pulling back with a mighty swell, and thundering once again on the coastline—we behold massive power capable of altering an entire landscape. Change happens slowly, over countless years. The natural beauty of the seashore arises through minutiae, as grains of sand get pressed together by the crashing of the waves, or as wind strikes relentlessly against the land, or as rain and sun alternate to bake the exposed earth into majestic outcroppings. Movement creates the majestic grandeur of the seashore.

Second, consider the making of alloys. Metals of various organic compounds are heated together in ovens, melted into liquids, then pressed together with tremendous force into a new solid. The new solid is then cooled rapidly to increase the cohesion of the particles into each other. Such movement (in terms of liquid-solid, or heating-cooling) results in a compound of greater strength than the individual parts.

Let me offer one further example. Years ago I traveled to a remote village church in eastern Kenya to conduct research. I asked the pastor if I could interview a few women after the service. He arranged for eight lay leaders to meet with me under an acacia tree. I asked the group of women one question, and for the next forty-five minutes they spoke, disagreed slightly with each other, revised their statements, asked each other key clarifying questions, and eventually came to a consensus of agreement pertaining to my question. I never spoke again during those forty-five minutes. To this day, it is the best interview I ever conducted, largely because I let them talk and because their comfort with each other helped nuance their answer. The women provided me what Clifford Geertz calls "thick description."[15]

In all these examples, back-and-forth movement results in thickness, whether the density of sand particles pressed into a seashore, the compounds combined to form alloy strength, or the collaborative voices of the women that give nuance to meaning. Back-and-forth movement results in a thickness of identity. And the ensuing thickness serves a purpose or mission. The seashore produces a diverse, integrated ecosystem for billions of creatures. Alloy metals form the frame of an airplane carrying people around the world. And the interview with the women helped nuance a critical cultural concept. In each of these examples, the thickness associated with movement produces a good. I want to explore what good the thickness of local congregations accomplishes within and for the public realm.

Why Is This Important?

Let me suggest two reasons why it is helpful to talk about thickness and congregational witness. The first reason is theological. In God's trinitarian nature we find a thickness of identity. I will explore this further in chapter 3, but for the present let me refer to the Trinity as integrated persons who, through eternal back-and-forth movement of sending and receiving, represent a thick, divine community of love. Who God is directly leads to what God is accomplishing in the world. The second reason is sociological. Publics have a thickness to them. The thickness of the public realm arises from the multiplicity of overlapping and interpenetrating publics. For some the thickness of the public realm is a thing of beauty; for many others it is a labyrinth of despair. Another way of speaking about thickness is to refer to complexity, and for the rest of the book I will be using these terms interchangeably.

Here is my basic point: it is not possible to witness to anything as thick (or complex) as the public realm with a thinness (or simplicity) of identity. We may think of a local congregation as a fairly simple entity, but it is actually

15. Geertz introduces this phrase in his essay "Thick Description: Toward an Interpretive Theology of Culture" and then illustrates it in the essay "Deep Play: Notes on the Balinese Cockfight," in *The Interpretation of Cultures: Selected Essays* (New York: Basic Books, 1973), 3–30, 412–53.

a complex organism. Or as Martyn Percy explains, "As anyone who has ever studied churches or denominations will know, the complexity, density, extensity and intricacy of a congregation contains manifold layers of complexity."[16] There are no simple congregations!

Rather than be discouraged by this fact, I ask us to embrace it. Complexity is not the enemy of Christianity and might just be our greatest ally. As I will share in chapter 3, complexity is a gift arising from the Trinity and flows into our world to create fruitfulness for all of life.

Of course, there are different kinds of complexity in the world. Complexity does not always lead to fruitfulness and in some cases results in great evil. John Wesley speaks of "complicated wickedness" to describe how many people experience the public realm. In her treatment of Wesley's concept, Christine Pohl refers to it as "a complex intertwining of several fundamental problems: the absence of true religion, a deep social alienation, degradation and oppression, and acute physical need."[17] We see this all around us in the world today. The distortion of God's nature leads to atrocious social evils such as slavery, racism, sexism, and tribalism, along with corresponding economic and environmental ills such as poverty, malnutrition, homelessness, deforestation, and global warming. One of the reasons it's complicated is that humans experience these less as singular ills and more as "complex, intertwining" social realities.

In the face of "complicated wickedness," evangelicals have historically sought succor in the arms of romanticized visions of simplicity (whether as a return to a previous era or a retreat altogether from public life). N. K. Clifford explains, "The Evangelical Protestant mind has never relished complexity. Indeed its crusading genius, whether in religion or politics, has always tended toward an over-simplification of issues and the substitution of inspiration and zeal for critical analysis and serious reflection."[18]

But there is another kind of complexity in this world, what Wesley calls a "complication of goodness," and that, I propose, is what we find in the local congregation. As we stand before the dizzying complexity of the public realm with its mixing and intoxicating appeal, can we really expect God to do anything less than give us a different kind of complexity by which to witness to the public realm? We can throw up our hands in discouragement

---

16. Martyn Percy, *Shaping the Church: The Promise of Implicit Theology* (Surrey, UK: Ashgate, 2010), 2.

17. Christine Pohl, "Practicing Hospitality in the Face of 'Complicated Wickedness,'" *Wesleyan Theological Journal* 42, no. 1 (Spring 2007): 11.

18. N. K. Clifford, "His Dominion: A Vision in Crisis," *Studies in Religion* 2, no. 4 (1973): 323. Of course, we need not bifurcate zeal from critical analysis as this quotation suggests, but it does highlight a problem that has long haunted Western evangelicalism.

with local congregations, or we can look beneath the surface to see what God is doing through the various movements taking place within and around the church.

What I Am Not Saying

Let me be clear about what I am not saying. When I talk about thickness (or complexity), I am not attempting to hide behind the obscure in order to say something profound. Nor am I suggesting that complexity or thickness lacks an order—that it's nothing but a free-for-all of movement. I am also not suggesting that only academic elites can witness to the public realm. The complexity I'm discussing in this book is thus not an intellectual complexity, like some giant Rubik's Cube. Instead, it's a complexity of movement, and I learned it from living in a rural Tanzanian village. Furthermore, at times complexity and simplicity might be intimately interrelated. For example, it is possible to experience a simplicity on the other side of complexity. That is perfectly compatible with the primary argument offered in this book.

I am also not saying that everything in God's mission is reducible to local congregations. I merely want to highlight that in local congregations we find all the resources necessary for public witness, which is why I refer to this book as a public missiology of the local congregation.

Finally, I am not putting forward one particular model of public witness. Every congregation exists in dynamic relationship with its surroundings, which is why sociologists speak of the church in ecological terms—much like an organism existing in a particular ecosystem.[19] In the second half of the book I offer three case studies to show diverse ways that actual congregations are doing public witness. These case studies are in no way meant to suggest what other churches should do. I am seeking merely to describe their public witness through movement and thickness. Every congregation is uniquely situated within and for its own context or ecosystem.

Parishioners as Evangelists in and through Their Publics

Throughout this book I will highlight the critical role of parishioners in God's mission. By talking about the local congregation as the agent of a new society,

19. See, e.g., Nancy L. Eiesland and R. Stephen Warner, "Ecology: Seeing the Congregation in Context," in *Studying Congregations: A New Handbook*, ed. Nancy T. Ammerman et al. (Nashville: Abingdon, 1998), 40–77.

I am referring to every person in the church, and especially the scattered church as a collective witness of God's reign within and for society.

Admittedly, clergy have a unique role in public witness. But this book is predicated on how parishioners utilize everyday life and work as the means of doing so. John Stackhouse refers to this as vocation: "Vocation is the divine calling to be a Christian in every mode of life, public as well as private, religious as well as secular, adult as well as juvenile, corporate as well as individual, female as well as male."[20] It is common for us to think of vocation through the lenses of a person's profession—and nothing I say in this book should question that. But vocation is much broader than a person's employment. Vocation happens in and through the ways the collective body of Jesus Christ inhabits public life.

Ultimately, I am making the case that parishioners serve as evangelists within and for the totality of public life. Perhaps another way of saying this is that when we share the gospel of Jesus Christ with another person, we do so through the basic resources of our humanity. We might conceptually witness to Christ in a wooden or transactional way—like giving people a get-out-of-hell-free card— but that is not what salvation really means. We are not saved *from* life but saved *in* and *for* the fullness of life. If this is true, and if the public realm emerges from the resources of the image of God entrusted to humans in creation, then this means that all of the things that emerge from human imaging (such as work, family, technology, power, and media) provide us with the means of extending salvation back into the public realm, for the flourishing of everything.

My Own Social Location

Let me explain my own social location. This is essential, since public theologians and public missiologists alike acknowledge the critical role self-knowledge plays in how people do theological or missiological activity (what social scientists call "reflexivity"). No one hovers over the world as a disembodied spirit. We all occupy real space in the world, which means we inhabit a story and are located in time, place, and a particular community.

Speaking of social location in the singular implies that people interpret life from a sole social location. However, increasingly, people do not possess one discrete social location but overlap *between* stories, spaces, and communities in a world defined by migration and transnationalism. Hence, social location can also mean movement between social locations. For example, I

---

20. John G. Stackhouse Jr., *Making the Best of It: Following Christ in the Real World* (New York: Oxford University Press, 2008), 222.

am a third-generation missionary, raised with a foot in both East Africa and the United States. I was born in Kenya, grew up in upstate New York, studied in Wheaton, Illinois, and Leeds, England, lived extended periods of my adult life in East Africa, and am now back residing in Kentucky. What does this mean for my social location? In a word: confused! Admittedly, I am a white man and have benefited from being a white man in society. But I have also drunk deeply from the incredible streams of African Christianity.[21] And as a family we have experienced eleven international moves between four countries—Tanzania, the United States, Kenya, and England—while living on three continents. This back-and-forth movement has unsettled any feelings I have of operating out of a fixed identity.[22]

Perhaps an analogy would be helpful. I think of myself as belonging to an international airport. Of course, no one really lives in an international airport—and that is precisely the point. At an international airport, one hears different languages spoken by diverse groups of people, but no language, culture, or nation "owns" the place, unless you consider the country where it's located—but then only nominally. People are on the move in an international airport. They experience liminality, moving fluidly between a number of places. And that is how I can best describe myself.

Why is this important? Theologians and missiologists write out of their own social location. Most of my public missiology colleagues do so out of conditions of secularity and the privatization of religion in the West. While I will also reflect on these realities, my concerns are much broader. I draw readily on Western and African literatures in my discussion. And as one might expect from a person who has moved internationally eleven times, I am reflecting on the conditions of movement in the world—not just in terms of migration but in terms of how movement results in a thickening of identity. This book, in part, reflects on my own experience in the world. As I have benefited from movement and its resultant thickening, so I am calling local congregations to witness through the same.

The Structure of the Book

This book is divided into two parts. The first part, "Public Witness" (chaps. 1–5), lays out a theoretical framework for congregational witness, and the

21. Brian Stanley goes so far as to talk about "missionary conversion" to describe how missionaries travel to another country to convert others, only to find themselves converted to the ways people in that location do theology. See "Conversion to Christianity: Colonization of the Mind?," *International Review of Mission* 92, no. 366 (2003): 315–31.

22. I don't mean to suggest I don't have a default identity. But even my default identity (American?) can easily get confused by the different contexts in which I have lived.

second part, "Congregations and Public Witness" (chaps. 6–9) describes in vivid detail what this looks like. After describing how we can study local congregations (chap. 6), I will offer case studies of three specific congregations: the first in Kenya (chap. 7), the second in Montreal (chap. 8), and the third in Nashville (chap. 9). Hence, the book starts broadly, examining a theoretical rationale for a public missiology, and then enters the churches to see what it looks like in living color.

In chapter 1 I am problematizing. I want to show why and how Christians in the West struggle with what to do with complex social problems. The purpose of this chapter is to draw the reader into a complex dilemma. It's not just an intellectual problem, like some grand puzzle, but something we experience with our bodies, within and for local communities around the world.

After problematizing, I will explore the nature of contemporary publics. We have good resources for the study of culture, but almost nothing for explicating the complexity of the public realm. I will differentiate the public realm—in its broad expanse—from smaller publics and show how the former is composed of the latter. The goal of chapter 2 is less an exegesis of publics and more an introduction to the thickness of publics.

In chapter 3 I will narrate the complex story of God's mission in the world and show how various kinds of back-and-forth movements contribute critically to that story. I will tell the story of God's mission through the imagery of movement and thickness. God is taking us on a journey from particularity to universality, but without ever leaving particularity behind.[23] God is thus fashioning a thicker humanity in the world, and he is doing so through different kinds of movement.

In chapter 4 I will lay out my thesis in full detail. I define what I mean by public missiology. I will relate this to public theology, showing similarities between the two disciplines while highlighting key differences. Chapter 5 will then focus on local congregations. I will study the various kinds of movement happening within and around local congregations and show how local congregations enter into the "open weave" of their surrounding publics through resources of liturgy, sacrament, and song. If chapter 4 is more theoretical in nature, chapter 5 shows what this looks like within local congregations.

In the second part of the book, I will transition to a more empirical focus. Rather than talking in the abstract about congregational witness, I describe what it actually looks like in three case studies. Chapter 6 will introduce

---

23. Richard Bauckham, *Bible and Mission: Christian Witness in a Postmodern World* (Grand Rapids: Baker Academic, 2003).

the reader to the study of congregations, which moves us from theology into ethnography. In chapters 7, 8, and 9 we will journey into three specific congregations. The different locations reveal different kinds of movements taking place in and around local congregations. In those chapters, we will be introduced to "thick doxology" and its connections with agricultural development (in Kenya); "thick place" and witness to the city of Montreal; and "thick identity" and witness to race and ethnicity (in Nashville).

Let's begin this journey by discussing why we need a public missiology of local congregations.

Part 1

Public Witness

1

Why Congregational Witness?

> The problem is not simple and the answer is not going to be
> simple either.
>
> —C. S. Lewis, *Mere Christianity*[1]

Why witness to the public realm? And why do so through local congregations? Those are two of the questions I will be asking in this opening chapter. My intention is to draw the reader into a complex dilemma involving the public realm and make the case for why we need to witness to it—within and through local congregations.

As I shared in the introduction, "public" has become all the rage these days. And so it should be. In the public realm, we work, shop, eat, and play. It's where we laugh, cry, and relate. We participate in the public realm with our bodies and experience it with our affections. However, the public realm is not just empirical, something we can point to and say, "That's the public realm!"— such as with a coffee shop down the street—but it operates at another level of existence. Charles Taylor refers to a "social imaginary," which he defines as "the ways in which [ordinary people] imagine their social existence, how they fit together with others, how things go on between them and their fellows, the expectations which are normally met, and the deeper normative notions and

1. C. S. Lewis, *Mere Christianity* (New York: Collier, 1943), 33.

images that underlie these expectation."[2] Hence, although we experience the public realm as a proximate place (such as where people physically gather), it is also notional (how people imagine public life).

Bringing together physical and imaginative dimensions is critical for what I am arguing in this chapter. We have developed good resources for confronting the more empirical aspects of public life, such as development for addressing physical dimensions of poverty or advocacy for confronting political issues. But we do not really know what to do with the imaginative (invisible) dimensions of public life, and we possess almost nothing for making sense of thick publics, especially those formed through interpenetration and overlap.

And yet the public realm exerts great influence on humans. It's the stuff of nation-states, Wall Street, Hollywood, and the United Nations, while no less the site of parks, coffee shops, malls, and restaurants. The public realm spans far and near. And if a proximate public, such as a city park, shapes human existence, then social imaginaries, such as notions of progress or freedom, do so with greater power. We interact with the public realm every time we turn on the television or scroll through the internet. It's the stuff of daily existence and where we are human together with others.

I will explain in chapter 2 what the public realm is and how it operates. But at this point let me underscore its complexity or thickness. We like to think of the public realm in simple ways, such as the coffee shop down the street or prominent domains such as politics. We then correlate particular domains of public life with key locations, such as politics with Washington, DC, economics with Wall Street, and media with Hollywood. At one level, these correlations are accurate. A coffee shop resides in the public realm, and Washington, DC, is certainly associated with politics. However, publics do not stand still.[3] The public realm is composed of many elements that interpenetrate one another in a wild dance. Wall Street is heavily influenced by decisions occurring in Washington, DC, as well as conflicts taking place across the globe in the Arabian Peninsula. Meanwhile, Hollywood has great economic power and shapes people's social imaginaries. Hence, the public realm may seem like a simple thing, but it owes its existence to different kinds of movement. People experience the public realm thickly.

We enjoy some of this thickness, such as visiting downtown London on a warm summer day and hearing the sounds of laughter, walking through shops, and riding the Underground. Other elements of thickness feel different.

2. Charles Taylor, *A Secular Age* (Cambridge, MA: Belknap, 2007), 171.
3. I will use the language of "publics" to refer to the multiplicity of overlapping and interpenetrating publics, and the "public realm" to refer to the collective whole where all of these publics exist.

When sin worms its way into the public realm, it does not sit comfortably in any one domain. For example, a transnational company seeks to increase its profit share by outsourcing manufacturing costs to a business located in East Africa. That business is able to win the contract because the owner is the son of a leading politician, and the business gains its own profits by hiring day laborers at a salary of one dollar a day and by securing rights to access the city's water supply. Day laborers cannot afford to commute and therefore set up a squatter camp next to the factory. They end up cutting down all the trees in the vicinity to cook their meals. Meanwhile, the nearby city experiences a dire water shortage due to decreased supply, raising the cost of living for all its residents. In this example, economics interrelates with politics and affects the environment, which subsequently influences economics across the entire city. The sin of greed brings forth more greed, resulting in increased poverty and environmental decay across the entire region. Hence, if publics arise through movement, sin spreads through movement, resulting in what John Wesley calls "complicated wickedness."

In this chapter I will explain why we need a public missiology. To do so, I will problematize. I want to show why we struggle to engage the public realm theologically and missiologically, especially as sin enters into the thickness of the public realm.

But first, let's begin with a story.

A Story of Publics

Growing up, I never spent time thinking about the public realm. I probably viewed it as a natural (albeit sinful) part of "the world." The public realm certainly was not anything my local congregation saw any value in considering, except to repeatedly warn people of its potential hazards.

And yet I was daily immersed in the public realm. I attended public schools, rode my bike around the neighborhood, shopped in malls, watched television, played sports in local parks, ate in restaurants, voted in elections (when I was old enough), and studied psychology and theology at a Christian liberal arts college. After graduating from college, I devoted more than a decade to working with American youth culture but still did not give much thought to the public realm. I dabbled in the study of culture (such as reading *Rolling Stone* magazine and watching MTV to better understand current trends in youth culture) but devoted most of my time to doing evangelism and discipleship with individuals, without connecting these activities with the public contexts in which the youth lived. I did not consider the public realm or think about how to witness to it with the gospel of Jesus Christ.

I first gave any consideration to the public realm when my family moved to a rural village in Tanzania. This may sound surprising to some. Yet the public realm is as much the stuff of rural African life as it is of urban American culture. In fact, that's where I first became aware of the public realm and especially the density of publics.

Before moving there, I nurtured romantic visions of life in Africa. I envisioned sitting with neighbors around a fire and telling stories as elongated shadows danced across the African landscape; or I saw myself farming a small plot of land into abundance, while acacia and baobab trees rose majestically across the sprawling plains. Looking back, these visions were not just romantic; they were simple. I can't put a finger on the reasons for desiring simplicity. Perhaps I felt disillusioned with Western forms of complexity, or maybe I wanted to return to my family heritage (as a third-generation African missionary). I'm really not sure. I only know that any visions of simplicity were quickly vanquished by real life in the village.

The village of Selare abuts the Maasai Steppe in north-central Tanzania.[4] The people living there are Warangi: Bantu by ethnolinguistic decent and socioreligiously Muslim. Our village had approximately fifteen hundred people. The landscape was arid and hard. People worked tirelessly from sunup to sundown and, because of the scarcity of food, had little nourishment to feed their meager frames. The women started every day by making a fire and sweeping the dirt outside their homes; the men set off to the fields, driving hoes relentlessly into the hard, red earth. Young boys led cows and goats in an endless search for anything green, while girls assisted with household chores, such as collecting water and wood or cooking food.

I knew life would be hard. It was rather the complexity of public life that surprised me. We lived eight hours from the nearest city of Arusha. There was no electricity or phone service anywhere within a three hours' drive. We had no internet or banks and only one small shop in the center of the village, where we purchased basic items such as matches, kerosene, and maize. All the things we normally associate with public life in the West were conspicuously absent. But public life in the little village of Selare was anything but simple.

I also first became aware of what Wesley calls "complicated wickedness" when living in the village—though I have come to see that it was always there

4. Some of this material first appeared in Gregg A. Okesson, "Public Theology for Global Development: A Case Study Dealing with 'Health' in Africa," *The Asbury Journal* 67, no. 1 (2012): 56–76.

in front of me, whether growing up in the American suburbs or pastoring American youth. There was nothing more "wicked" about public life in Africa than what I experienced in the States, only the people were more vulnerable to its effects, and we shared in their vulnerability. As a white male, I had never bumped into complicated wickedness before (and it is usually with our bodies that we experience complex forms of sin). But in the village we toiled alongside our neighbors in the fields; my entire family became sick with malaria, worms, and tuberculosis; and we felt the ravages of malnutrition. Of course, we did not experience any of these to the degree our neighbors did. We had a vehicle and money to seek medical help in the city of Arusha eight hours away, and we could purchase fruit and vegetables to supplement our diet. Nevertheless, we felt complex forms of public life with our bodies.

What we experienced opened my eyes to sin in public places. Our neighbors were trapped in a labyrinth. In the beginning, I searched frantically for simple solutions to alleviate their poverty. I experimented with irrigation and purchased new technologies from the city. I brought back supplies to help improve the water supply to the village, only to find that each of these "solutions" engendered new dilemmas. A new faucet required a change in community behavior and was soon broken. Advanced technology for tilling soil required financial investment and led to increased division between family groups. I felt frustrated. I watched people die daily and grasped for any "solution" I could find, only to discover that my neighbors had tried all of them. And then they told me of a hundred other things they had attempted and why those didn't work. Theirs was not a deficiency of intellect, innovation, or effort. Quite the contrary, their capacities astounded me. It was rather how sin entered into their everyday public life that made their plight so dire.

The rains would come only to end abruptly, and everything would die. On the off chance the rains continued, caterpillars, locusts, and birds infested the crops, devouring everything in sight. And when the villagers managed to harvest crops, so did many others, and the price of maize or sorghum would plunge because of supply and demand. A few well-to-do family groups had the luxury of storing produce until they could sell it at a higher price, but even for them, insects ravaged the crops while in storage. Meanwhile, unscrupulous middlemen descended on the village at various points each year, offering to purchase maize or sorghum at insultingly low prices, taking advantage of the people's desperation.

Most of the homes were constructed of mud, making them susceptible to insects, damp, and disease. The rains would come and bring relief from heat, while bringing waves of sickness to the region. People died of malaria, typhoid, pneumonia, tuberculosis, and most commonly, as I discovered later,

HIV/AIDS. Funerals occurred several times a week. In the beginning, they told me the cause of death was malaria or pneumonia, only to admit later that people died as the result of "the sickness nobody talks about." My "job" in the community was that of ambulance driver. People would come to my house in the middle of the night, usually when a person's fever was highest and all other traditional efforts had failed. We filled the vehicle with family members and raced off over tenuous roads to the nearest government hospital three hours away. Many of the sick survived; some did not. Mothers gave birth in my truck. I also transported corpses so they could be buried in the family homestead, a socioreligious value held by the people living in the village.

Community leaders requested my help with informal training programs to raise awareness of health-related needs. We walked throughout the village discussing things like sanitation and dietary issues with family groups. Each of the solutions engendered socioeconomic implications and necessitated religious and cultural rationale. To boil water to purify drinking water, the people needed to collect firewood from the mountains; not only was this illegal, but it required them to enter into the ambiguous domain of the spirits (and cutting down trees led to deforestation). Or if they bought mosquito nets, they had less money for daily needs, and it required changes to how they lived, since most of the people did not own beds. Hence, "health" was not an autonomous domain but was combined with economic, environmental, and spiritual issues. Agriculture was also economic, as well as intensely political, because of the absence of property boundary markers. Each of these domains did not just sit on top of the others but burrowed into other facets of life. Furthermore, this sleepy little village was surprisingly well connected with national and global stages. People listened to the Swahili BBC and actively aligned themselves with religious groups in Saudi Arabia and Zanzibar. Local and global were locked in a complex dance of movement and melody, of which I could make little sense.

I listened to my neighbors' questions as we drank strong coffee or walked through their fields. Their queries led me deeper into the swirling complexity of public life. Where were the rains? How should they feed their children? Should they spend any money to send their children to school or have them work in the fields? After I earned a certain amount of trust in the community, they confided in me their spiritual fears. How should they ward off evil? What were the causes of sickness? And when my own infant son experienced demonic attacks, everything took on a new level of meaning. Theirs was a cosmology far larger than anything I had experienced in the West.

Here is my main purpose in narrating this story: little in my theological education prepared me for what I experienced in the village. I held degrees in psychology, theology, and intercultural studies and prided myself on living within the confluence of multiple disciplines. However, the complexity of public life in that rural village astounded me. Our intentions were to plant a church, and thus I was constantly thinking about gospel and culture. Even here I encountered difficulties. How does the subject of God relate to development, salvation to agriculture, or ecclesiology to health? And then there were the "invisible" things we bumped up against in our pursuit to alleviate human suffering. My theological training might have provided a few meager insights for encountering evil spirits, but it offered me almost nothing for dealing with sin in systems and structures. White evangelicals living in North America do not consider such things. Systems and structures usually work for us. But in Tanzania I felt them alongside my neighbors. And thus I "saw" public life as if for the very first time.

Of course, I had always lived in the public realm. In one sense, none of this was new to me. My neighbors merely bestowed on me the great honor of seeing life through their eyes. I was shocked by what I experienced. Their lives ultimately led me in the direction of public missiology.

I learned that there are no simple societies. Our theological training in the West often struggles to interpenetrate the thick webs of public life. Once I saw the public realm—or better yet, experienced it through my neighbors and my own body—I was led on a journey that became this book.

We all experience life thickly. In one sense, thickness is a natural part of living together with others in public life. But it's also one of the main reasons we fail to witness to publics. We have been trained (whether explicitly or implicitly) to think of the gospel simply (or thinly) and thus approach the subject of witness by focusing on the lowest common denominator: the conversion of individuals. Let me say up front: we should never neglect the "for me-ness" of the gospel! However, salvation is more than individual conversion. Public missiology requires a robust understanding of salvation (what David Bosch refers to as a "total comprehensive salvation"[5]), along with a complex analysis of public life. Hence, I will argue that public missiology is thick witness within and for a thick society.

Before I unpack what this looks like, let me explain why it is necessary.

Why Public Missiology?

My previous story provides the point of departure for my journey into public missiology. When I moved to Tanzania, I did so as a missionary, a church

5. David Bosch, *Transforming Mission: Paradigm Shifts in Theology of Mission* (Maryknoll, NY: Orbis, 1991), 399–400.

planter, and a theologically trained development practitioner. I had devoted years to sharing the gospel with youth and serving as the deacon of outreach at my local congregation. I knew the gospel (or so I thought), and I certainly knew how to share the gospel with individuals—just not within and for thick publics.

Nothing in my life or theological training prepared me for what I experienced in the village. I reached frantically into my theological tool belt to find anything that would help my neighbors, but to little avail. Their predicament forced me to think anew about my theological heritage. It caused me to read Scripture afresh through a larger understanding of salvation. None of this moved me away from the gospel, or evangelism, but always more deeply into it. And it has not lessened my interest in missiology but expanded it into what some of us are calling "public missiology."

If we believe God created everything "good," and redemption is the reconciliation of all things to the Source of that goodness (Christ himself, as we see in Eph. 1:10), then we cannot restrict salvation to individuals but instead extend it to everything that emerges from human imaging (work, family, and other institutions of human life), along with the realm of creation (Paul explains we are eternally linked to the redemption of creation—e.g., Rom. 8:19–25).

The church is called to "make known" God's wisdom to the rulers and authorities in the heavenly realms (Eph. 3:10), which, as Walter Wink makes clear, must involve both spiritual and material realities, refusing to separate the two.[6] By highlighting the church in Ephesians 3, Paul foregrounds the reality that God redeems the world through communities that embody the kingdom of God in all aspects of their lives. Hence, we need a gospel thick enough to interpenetrate the public realm, where people live, work, eat, and relate. Where life happens!

Unfortunately, I did not possess that when we moved to Tanzania, and maybe you are wondering whether you do as well.

Simple answers did not help my neighbors. And sharing the gospel as a private, individual message of propositional truth did not do anything to address the dire predicament of poverty in which my neighbors lived. Developing a public missiology is also critical for those of us living in the West, where complex forms of racism, poverty, human trafficking, sexism, and the intermingling of economic and political ideologies with religious resources daily vexes public life. We have been trained to witness to individuals but not

---

6. Walter Wink, *Naming the Powers: The Language of Power in the New Testament* (Philadelphia: Fortress, 1986), 5.

to the complex publics that spin, turn, and merge together as if participating in some large ballroom dance.

Let me lay out five problems that have contributed to our current situation.

Problem 1: Theology Divorced from Life

Those of us in the West have been trained to associate theology with the private realm, divorced from all public realities. Theology happens in churches and seminaries (if we assume those to be "private" locations), done by specialists we call pastors and theologians. And the primary goal of theology is to address spiritual aspects of life, while guarding theology from being tarnished by the public realm.

Of course, this is a particular problem for Western societies, where the Enlightenment project gradually expanded the scope of the public realm through scientific inquiry, while marginalizing religion in the process.[7] As public domains enlarged in scope and legitimacy, the private domain shrunk and was questioned. As the secular realm became synonymous with all things public, the sacred diminished in scope and at times retreated into the safety of private ghettos. Christians of various stripes reinforced this divide by interpreting the public realm as synonymous with sin and corruption, and the private realm (erroneously associated with the church) as associated with salvation and purity. This binary cartography continues to haunt us. The task of theology, according to this very limited cosmology, is to protect the purity of the church by guarding the frontiers where the church meets the public realm.[8]

For theological institutions, this means the theology we teach usually revolves around private and spiritual concerns, with limited contact with public domains. We see this in the different categories of systematic theology (God, salvation, church, and eschatology) and the struggles we in the West experience relating them with public life. We need more attention given to movement. How does the doctrine of God provide resources for encountering injustices in the world? How does salvation relate to global poverty? How might our doctrines of ecclesiology address economic or political ideologies?

---

7. I am simplifying things for the sake of argument. For a more complete picture, we would need to talk about scholasticism, the influence of the Reformation(s), and the ensuing ecclesiastical wars, along with other developments associated with the Enlightenment, the rise of Pietism, and many other influences.

8. Let me make clear that boundaries are critical. No church is utterly open to its surroundings. I am not arguing we should do away with boundaries. I am merely suggesting that the Enlightenment cartography of drawing boundaries according to simplistic binaries is a project we need to reconsider.

And what connections can we make between eschatology and God's intentions for all of creation?

This problem bleeds into the churches, where we attempt to keep all the messiness of the public realm on the outside so we can "do church" in a purer manner. Let me say that I believe deeply in purity, but the church is pure not by distancing itself from public life. The church is a different kind of public in the world, and its publicness relates to a different way of being human. But that is not how we normally think about the church. We think of it as a "private" entity, removed from public life. And thus the "theology" we do in local congregations is often intentionally distanced from the everydayness of life that people experience in the public realm.

The great irony is that publics are always entering churches with parishioners (and also with clergy)! Publics walk through the doors in the form of invisible ideologies and social imaginaries, which shape the affections of people sitting in the pews. We allow some of the elements into the church, such as our allegiance to a local sports team (where we celebrate a victory from the pulpit or wear a sweater with the team's logo). Churches actively court other public dimensions, such as endorsing various forms of capitalism as it relates to a forthcoming church building project or helping people get out of debt. But then we attempt to restrict other forms of public life. How do you decide which forms of public life to preach about, sing to, pray for, or liturgize and which to guard against?

The lingering assumption behind our theological heritage is that theology is a sacred discipline having nothing to do with the secular world. We have established it as an academic discipline located within the faculties of cognition but not embodiment, affections, or social realities. And we think of theology as associated with spiritual specialists, the theologians or pastors, but not pertaining to average people sitting in the pews.

And yet parishioners are doing theology all the time, and doing it in public places. We may not readily call their tweets, posts, discussions over a cup of coffee, or stories around the water cooler by the name theology. But parishioners are actively trying to make sense of their worlds and doing so through resources of God, creation, and eschatological visions of where the world is heading. People do so politically by venting frustration at the current legislative crisis, economically as they ponder the latest round of layoffs, and in relation to public issues—such as nationalism, immigration, or the latest movie hitting the theaters. None of this implies their theology is faithful to Scripture. Undoubtedly, they might use their theologizing to endorse secular eschatologies of materialism or as a means of baptizing quasi-religious forms of nationalism. At this point, I am not interpreting the merits of their theology. I am just highlighting the simple fact that parishioners are always doing theology in public spaces.

Here's the problem. On one side of a chasm, we find theology "proper." This is what we teach in our seminaries and churches. The theology done on this side arises from spiritual specialists—pastors, theologians, historians, and biblical scholars—and leans toward private, sacred, cognitive, and theoretical characteristics. On the other side of the chasm is "ordinary" theology. It's done by people sitting in the pews as they make sense of their public lives. And they further do it in public spaces and by drawing on secular, embodied, experiential, and even mystical resources (see fig. 1.1).

Figure 1.1
The Divide

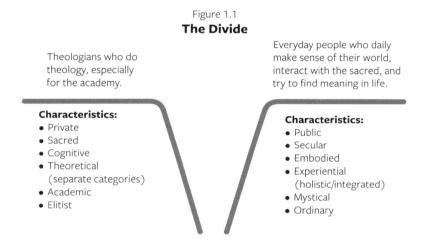

Theologians who do theology, especially for the academy.

Everyday people who daily make sense of their world, interact with the sacred, and try to find meaning in life.

Characteristics:
- Private
- Sacred
- Cognitive
- Theoretical
  (separate categories)
- Academic
- Elitist

Characteristics:
- Public
- Secular
- Embodied
- Experiential
  (holistic/integrated)
- Mystical
- Ordinary

What does this mean for theology? If you restrict theology to the vocation of specialists who do theology in carefully sequestered locations, then you will inevitably end up only talking about what matters to those spaces. This does not mean you won't discuss important things. You may very well engage critical issues, such as God's nature, place, and human identity (all topics I will address later in the case studies), but you will discuss those topics in ways that restrict them to sacred antecedents. Hence, when we teach God's nature (e.g., the Trinity), we will primarily relate the Trinity to what we do inside the church and not what we experience in public life.[9] This is the legacy we have received, and it is hard to unlearn those lessons. And it

9. A couple years ago I taught a Sunday school class in my local church where I dealt with the public significance of the Trinity. It was a fun and helpful exercise for me (and hopefully for the parishioners) to grapple with how the Trinity moves us out into the public realm. For more on this, see Lesslie Newbigin, "The Trinity as Public Truth," in *The Trinity in a*

makes it virtually impossible to engage Hollywood, racism, globalization, or local issues confronting your hometown—or the dire, complex problems facing my village in Tanzania.

Problem 2: Missiology Divorced from Theology

Not only is theology divorced from life, but this problem is exacerbated by the separation of theology from missiology. Theology's flight from missiology occurred slowly over time, as the missionary impulse took place at the frontiers of Christianity (what we might call the margins), while theology gradually became associated with the center of Christendom (the places of power). This separation of the margins from the center deprived theology of the invaluable resources of Christian witness as it has always taken place in public spaces.[10]

To narrate the story of theology's separation from missiology, we need to begin with the early church. David Bosch calls mission "the mother of theology"[11] and explains that throughout the first few centuries "theology was not a luxury of the world-conquering church but was generated by the emergency situation in which the missionizing church found itself."[12] As theology responded to the emergency situation of the missionizing church, it invariably faced public realities, such as persecution, poverty, slavery, and civil forms of religion (e.g., emperor worship). Daniel Treier refers to theology during the premodern period as "an aspect of *paideia* or *humanitas*, the Greco-Roman emphasis upon forming people for public life."[13] Early on, both theology and mission were focused on public life.

Throughout the growth of the early church, theology and mission related to each other in an intimate dance: theology as public wisdom responding to the issues that the "missionizing church" encountered from the margins, such as witness amid persecution. The early church also did not separate what believers did in their gathering from what they did in their scattering. How the church formed itself *from* worship became the church's primary witness

---

Pluralistic Age: Theological Essays on Culture and Religion, ed. Kevin J. Vanhoozer (Grand Rapids: Eerdmans, 1997), 1–8.

10. Andrew Walls calls this the "gospel test," referring to Kenneth Latourette's reflection on "the effect of Jesus on individual lives and civilizations." See *The Cross-Cultural Process in Christian History* (Maryknoll, NY: Orbis, 2002), 18; Walls quotes Latourette, *A History of the Expansion of Christianity*, vol. 7 (New York: Harper and Brothers, 1945), 418.

11. Bosch, *Transforming Mission*, 15–16.

12. Bosch, *Transforming Mission*, 489. Here Bosch is paraphrasing a point made by Martin Kähler; see *Schriften zur Christologie und Mission* (Munich: Kaiser, 1971), 189.

13. Daniel J. Treier, *Virtue and the Voice of God: Toward Theology as Wisdom* (Grand Rapids: Eerdmans, 2006), 5.

amid public life.[14] Or as Morna Hooker explains, "Holiness [was, for the early church,] about transforming *this* world."[15] The house fellowships served as the primary means for the public transformation of society.

Through the years, this changed. I won't take the time to explain how and why it changed. Suffice it to say that the center of theologizing activity became separated from the margins of mission through the alliance of the church's power with the state after Constantine's conversion. With the rise of the Enlightenment project, we see further changes. Not only do we find the dichotomizing of sacred and secular, along with private and public, which I discussed in the previous section, but theology began to mirror the hard sciences in regard to specializations. Up to this point, "there was only one discipline of theology, without sub-divisions."[16] Now we find the development of subfields of biblical, dogmatic, historical, and practical theology—but little integration between these fields, and virtually no room for mission. Eventually mission was added, but it did not fit comfortably into any of the specializations, leading Bosch to say, "Missiology became the theological institution's 'department of foreign affairs,' dealing with the exotic but at the same time the peripheral."[17]

The separation of theology and mission carries three implications for the subject material of this book. First, theology after the Enlightenment concerns itself with what happens in private, spiritual places, far away from the public realm. Meanwhile, mission always happens in public life, leading some scholars to rightfully question whether public missiology is nothing other than a redundancy of terms. As a multidisciplinary field, missiology is focused on movement *into*, conversion *of*, and integration *with* the entire realm of God's redemptive work. Apart from mission, theology in the West has historically struggled to know what to do with the full scope of public life or to witness to it in and through the gospel.[18]

Second, theology in the West is associated more with various centers of Christian thought and less with what is happening on the margins, where

14. For an excellent treatment of the habitus of the early church, see Alan Kreider, *The Patient Ferment of the Early Church: The Improbable Rise of Christianity in the Roman Empire* (Grand Rapids: Baker Academic, 2016).

15. Morna Hooker and Frances Young, *Holiness and Mission: Learning from the Early Church about Mission in the City* (London: SCM, 2010), 25.

16. Bosch, *Transforming Mission*, 489.

17. Bosch, *Transforming Mission*, 492.

18. With the recent rise of public theology, some of that is changing, and not surprisingly, public theology is actively courting the voices of missiologists. Recently, William Storrar and Dirkie Smit have invited our working group of public missiology to discuss shared interests with them at Princeton Theological Seminary. This gives hope that theologians and missiologists might work more closely in the years to come.

the gospel confronts unbelief. Not only does this lead theology to speak to itself in theological echo chambers, but it deprives theology of the benefits of "emergency situations" around the world. The growth of world Christianity as a scholarly field of study has helped us see that without the margins (as they are called), the "center" can easily become dangerous and even toxic in nature, defining theology for all people everywhere according to its own cultural suppositions. We need a healthy relationship between centers and margins—and this is something missiology offers theology.[19]

Finally, the separation of theology and missiology leads to a situation where theology struggles to do anything with publics other than "engage" them. It's true that some public theologians, such as Duncan Forrester and Max Stackhouse, use the language of witness, but it's unclear what they mean by this word. It is further uncertain how this language relates to salvation. Whatever the reasons for the hesitation—and some of it is undoubtedly due to a desire to use accessible language, along with legitimate concerns arising from the colonial heritage of Western missions—missiology offers theology a robust soteriology within and for the public realm.

Problem 3: The Thickness of the Public Realm

I won't spend much time with this problem since it is the subject of the following chapter and I have already hinted at the problem previously in this chapter. But let me explicitly state my concerns here.

We live in the public world but rarely consider it, and when we do, it is usually one dominant aspect of the public realm (say, politics or economics). We avoid considering the overlap and interpenetration occurring within the public realm, since that intimates great complexity. It is easier to think of publics one-dimensionally. We also like to treat them empirically. But the public realm is both empirical *and* notional, with an implicit spirituality behind the public realm that influences people far more than they would like to admit. Furthermore, we rarely connect theology with the public realm, and when we do, it is with singular domains (not with all the messiness that happens in everyday life).

And yet we are immersed in the public realm daily. It is the stuff of human life. In it we experience the building blocks of identity: ethnicity, race, place, family, education, and social status. We carry such things with us wherever we

---

19. The language of margins is critical in light of shifts taking place in today's world, and especially with the secularization of the West. It may soon happen (and some argue it already has) that the West will be become the margin—and it is my hope that public missiology will help prepare us for witnessing to all of life from the margins.

go, intuitively knowing when to allow certain publics inside us (opening our affections to the influence of a corporate brand) and when to restrict others from entering (tightening the boundaries of identity to the sway of a rival political ideology). The public realm is also filled with sports, leisure, food, and entertainment—all aspects that feed our thirst for pleasure and escape. And the public realm is the site of competing, clamoring narratives that claim authority over the whole of our lives.

We can observe these narratives in movies, novels, and other media. Some of these narratives come in bits and pieces: we hear something on the radio we find interesting or observe an event that strikes us at a visceral level. However, the more powerful narratives are those that provide a comprehensive framework, such as the freedom of the individual or the rugged muscularity of male gender. Anything that might bump up against these narratives gets brandished as toxic, whether it is a political issue such as gun control in the United States (as it implies the restriction of individual rights) or, more subtly, a sixteen-year-old male trying to find his identity within a culture that constantly reinforces traits such as toughness, male dominance, and sexual aggressiveness, while scorning anything that smacks of gentleness, kindness, and self-control. Certain narratives possess more power than others and feed the dominant expressions of the public realm in a particular place.

All of what I have just described happens within any given location. Publics will not sit still but overlap and merge into each other. The realm of economics simultaneously bumps up against and conflates with other realms, such as politics. Nationalism feeds off a complex, intertwining story that incorporates race, military power, and sports culture, and does so via narratives told through media, while mixing with religion, to sacralize the whole.

One of the reasons we in the West struggle to deal with social, cultural, and societal sin is that visible aspects of public life (such as poverty) are sourced deeper down by invisible referent points (what biblical authors describe as "powers"). In Tanzania I encountered physical dimensions of poverty the likes of which I had never seen. I sought to combat poverty with physical solutions. I worked on the water supply in the village. I did agricultural training, using new technologies. I worked with local leaders on community-health issues. But it took time to realize that beneath these empirical realities lay deeply held religious and mythic beliefs. Poverty was not just physical but involved how people thought of the spiritual realm, combined with sociopolitical systems built around patron-client relationships.[20] While we might naturally expect

---

20. For more on this see, see Paul Gifford, *Christianity, Development and Modernity in Africa* (London: Hurst, 2015).

this to be the case for public life in Africa, spiritual powers are no less real in the West, taking the form of ideologies and myths (such as bootstrap individualism or our heritage of progress).

My point at this juncture is not to critique the ideologies but to identify that invisible, spiritual referent points lie behind poverty in America, just as they did poverty in my village. Most of our efforts to address forms of "complicated wickedness" in the West focus only on material referent points and neglect the spiritual (or religious) powers underneath the surface.

Problem 4: Thick Publics, Thin Religion

Let me begin to put the pieces together. I explained how we experience the public realm thickly via the interpenetration of many different publics and a deeper spirituality behind them. Meanwhile, our theological heritage in the West recoils from public realities and opts instead to focus on spiritual dimensions and the individual. We encounter the public realm thickly, while trying to witness to it thinly. This problem stems from two related issues: (1) a reluctance to enter into the complexity of the public realm, and (2) limitations in how we interpret (and embody) the salvation offered to us in Jesus Christ and through local congregations.

As I explained above, evangelicals in the West do not do particularly well with complexity. We favor simplistic and authoritative readings of identity that wrap everything up into a convenient whole. Robert Hunt explains how, in the past, people's identities were constructed from certain givens, such as ethnicity, race, or being born in a certain location (such as a farm community).[21] A person was handed their identity from their parents, and that identity became reified over time through ethnic ties and communal bonds. Because of the power of the local community, these older identities bore exclusionary characteristics, revealing not only who belonged to the community but also who did not. For the reasons I just explained, these previous identities were authoritative. No one questioned them.

Hunt then contrasts these older identities with newer forms. Newer identities arise from three causes: "the breakdown of stable public identities, the consciousness that identity and affiliation are chosen rather than given, and the development of narrative as the basis of identity."[22] As people move away from "stable" identities given to them by their parents, they are forced to choose new pathways from an infinite menu of options, where each option

---

21. Robert Hunt, "Public Missiology and Anxious Tribalism," *Missiology* 44, no. 2 (2016): 129–41.

22. Hunt, "Public Missiology," 131.

competes with others for a person's allegiance. These newer identities lack the stability of the older varieties, thus feeding what Hunt refers to as "anxious tribalism." The anxiousness arises in part because of people's choosing them (rather than being given them), along with their comparing them against all available options out there in the world. The newer identities lack the authority that the older ones held.

How do people respond to complex forms of identity in the world? In some cases they seek simplicity, especially by appealing to an all-powerful socioreligious identity that wraps up everything into a totalizing whole. We want the pastor to just tell us what to believe. Or we carve the world up according to nice, neat binaries of sacred/secular, private/public. Alternatively, we actively court a return to a romanticized and socially constructed past, such as how we remember our childhood or imagine life for the early church (though it was highly complex for people living during that era). In the face of competing, swirling options available in public life, people actively desire a simple, authoritative identity to manage the scope of complexity in the world.

But here's the problem. Such aforementioned forms of identity are nothing but a veneer and, as such, prove to be dangerously thin. Scott Appleby says something similar, drawing on what he calls "strong" and "weak" religions.[23] He says a religion is strong if it boasts a robust "religious literacy," along with a mature institutional presence. Meanwhile, weak religions lack such literacy and suffer under fear and insecurity, constantly threatened by the presence of contrasting viewpoints. A strong religion is able to hear different perspectives. It continually evaluates everything according to its center (for Christians, Jesus Christ), guarding people from running after ideologies or idols of materialism. In contrast, as Appleby explains, "a 'weak' religion is one in which the people retain meaningful contact only with vestiges of the broader religious worldview and network of meanings and resources, in which they are isolated from one another and from educators and spiritual-moral exemplars."[24] Hence, when religions lose interconnections with public life, they become susceptible to nationalistic or ideological thinning; or, to use Hunt's language, Christians become prey to anxious tribalism.

Meanwhile Miroslav Volf explores differences between what he calls "thin" and "thick" faith, getting more to the heart of my central thesis.[25] He explains that solving the problem of religious violence will require not less religion

---

23. R. Scott Appleby, *The Ambivalence of the Sacred: Religion, Violence, and Reconciliation* (Lanham, MD: Rowman & Littlefield, 2000), 77.

24. Appleby, *Ambivalence of the Sacred*, 77.

25. Miroslav Volf, *A Public Faith: How Followers of Christ Should Serve the Common Good* (Grand Rapids: Brazos, 2011), 39–41.

but more religion, but of a kind integrated into the whole of public life. Volf says it this way:

> The more we reduce faith to vague religiosity that serves primarily to energize, heal, and give meaning to the business of life whose course is shaped by factors other than faith (such as national or economic interests), the worse off we will be. Inversely, the more the Christian faith matters to its adherents as faith that maps a way of life, and the more they practice it as an ongoing tradition with strong ties to its origins and history, and with clear cognitive and moral content, the better off we will be. "Thin" but zealous practice of the Christian faith is likely to foster violence; "thick" and committed practice will help generate and sustain a culture of peace.[26]

Thin faith draws heavily on religious language, but religion is nothing but a thin veneer to make us feel well fortified against public life or to baptize existing interests in the name of faith. Hence, Christians fall victim to tribalism, ideologies of various kinds, or self-protectionism. By way of contrast, thick faith is woven into the fabric of public life. It provides, as Volf says, a map for a way of life.

It is easy to see how Christians in the West suffer from anxious tribalism, while opting for weak or thin expressions of faith. Thin faith gives Christians every appearance of totalizing authority, something we desperately crave. We witness to individuals, but not to the publics around human life. We focus on getting people into heaven, but not on holistic discipleship involving every aspect of public realm. We attend to Christ's death for cleansing our sins, but not as it relates to the redemption of public life. We spiritualize the faith while neglecting its material and structural significance. Or else we baptize existing ideologies through biblical resources. Christians experience the public realm thickly while trying to witness to it thinly.

In an interesting turn of events, millennials in North America are currently rejecting the institutional church in large part because they don't believe it's preparing them for living in a complex world. David Kinnaman and Aly Hawkins explain, "To young Christians, the church can feel rigid and unreal. Christians' black-and-white views seem not to reflect the world as it really is. . . . For these young people, matters concerning 'the world,' relationships, and faith are rich and textured."[27] Millennials compare the complexity they experience in the world with what they find in local churches and are discouraged by the disconnect. They yearn for thick faith to help them make sense of complexity in the world.

---

26. Volf, *Public Faith*, 40.
27. David Kinnaman with Aly Hawkins, *You Lost Me: Why Young Christians Are Leaving Church . . . and Rethinking Faith* (Grand Rapids: Baker Books, 2011), 98.

Problem 5: Individual, Technological, and Problem-Solving Solutions to Complex Social Problems

Let me conclude with one final problem. We too often opt for quick, ready-made solutions to complex problems. Carver Yu accuses the West of "technological optimism and literary despair,"[28] and Emmanuel Katongole accuses the West of what he calls, "prescriptive haste."[29] Since we have not been properly trained to theologize in and for public life (problem 1 above), or integrate theology with missiology (problem 2), or properly wade into the messiness of public life (problem 3), or witness thickly to the complexity of the public realm (problem 4), we tend to revert to individual, technological, problem-solving solutions in the face of highly complex social problems.[30]

In the West we interpret public life through the lowest common denominator: the individual. Our view of social change boils down to electing the right president, hiring the proper senior pastor, discovering the innovative "social entrepreneur," or leveraging the financial resources of the billionaire. According to this way of looking at things, one changes society by changing individuals. And this carries over into how we undertake Christian witness. Christian Smith calls this the "personal influence strategy."[31] He suggests this strategy reflects the primary heritage of American evangelicals, spilling over into how they understand social engagement. However, complex social problems found in publics require complex social answers.[32]

Not only do we approach issues through the individual, but we struggle to integrate spiritual resources into material realities. We know how to address spiritual problems, such as combating idolatry with biblical preaching. And we also know how to address material problems, such as healing diseases with

28. Carver T. Yu, "Truth and Authentic Humanity" (plenary address at the Gospel and Our Culture Network consultation, Swanwick, 1992).

29. Emmanuel Katongole, *The Sacrifice of Africa: A Political Theology for Africa* (Grand Rapids: Eerdmans, 2010), 32.

30. Some of this is changing. Millennials are becoming more likely to actively engage such realms, though older generations such as mine have not bequeathed them a good heritage for doing so. They either have left the church altogether (while maintaining a thirst for spirituality) or still attend the church and look for complex answers to social problems via social activism and other sources.

31. Christian Smith, *American Evangelicalism: Embattled and Thriving* (Chicago: University of Chicago Press, 1998), 187, 193.

32. James Davison Hunter critiques such a tendency to focus solely on individuals, arguing that it neglects a more sophisticated understanding of power and how change works best with "overlapping networks of leaders and overlapping resources, all operating near or in the center institutions and in common purpose." *To Change the World: The Irony, Tragedy, and Possibility of Christianity in the Late Modern World* (New York: Oxford University Press, 2010), 44.

medicine. But how does idolatry relate to disease, or preaching to medicine? We don't have resources for crossing the domains. In my last year living in Africa, I was posted to a nursing college with the goal of integrating theology into a medical curriculum. When doctors and nurses (who were trained from a Western missionary perspective) asked me why I was there, most were confused, and a few directly asked me, "Why do we need that?" Deep down, we have been trained to think that material problems require material solutions, and spiritual problems demand spiritual resources. Integration, however, requires delving into complexity, and we have not been trained for that.

Furthermore, our Western predisposition to solve problems with *technē* (the root word of technology) colors how we go about public change. We strategize, create programs, launch campaigns, raise capital for poverty alleviation (because money is, after all, the highest form of *technē*), and leverage technology for solving complex social ills. Just walk through the labyrinth of booths at the Justice Conference, and you will find a wide range of water-treatment systems, direct-trade markets, coffee-roasting companies, and small business ventures. Now, please understand me: each of these holds a valid place in combating "complicated wickedness." I myself have started a business, been a part of a microenterprise scheme, experimented with agricultural technologies, and supported direct-trade coffee imports. I merely want to show that in light of our theological heritage of separation, along with our discouragement with the church, we revert to quick-leveraged, material solutions.

At the root is a need to problem-solve. I was guilty of this same thing (as my earlier narrative betrays). When we problem-solve, we do so with specific cultural readings of the universe fed by mechanistic understandings. For example, if the world is nothing but a grand machine with gears, nuts and bolts, and hoses, then our answers to the greatest problems will be found in ratchets (technologies), mechanics (specialists), and strategies (techniques). Hence, poverty, malnutrition, disease, and warfare are too often understood as problems to be solved, rather than as concerns involving people living within complex social, economic, and political systems. Little or no attention is paid to implicit theologies and how they inform how people look at the world.[33]

In one sense, problem-solving is natural. We all seek solutions to dire public problems. The question is how. Keith Clements suggests that Western societies do so through the lenses of a mechanistic, technological universe, by reducing complex social problems to one or two things. He explains, "Single 'answers'

---

33. Hunter says something similar: "The near exclusive focus on the explicit, visible, and conscious aspects of culture minimizes the more implicit, intangible, preconscious, inherited, and thus more encompassing nature of culture." *To Change the World*, 30.

are sought to 'problems' as entrenched as 'the Irish problem,' juvenile crime, the global population explosion and third-world poverty."[34] At the root of this reductionism is the belief (theology?) that humanity is "something to be managed in a rational way which secures the dominance of the already-powerful over the less-powerful, and over nature."[35] For those sitting in global places where complex public issues daily vex the limits of human nature, it is hard not to see Western problem-solving as anything other than a veiled form of neocolonialism, the arrogant leisure of the wealthy, or, worse yet, what Steve Corbett and Brian Fikkert refer to as the "god-complex."[36]

How then should we witness to publics, especially in the face of "complicated wickedness"? That's what I would like to address throughout the remainder of this book.

How Do We Get Out of This Morass?

I have stated the problem. We have separated theology from the public realm, we have divorced theology from missiology, we do not possess sufficient understandings of the public realm, we seek thin forms of witness in the face of thick interpenetrating publics, and we problem-solve using individual technological answers to address complex social problems.

How do we chart a course forward? The answer is public missiology, especially of the kind focused on the local congregation. For the remainder of this book, I will show how missiology offers a wealth of resources for addressing complex publics. In the next four chapters, I will present a theoretical case for a public missiology; then in the final four chapters, I will offer various case studies to show what it looks like within local congregations.

Let's start by going deeper into the public realm. What is it? How does it function? And what does the public realm mean for missiology?

34. Keith Clements, *Learning to Speak: The Church's Voice in Public Affairs* (Eugene, OR: Wipf & Stock, 2000), 65. He then says, "The ultimate in 'solutions' is of course the most mechanical of all, that is, the use of military force which is becoming ever more technological, and ever more costly in every way."

35. Clements, *Learning to Speak*, 66. Clements proceeds to argue that "the New Testament proclamation is not about 'solving' problematic situations by rearranging human affairs, but about a critical confrontation and transformation of the human condition through death and resurrection" (74).

36. Steve Corbett and Brian Fikkert, *When Helping Hurts: How to Alleviate Poverty without Hurting the Poor . . . and Yourself* (Chicago: Moody, 2014).

2

What Publics? Where Publics?

Public discourse craves attention like a child. Texts clamor at us.
Images solicit our gaze. Look here! Listen! Hey!

—Michael Warner, *Publics and Counterpublics*[1]

What are publics? That's the question I will unpack in this chapter. I want to show how the public realm, which we refer to in the singular, is composed of many overlapping, interpenetrating publics.[2] We experience it thickly.

Let's return to my earlier narrative. In the Tanzanian village, I found myself immersed in a world of publics, as if for the first time. It's an odd place for one to discover the public realm. In Selare we did not have televisions, telephones, or social media. Letters would take upwards of three weeks to reach us from distant family members. Our sleepy little village did not have a financial district or a political seat of power, and by all outward appearances it had no technology—at least how we normally define it in the West. Yet we had a complex public realm made up of interpenetrating publics.

1. Michael Warner, *Publics and Counterpublics* (New York: Zone, 2005), 89.
2. My goal in this chapter is not to exegete the public realm. I am not a sociologist and will therefore speak of the public realm differently from someone trained in the social sciences. For me, it is a way of thinking about culture with greater movement between the different elements, and where the focus is on public life.

Though eight hours from the nearest city, our village was surprisingly connected with the outside world. We listened to the BBC and Voice of America every morning on shortwave radio, and our neighbors did the same, though in Swahili. People received news of family members living in distant cities such as Dar es Salaam through sophisticated networks of radio communication or carried by word of mouth via public transportation. One also does not need to have a financial district to possess economics. Everyone in the village participated freely in what Patrick Chabal calls an "economy of affection,"[3] where people exchanged goods and services with each other through highly organized webs of social belonging. Our little village likewise had plenty of politics, though not in the form we typically think of it. We had political and religious leaders, but more importantly families of distinction ("patrons") who influenced affairs within the community. For a remote village we had surprisingly strong religious ties, stretching as far as Zanzibar and Saudi Arabia.

We also had public spaces. I would sit in the village "square" and listen to stories, or drink strong coffee with village leaders in a mud-walled coffee shop. Women exchanged news at the lone water tap. Weddings and funerals functioned as critical means for people to come together and exchange news and strengthen filial ties. Our village had specific "spaces" where public life took place.

Here's my point: we in the West tend to associate the public realm with urban centers in Western countries or interpret it through the lenses of one overarching domain, such as economics or politics. Because of this, we tend to assume that Western societies possess more publics, or at least more influence on the public realm. Later in this chapter I will talk about globalization's uneven influence on the public realm. But for now I merely want to show that all societies participate in public life, and the public realm arises from the movement of many different parts. I will speak of the public realm in the singular to show how it is composed of many elements (what I am calling "publics"), lending it a thickness of identity.

What Are Publics? A Preliminary Definition

The public realm makes life possible (and enjoyable) for people throughout the world. We give particular aspects of the public realm our soul, such as with economics, and entrust others with savior-like characteristics, such as with technology or politics. It is impossible to imagine human life without them. While we typically gravitate toward the larger aspects, to which the

---

3. Patrick Chabal, *Africa: The Politics of Suffering and Smiling* (London: Zed, 2009), 110.

entire weight of humanity seems to be drawn like some invisible force, the smaller parts, such as coffee shops, street corners, and city parks, prove every bit as critical. They help us interact with the public realm in solid, earthy ways.

What then is the public realm, and how is it related to publics? As I explained above, I will speak of the public realm in the broadest possible manner to refer to where public life occurs. What then are publics?

Let me say up front that publics are not easily defined. As one of my colleagues likes to say, we have no clearly articulated "publicology."[4] We have well-crafted methods for the study of culture, social life, and civil society, but few resources for exegeting publics.[5] We have discrete disciplines for thinking about specific public dimensions, such as political science, economics, and communications, but little for considering how they interpenetrate each other, and nothing for how we should witness to them.

Perhaps the beauty of the term *publics* is found precisely in its ambiguity. As Michael Warner writes, "Publics are queer creatures. You cannot point to them or look them in the eye. You also cannot easily avoid them. They have become an almost natural feature of the social landscape, like pavement."[6] Perhaps the analogy of pavement is fitting since we often think of publics by virtue of their place, as located in a bank, shopping district, or urban center. But any emphasis on location is also misleading since publics can correspond to symbols, such as "economics" when we see the stock ticker in Times Square, or "entertainment" as we drive past the Hollywood sign.

For the purposes of this book, I will define publics as common spaces of togetherness where people participate with one another in life and form opinions through the circulation of different texts.[7] Andrew Morton likewise defines a public as "togetherness but with large spaces in it; its weave is open."[8] That might be as good a place as any to begin.

---

4. I am grateful to Greg Leffel for some of these thoughts, first presented at the 2015 American Society of Missiology meetings.

5. Anthropologists and sociologists alike have long engaged the public domain. Nevertheless, I would suggest that contemporary "publics" present a new challenge that requires all the resources of missiology. This is especially the case if one take takes seriously (as we must) the invisible and religious dimension behind publics.

6. Michael Warner, *Publics and Counterpublics* (New York: Zone, 2005), 7.

7. Charles Taylor at one point refers to "publics" as "horizontal, simultaneous mutual presence" to get at the same general idea of texts, but he broadens it beyond speech to include what he calls "mutual display." Hence, a public can be formed around fashion or other nonverbal means. See *A Secular Age* (Cambridge, MA: Belknap, 2007), 481.

8. Andrew R. Morton, "Duncan Forrester: A Public Theologian," in *Public Theology for the 21st Century*, ed. William F. Storrar and Andrew R. Morton (New York: T&T Clark, 2004), 25–36, here 29.

Let me briefly unpack this definition. First, publics are composed of "common spaces of togetherness." These can be physical places where people meet, such as a coffee shop, a city park, or a village water tap. They can also be virtual spaces where people interact with each other across time, such as Facebook, Twitter, or a chat room on the internet. The common space facilitates a shared community, even including complete strangers. Second, publics possess an "open weave." In other words, there is room for people to bring in their differences. Morton explains this as a good thing. In a closed community, people align around similarity. Differences are frowned on, and people police the boundaries of togetherness to maintain ethnic, religious, or ideological purity. However, it is much harder to police publics—though people still try. Finally, publics are formed through many different elements. They are comprised of various "texts" that feed a larger, thicker narrative.

A Short History of the "Public Realm" and "Publics"

Let me provide a short history of how the public realm has evolved over the centuries, drawing on research from the seminal scholars. In this section, my purpose is to broadly sketch some of the main changes to the public realm in order to help us understand how we experience it in contemporary society.

From Something Controlled by Elites to Independent "Space"

In ancient Greece, the public realm was associated with the polis and located in public meeting places, such as the agora. In these places, male citizens met to discuss things of interest to the entire community. Hence, the public realm is not a new evolution come into the world; it has always existed. Throughout the world, and at all points in time, people have met together to form opinions and share life together. The public realm arises from creation, and especially image-bearing powers entrusted to humans.[9] It is rather the shape and nature of the public realm that has changed over the years.

The public realm has long represented contested space. In ancient Greece, women and slaves were excluded from participation. Male citizens debated viewpoints. Years later the public came to be associated with various elites. Jürgen Habermas narrates the transition of the public realm from a free, open (at least for male citizens) "space" in ancient Greece to what occurred during the medieval period, where ecclesiastical elites cast their long shadows

9. In the Old Testament, the city gates were one of the most critical locations for public life, for it was there that people gathered to make decisions, sell goods, and enforce laws.

on the people. During those years, everything took place under the influence of royalty and clergy. Decisions were made and opinions were constructed from fiats issued on high. In a manner of speaking, during the medieval period, there was only one public in the world: that controlled by the elites/ church.

Habermas then describes the emergence of an "independent" public sphere during the medieval period through the rise of commerce. People began to carve out independent space through financial transactions.[10] But the introduction of early forms of capitalism was not sufficient to create a variegated public realm. It carved into the landscape certain conditions that allowed people to act with greater freedoms of decision, unencumbered by the elites. But more was needed. And that more came in the form of the printing press, along with physical spaces for the formation of public opinion. Habermas describes the rise of coffeehouses, newspapers, reading clubs, and other conduits necessary for forming opinions, debating subjects, and offering critique in the face of the elites. This, he argues, is the formal beginning of the modern "independent" public sphere.[11]

From Religious Collective to Secular Individual

With this new, "independent" public sphere, which arose during the medieval period and was later reinforced by the Enlightenment, we discover two further characteristics we now take for granted. The Enlightenment individualized what had previously been a collective entity (such as in ancient Greece), and it secularized what had been associated with religion (under Christendom). Ever since the Enlightenment, the public realm has become the site of individual agency. This is what makes Western contemporary publics more diverse than ever, and sites of greater contested powers. Ever since the Enlightenment, the public realm has largely excluded religion (though, as I will later show, it was still fed by myths, traditions, and symbols carrying quasi-spiritual meaning). Charles Taylor says that "secularity" defines Western forms of public life. It is made up entirely of the actions of its members, and these actions are not preconditioned on any belief in God or higher transcendent order.[12]

10. This was due to the rise of contract laws requiring all persons involved in commerce to treat each other with equal status.

11. Jürgen Habermas, *The Structural Transformation of the Public Sphere: An Inquiry into a Category of Bourgeois Society*, trans. Thomas Burger with the assistance of Frederick Lawrence (Cambridge, MA: MIT Press, 1991).

12. Taylor, *Secular Age*, 192. He explains further, "The eighteenth century public sphere thus represents an instance of a new kind: a metatopical common space and common agency

From Proximate Space to Notional "Social Imaginaries"

Benedict Anderson builds on Habermas's work. He explores the rise of the nation-state as an "imagined community"[13] and the critical role that the novel and the printing press played in the development of a shared common national identity—despite the fact that most citizens did not personally know each other. We can experience this today. Imagine meeting a fellow citizen in a distant land. You immediately feel a sense of belonging. Though thousands of miles away from home, you instantly talk about shared realities, such as missing a certain food, while drawing on colloquial language to express common sentiment. You feel a sense of belonging together that transcends physical space. Alternatively, imagine walking out of a sports event surrounded by complete strangers and carrying on an animated conversation as if belonging to the same "tribe." The emphasis on the "imagined community" gives rise to many different publics within the public realm. A public brings diverse people together through a common space, whether around a national identity or through allegiances to a sports team. Hence, the public realm is composed of many different imagined communities.

In one sense then we can speak about the public sphere in the singular as "a common space in which the members of society are deemed to meet through a variety of media: print, electronic, and also face-to-face encounters; to discuss matters of common interest; and thus to be able to form a common mind about these."[14] But this one "common space" is made up of many competing interests. This is where Taylor's language of social imaginaries is particularly helpful. The public realm shapes how people imagine their social existence, which then feeds back into the greater whole. For example, a person reads about a topic in the newspaper, discusses it with friends while seated in a coffee shop, listens to the topic debated on the radio while driving, talks about it further with a complete stranger while getting a haircut, and the story broadens its discourse across time and space. This is what Taylor means by the public sphere. Along the way, this one common space is filled with many interpretations of reality, which is why we can speak of the public realm as a whole, along with a plurality of publics.

---

without an action-transcendent constitution, an agency grounded purely in its own common actions" (194).

13. Benedict Anderson, *Imagined Communities: Reflections on the Origin and Spread of Nationalism* (London: Verso, 1983).

14. Taylor, *Secular Age*, 185. Taylor contends that the public space should always be referred to in the singular because of the way that media circulates: "The discussion we're having on television now takes account of what was said in the newspaper this morning, which in turn reports on the radio debate yesterday, and so on" (185).

From Sphere Language to the Fluid Movement of Publics

In the past, it was common to speak of the public realm according to carefully delineated "spheres" (such as politics, economics, or family systems). There is a good rationale for this, and it acknowledges that each of these spheres possesses its own discourse and methodology. However, it is increasingly problematic to maintain this sphere language in contemporary society. Each of these spheres overlaps and interpenetrates with the others, which is why I think it is better to speak of publics.

Karin Barber speaks of a public as made up of an audience and composed of many different "texts."[15] Her contribution is important because of the non-Western context of her writing (where she is analyzing different kinds of texts and publics in Africa). Barber defines a public as "an audience of a distinctive kind. It is an audience whose members are not known to the speaker/composer of the text, and not necessarily present, but still addressed simultaneously, and imagined as a collectivity."[16]

Thinking about publics as audiences is helpful for this discussion in three ways. First, as Barber's work points out, it allows for a variety of "texts." In the West, we tend to think of written texts, but Barber's work shows they also can be oral or embodied. She defines a text as a sort of "weaving or fabricating—connectedness, the quality of having been put together, of having been made by human ingenuity."[17] This definition allows for multiple genres in the construction of texts and moves nimbly between oral, written, and embodied frames.

Second, speaking of publics shifts the scope away from associating the public realm with one particular domain. It is not necessarily wrong to speak of sphere sovereignty, and we could certainly add that the differentiation of domains is a valuable aspect of the social sciences. Abraham Kuyper introduced the language of sphere sovereignty to safeguard such entities as family, church, and business from intrusion by the state, while preventing the various spheres from being amalgamated into one amorphous whole.[18] By talking about publics, I am not suggesting the public realm is just a free-for-all of movement, where one specific domain such as politics or economics can overstep its scope (although this is a real danger in our contemporary

---

15. Karin Barber, *The Anthropology of Texts, Persons and Publics: Oral and Written Culture in Africa and Beyond* (New York: Cambridge University Press, 2007).

16. Barber, *Anthropology*, 139.

17. Barber, *Anthropology*, 21.

18. Abraham Kuyper's language of "sphere sovereignty" built on Calvin's writings; see *Lectures on Calvinism: Six Lectures from the Stone Foundation Lectures Delivered at Princeton University* (Peabody, MA: Hendrickson, 2008).

world and something we need to guard against). I am merely highlighting the diversity of contemporary publics through the interpenetration of many different "texts."

Finally, publics are not passive; rather, they "act back" on the message being delivered. Think of an interactive theater in which the entire audience participates in the different scenes of the play. It's challenging for people to think of themselves as influencing the public realm, especially with dominant narratives such as nationalism. But it's easier for them to envision their agency in an interactive theater. Public life is composed of many different theaters (publics) within a shared space of togetherness (public realm).

From "Neutral" Space to the Contestation of Power

Another historical shift highlights the power dynamics I referenced earlier. We see the public realm moving from what Habermas and others call an "independent" space to the contested sites of power in our contemporary world. Power dynamics have always informed the public realm (think back to ancient Greece, where only male citizens could make decisions). The contestation of power is not a new feature on the landscape. It is rather the accessibility of every person on the planet to engage the public realm through Twitter, Facebook, and other social media platforms that heightens the power dynamics of contemporary publics. Warner explains, "Public discourse craves attention like a child. Texts clamor at us. Images solicit our gaze. Look here! Listen! Hey!"[19] Just peruse social media after a legal ruling on immigration. Or look at your Twitter feed after a national election. There are no neutral spaces within the contemporary public realm, and specific publics are always seeking to increase their powers. Think of political ideologies of nationalism and race or the deeper myths of progress that continue to underwrite cultural narratives. To witness in and through publics, we need to embody together a different kind of power in and for the world.

From Slow Evolution of the Public Realm to Rapid Change

One final characteristic is perhaps the most obvious of all. Never before in history have we seen such rapid changes within the public realm. While in an earlier era the rise of early forms of capitalism and the invention of the printing press ushered in the early development of an "independent" public realm, today innovations such as air transport, the internet, and smartphones are changing the public realm like never before. One of the reasons people feel

19. Warner, *Publics and Counterpublics*, 89.

overwhelmed with contemporary publics (and seek a retreat into the socially constructed memories of a simpler time) is precisely the pace and scope of change occurring in the public realm. We struggle keeping up with it all. The pace of change also triggers a desire to return to the past and a time when things were simpler. While some of this can be healthy, other aspects need to be scrutinized.

Globalization and "Thick Publics"

If everything I've said so far is not sufficient to highlight the thickness of the public realm, perhaps globalization, which makes life denser, will be. I won't take the time to explain all the dynamics that go into globalization, since this is something other scholars have done with great aplomb.[20] I want merely to show how globalization involves many different strands combining to create thick, transnational publics.

Globalization involves something of a paradox. It is simultaneously a process of *complexifying* everything while bringing the entire world into a heightened state of *compression*. On the surface, complexity and compression make strange bedfellows. Complexity implies incredible diversity (as if the world were splintering into a million pieces), while compression suggests mass homogenization (where we think the entire world is coming together into one particular shape). These push-and-pull forces lie at the very heart of globalization. Roland Robertson defines globalization as the point where these twin forces meet. For him, it entails a particular kind of compression in which local diversity and global homogeneity give rise to *glocalization*.[21] Hence, Robertson understands it as a multidimensional process involving a dizzying array of "sociocultural density" accompanied by "rapidly expanding consciousness."[22]

Involved in this process are many different elements. Bryant Myers defines globalization around five domains: technology, economics, governance,

20. For good treatments of globalization, see Roland Robertson, *Globalization: Social Theory and Global Culture* (Newbury Park, CA: Sage, 1992); Arjun Appadurai, *Modernity at Large: Cultural Dimensions of Globalization* (Minneapolis: University of Minnesota Press, 1996); and Bryant Myers, *Engaging Globalization: The Poor, Christian Mission, and Our Hyperconnected World* (Grand Rapids: Baker Academic, 2017).

21. Roland Robertson, "Globalization and the Future of 'Traditional Religion,'" in *God and Globalization*, ed. Max L. Stackhouse, vol. 1, *Religion and the Powers of the Common Life*, ed. Max L. Stackhouse and Peter J. Paris (New York: T&T Clark, 2000), 53–68, here 53–54.

22. Robertson refers to globalization as homogenization versus heterogenization, or the "universalization of particularism and the particularization of universalism." "Globalization," 56.

culture, and human beings.[23] Arjun Appadurai also focuses on five: eth-noscapes, mediascapes, technoscapes, financescapes, and ideoscapes.[24] The language of "-scapes" helps us envision the domains in terms of movement, such that Appadurai refers to them as "streams," "fluid" encounters, or "global flows."[25] The imagery of movement is helpful to show how global-ization is fed by different streams, like water emerging from tiny cracks in a lofty alpine summit, slowly making its way down the mountain to connect with other streams, and ultimately producing a mighty torrent of a river cascading through the valley. Whether we use the language of texts (as ex-plained by Barber) or the idea of flows (through Appadurai's writings), the result is very similar: movement produces a thicker, more complex reality in the world.

Of course, people will invariably interpret globalization according to one particular domain (usually economics) and describe it as the forceful imposition of that domain (e.g., global capitalism) onto the rest of the world, and there are valid reasons for doing so. Just travel to Hyderabad, India. You pass skyscrapers filled with multinational tech companies, and then stroll through shopping malls past Gucci, Nike, and Apple stores, and then settle down in the food court where you can drink a Coke from a McDonald's. Globalization has made the world a smaller place, defined in large part by Western companies. However, such a reading tends to privilege the "rapidly expanding consciousness" at the expense of "sociocultural density." So even as you eat at a McDonald's in Hyderabad, you will not find any hamburgers in a Hindu nation, and you will inevitably encounter local impressions, such as a McSpicy Paneer or the Veg Maharaja Mac. According to this way of looking at things, globalization homogenizes cultural forms while facilitating local agency to impart new meanings into global forms.

Once again, globalization can best be understood by the imagery of flows. Appadurai refers to it, in part, as "a complex, overlapping, disjunctive order that cannot be understood in terms of existing center-periphery models (even those that might account for multiple centers and peripheries)."[26] Meanwhile, Mike Rynkiewich defines globalization as "a widespread engagement of people with an expanding worldwide system of communication, commerce, and culture that is producing broad uniformities across selected sectors of many societies as well as generating multiple hybrid cultures in various stages

23. Myers, *Engaging Globalization*, 44–51.
24. Appadurai, *Modernity at Large*, 33–36.
25. Appadurai, *Modernity at Large*, 45–46.
26. Appadurai, *Modernity at Large*, 32.

of reception, rejection, and reinvention of innovations."[27] Vinoth Ramachandra describes it as "dialectic interplay between the universal and the particular, between what they all share and what is culturally specific."[28] Each of these definitions explains globalization through the language of movement (physical and imaginative), with the result being greater density to the whole.

The language of density is also helpful for locating globalization in the subject material of this book, as it intimates some of what I have been explaining with my reference to thickness. Globalization involves many different elements brought together in a variety of ways. However, density or thickness does not explain *how* things come together; it only suggests that they do come together.[29] Globalization involves many different encounters, which we might think of as strands, some of which are heavier than others. And however much we might want to speak of local agency, globalization invariably involves an uneven process fraught with constant dangers, especially for the poor.[30]

This raises the sordid side of globalization. Let me illustrate through a story. I taught for more than a decade at an African theological institution. When I first arrived in Kenya, I participated in a graduation ceremony. I recall sitting as one of the only Westerners before a sea of faces. A bishop from Tanzania was the guest speaker. He delivered an impassioned speech about the need for high-quality theological education on the continent. At one point in his speech, he stopped, turned, and looked at me—the only white face on the stage—and said to the crowd, "I hate globalization!" I felt my heart stop. A thousand eyes fell on me. Besides the obvious feelings of discomfort at being singled out, this led me to consider how I, from the West, represented many of his concerns. The bishop saw globalization through the lenses of America exporting its worst culture into his home country, and especially into his churches. At that particular moment, I became the face of Hollywood, immodest clothing styles, Western pop music with sordid lyrics, and changing social mores influencing the youth in his denomination.

Globalization feels either really good or really bad, depending on where you're sitting. As an audience, globalization arises with many different "texts,"

---

27. Michael Rynkiewich, *Soul, Self, and Society: A Postmodern Anthropology for Mission in a Postcolonial World* (Eugene, OR: Cascade, 2011), 234.

28. Vinoth Ramachandra, *Subverting Global Myths: Theology and the Public Issues Shaping Our World* (Downers Grove, IL: IVP Academic, 2008), 135.

29. Robertson differentiates between integration and interdependence. He explains how globalization heightens global interdependence, but it does not lead to global integration, as if suggesting a state of "normative cohesiveness." "Globalization," 54.

30. Bryant Myers does well to capture these dynamics in his book *Engaging Globalization*; see esp. chaps. 9 and 10.

some louder than others; or as a flow, it is composed of many different "-scapes," not all equal in size and weight. Whether globalization benefits you or represents the Western imposition of culture on your context, there can be no contesting the fact that we all experience globalization thickly. How then does this relate to our understanding of culture?

Publics and Culture

During the 1960s, social scientists defined "culture" according to certain modernist assumptions, viewing it as an empirical, bounded set of beliefs, behaviors, and artifacts. In such a reading, culture constituted an entity one explores objectively from the outside, such as with an organism in a petri dish. Social sciences quickly moved away from such a view, yet such a view still lingers. People view culture as essentialized.[31]

Some of these older ways of thinking about culture carry over into how we interpret the public realm today. We look at the different parts of public life as bounded spheres with a "certain set of attributes." According to this way of thinking, politics, economics, and technology function as empirical realities one can point to and say, "That's the political realm," when gazing on the Capitol building, or, "Here's economics," while strolling down Wall Street, or, "I'm holding technology," while using a smartphone. Each of these does in fact represent politics and economics and technology, but not exclusively so. For example, I can use a smartphone to check the stock market, which fluctuates as a result of political decisions occurring around the world while being further influenced by earnings from transnational companies, and now the one domain (technology) overlaps with politics and economics.

A danger occurs whenever one particular domain gets elevated above the others. This was the primary concern for the Tanzanian bishop. I spoke with him after the graduation service, and he explained how the youth in his parish were caught up with American pop music, movies, and celebrities, resulting in changes to their dress and speech and, more importantly, in how they interacted with their parents and the church. Similar dangers arise from how we view economics. People ascribe secular eschatologies to money, implying

31. Patrick Chabal defines essentialism as "a two-step type of reductionism. The first is to claim that given groups of people are endowed with a certain set of attributes, which can be identified and classified. The second is to deduce from these alleged attributes types of morality, beliefs, thinking or behaviour, which are supposed to 'explain' why these groups act as they do." *Africa*, 181.

that a person's identity is equal to the sum total of their possessions. When this happens, economics risks commodifying all other aspects of life, even influencing personal relationships.[32]

Hence, the public realm of the twenty-first century is not a monolithic entity but more a spirited dance as free-flowing domains clasp hands, clutch one another in mad embrace, push apart, and spin across the ballroom, constantly seeking out new partners.[33] Talk about publics is talk about complex forms of culture, giving rise to concepts such as fluidity, bricolage, and cosmopolitanism.[34] One benefit of speaking of publics is that it forces us to jettison older ways of referring to culture,[35] where people treat culture or cultural domains "as discrete wholes."[36]

Publics and Religion

Finally, we need to relate all of this to religion. By talking about publics through the imagery of movement, it is easy to get the impression that publics are nothing but a free-for-all. And sometimes that's how it feels. If we stop to think about any public discourse—whether global poverty, immigration, the publics of my village in Tanzania, or the local coffee shop down the street—we feel overwhelmed by all the different flows.

Our analysis of the public realm becomes messier—while potentially more ordered—when turning to religion. To begin with, let's admit that religion can increase the problem—and that is one of the primary reasons people attempt to keep religion out of the public realm. A religious leader sanctions a political ideology, baptizing it with sacred power. Alternatively, people interpret a particular

---

32. I experienced this when my sister was killed. The insurance agency came to us with calculations to determine how much money we could receive, determined by their financial estimates of her life worth.

33. I am indebted to Brian Howell for this dance metaphor. He describes contextualization as "a complex dance of music and movement in which choices are made moment by moment and each new circumstance requires new response." "Contextualizing Context," in *Power and Identity in the Global Church: Six Contemporary Cases*, ed. Brian M. Howell and Edwin Zehner (Pasadena, CA: William Carey Library, 2009), 24–25.

34. Kwame Anthony Appiah, *Cosmopolitanism: Ethics in a World of Strangers* (New York: Norton, 2006). *Bricolage* is a term used in a variety of disciplines to refer to the construction of something from the many different parts available to people. It is used in reference to food, technology, and other aspects of culture.

35. I am not suggesting we should do away with the language of culture (although some social scientists have argued for precisely that), nor am I implying that "public" and "culture" always mean exactly the same thing. I merely think that the language of publics helps us think about culture differently and that this is important for missiologists.

36. For a helpful discussion related to this, see Howell, "Contextualizing Context," 14.

reading of economics through biblical texts. We witnessed the sacralization of politics in Nazi Germany, the Jim Crow laws in the southern United States, and apartheid in South Africa. Whenever a particular ordering of the world is baptized with religious warrant, it's hard for anyone to argue against it.

Not only does religion mix with publics, but when it does, it can create a violent response. Such is the case when any group draws on the remembered past (how it rehearses history) and interprets its own identity through a selective and privileged reading of Scriptures. The Palestinian-Israeli conflict provides a prime example from both sides. However, it is not just that people interpret official religious texts in a manner that underwrites violence; it is how these official texts combine with unofficial texts, such as local customs, traditions, superstitions, and even myths to elevate one group (and denigrate another).[37] Hence, we do not just need religion but *a specific kind of religion* in order to witness to the public realm.[38]

Let me say one final thing about religion. As we know full well, the public realm can be animated by something best described as a "spirit." We like to think of the public realm in secular terms, but underneath it lie what Max Stackhouse refers to as "principalities," or invisible forces that order the public.[39] He later describes these as "psycho-social-spiritual forces" that exist deeply buried within global societies, and he argues that only religion—and, more so, theology in public spaces—can adequately address these deeper spiritual forces.[40]

Scholars attempt to describe these "psycho-social-spiritual forces" in various ways. Walter Wink does so through the biblical language of powers. His analysis is beneficial if for no other reason than he refuses to "spiritualize" the powers and keep them separate from material aspects of life. Neither does he define the powers solely on the basis of their materiality. Instead he says, "Every power tends to have a visible pole, an outer form—be it a church, a nation, or an economy—and an invisible pole, an inner spirit or driving energy that animates physical manifestations in the world."[41] I would add that not only

37. R. Scott Appleby, *The Ambivalence of the Sacred: Religion, Violence, and Reconciliation* (Lanham, MD: Rowman & Littlefield, 2000), 69.

38. Miroslav Volf offers such a proposal in *Flourishing: Why We Need Religion in a Globalized World* (New Haven: Yale University Press, 2015).

39. Max L. Stackhouse, "General Introduction," in Stackhouse, *God and Globalization*, 1:1–52, here 36–39.

40. *God and Globalization*, ed. Max L. Stackhouse, vol. 4, *Globalization and Grace*, by Max L. Stackhouse (New York: Continuum, 2007), 233.

41. Walter Wink, *Naming the Powers: The Language of Power in the New Testament* (Philadelphia: Fortress, 1986), 5. In a similar way, Hendrikus Berkhof describes the powers as the "framework of creation, the canvas which invisibly supports the tableau of the life of men and society." *Christ and the Powers*, trans. John Howard Yoder (Scottdale, PA: Herald, 1977), 23.

are the powers spiritual and material, but there is constant movement back and forth between the poles.

Max Stackhouse builds on Wink's interpretation of the powers to analyze the spiritual roots behind globalization. Biblical authors use the language of *exousia* (power) more than one hundred times in the New Testament to describe human leaders, along with the "symbolic power of the offices and roles they play in the common life."[42] Stackhouse applies this concept to the underlying spiritual order behind public life, explaining how the powers become demonic when "preoccupied with their own value and declare independence from any transcendent source or norm."[43] We see this whenever publics become exclusionary, toxic, greedy, oppressive, and vulgar. At such times, publics deviate from God's specific "ordering" of the world (which biblical writers refer to as shalom in the Old Testament, or the kingdom of God in the New Testament), giving rise to all kinds of abuses against humans and the rest of creation.[44]

Here is a critical point. It is impossible to witness to the spirituality behind contemporary publics through secular means alone (whether through strategy, science, or technology). We require the resources of religion to address the demonic nature of publics. In the previous chapter, I noted the difference between "thick" and "thin" religion. Stackhouse argues similarly that religion—especially theological ethics in public life—needs to be that which "holds the whole together; it is decisive for shaping the ethos by which the spheres of society may cohere with one another and become coherent, both morally and spiritually."[45] With the words "holds the whole together" and "cohere," Stackhouse appears to be saying that religion contributes an important, integrative role in society. Religion can enter into the thickness of public life to hold things together in a different way.

The task of theological ethics, according to Stackhouse, is to inform and remind the various spheres of public life of their source and meaning in Jesus Christ in a way that reorients them from their destructive tendencies and leads them toward human flourishing.[46] I wonder, however, if this goes far enough. Stackhouse draws heavily on the language of guidance and reconstruction to

42. Stackhouse, "General Introduction," 35.
43. Stackhouse, "General Introduction," 35.
44. Miroslav Volf says, "The modern world, differentiated as it is into multiple and relatively autonomous spheres, is a world of many gods. Each sphere—be it politics, law, business, media, or whatever—imposes its own rules upon those who wish to participate in it." *A Public Faith: How Followers of Christ Should Serve the Common Good* (Grand Rapids: Brazos, 2011), 14.
45. Stackhouse, "General Introduction," 40–41.
46. Stackhouse later says, "The 'spirit' or 'mentality' or 'ethos' of a community can be transformed and renewed by the agency of those who have a calling and work with others

explain such a theological imperative. He does at times use more overt soterio-logical language such as conversion and sanctification to explain how religion engages the publics of globalization but is less explicit about what this looks like.[47] I hope, in the chapters to come, to build on such an important foundation to relate this to the salvation offered to us in Jesus Christ through the Holy Spirit.

Let me now bring all of this to a climax. Despite publics being formed by mixing and interpenetration, I want to show how they can be interpenetrated.

Interpenetration of Thick Publics

Let me conclude this chapter with three examples of the kind of thickness occurring in the public realm. As I stated earlier, my goal is to show how congregations can enter into the open weave of publics, and witness in and through them, via interpenetration. But before we get there, we need to analyze the kind of thickness existing in the public realm.

Back-and-Forth Movement between Public and Private

When I teach on this topic, I usually ask my students, "What is a public?" Someone will invariably answer by saying, "Anything that's not a private." And that is how we typically think of them, but it's not quite true.

Hannah Arendt narrates the history of publics back to ancient Greece, where the private realm related to the domestic condition and the public realm was associated with everything taking place in the polis.[48] However, what appeared self-evident in the ancient world has now become blurred under modernity and, we might add, further complexified under the conditions of globalization. Arendt therefore writes, "In the modern world, the two realms [private and public] indeed constantly flow into each other like waves in the never-resting stream of the life process itself."[49] The language of waves is helpful. We treat private and public as polar opposites, but they constantly "flow into each other" like the mighty billows of the sea.

---

covenantally, by coming to know Christ personally and by the influence of the Holy Spirit in communities of commitment that reach toward holiness." *God and Globalization*, 4:233–34.

47. Stackhouse, *God and Globalization*, 4:194–229.

48. See Hannah Arendt, *The Human Condition* (Chicago: University of Chicago Press, 1958), 28–37. A variety of feminist scholars have subsequently criticized Arendt for the ways her articulation of private-public exploits women and restricts them to the private realm. However, it seems to me that Arendt's fundamental point is that the freedom of the public sphere has historically depended on the private realm, which is now in danger of being entirely lost as the public sphere intrudes on the private (household).

49. Arendt, *Human Condition*, 33.

Let me give an example. Let's imagine that driving home from work, I pass a demonstration happening in my state capitol. It's related to the sensitive topic of immigration. People are out in the streets brandishing placards for and against an upcoming legislative vote aimed at increasing the number of asylum seekers in the country. As I continue driving, the topic is being discussed on public radio, with people calling from their homes to weigh in on the matter. I walk into my house and turn on the television, and media outlets continue the discussion. I hear a university economist talking about the financial implications of immigration; another correspondent cuts to footage of refugees crossing the Mediterranean (while showing the lifeless body of a young child washed up on shore). The broadcast returns to the demonstration happening in the city, with some people shaking fists, while others hold a prayer vigil.

In this illustration, I encounter a *public* demonstration, listen to *public* radio in the *privacy* of my car (with people calling in from the *privacy* of their own homes), and then enter into the *privacy* of my house. Here I see *public* images of immigration: a university professor, a seashore in Greece—but then the stark image of a dead boy (which might be *public* or *private* depending on one's cultural background). The scene ends with a *public* demonstration in my city, along with a *private* prayer vigil.

We experience this on a daily basis. Advances in media technology contribute to the blurring of private and public, where we find public media images constantly streaming into the privacy of homes (even into bedrooms, where people watch television or browse the internet); while people use media conduits such as Twitter, Facebook, and Instagram to project private thoughts, pictures, and videos into the immediacy of everyone else's public. It is not merely that the public realm intrudes on the private realm (which was central to Arendt's concern), but that the private realm is constantly enticed, coaxed, and paraded out into the open. We have become a world of voyeurs, giggling with delight when public persons get their most intimate secrets heralded before the world. We do not really want private and public to stay apart, even though we treat them as rigid binaries.

In the West, we interpret private and public according to Enlightenment maps, defining certain things as public (such as politics, media, and the arts) and other entities as private (such as sexuality, religious beliefs, and family). However, people negotiate them with far greater fluidity than this lets on. For example, politics might appear to be a public category, but sit down in the United States with a complete stranger and broach the topic of an upcoming election, and you will immediately feel the discord—as if you have crossed an invisible line separating public from private discourse. Or try to restrict sexuality to the privacy of bedrooms, and you will see that it does not want to stay there. It wants to go public: into talk shows, headlines, and watercooler discussions.[50] Cultural competence demands we know what kinds of things private and what kinds public should be, and when. That is precisely my point. It's not as if private and public have been destroyed, but rather that people reconfigure them in different ways.

I will resist efforts to define the public realm in contradistinction to the private realm.[51] None of this means they lose their identities—as if in response to the failed dichotomies of modernity we blur them together into one amorphous whole. There continue to be good reasons for talking about public or private[52]—it's just that we need more sophisticated tools than strict binaries allow. It is essential to see them less as binaries and more as "moveable slots" or contested sites that people use to negotiate agency in the world. Ultimately, I will be making the case for the church as a different kind of public in and for the world.

A Plurality of Interpenetrating Publics

Not only is there back and forth movement with public and private, but as we have seen throughout this chapter, publics also mix within themselves. James Davison Hunter explains that "culture—as ideas and institutions—is mixed together in the most complex ways imaginable with all other institutions, not least of which in our own day are the market economy and the state."[53] We see this in everyday life, such as economics mixing with politics,

50. As an example, Birgit Meyer shows how Pentecostalism in Ghana has moved the topic of sexuality from the private to the public domain in response to the tremendous scandals and sexual indiscretions of prominent public individuals. See "Going and Making Public: Pentecostalism as Public Religion in Ghana," in *Christianity and Public Culture in Africa*, ed. Harri Englund (Athens: Ohio University Press, 2011), 149–66, here 158.

51. Elaine Graham explains it this way: "We may be entering a time in which—rather like the boundaries between sacred and the secular—inherited conventions governing the fault-lines between the public and the private are being displaced by new understandings, new practices of everyday life, requiring us to learn a new vocabulary of public and private in relation to self and society." *Between a Rock and a Hard Place: Public Theology in a Post-secular Age* (London: SCM, 2013), 90. She goes on to say that the public and private are being delocalized: they are no longer attached to physical space through the influence of different forms of technology, such that they are "subject to constant negotiation" (91).

52. Indeed, I believe a great disservice has been foisted on Christianity by linking the public realm with science, technology, economics, and politics, while relegating religion to the private sphere. But I should hasten to say that an equally egregious error would be to make religion become utterly public.

53. James Davison Hunter, *To Change the World: The Irony, Tragedy, and Possibility of Christianity in the Late Modern World* (New York: Oxford University Press, 2010), 39.

the military with nationalism, or, as I explained earlier in this chapter, religion with the rest of life. Let me offer an example.

When I teach on this topic, I show students a Beats commercial made for the World Cup in Brazil.[54] It's a great example of thick publics. The commercial begins with music drawing us into a narrative that combines sports culture with Brazilian religious spiritism, accented with celebrity worship, and interlaced with nationalistic fervor. It makes for a powerful story. The commercial opens with a father talking to his son, Neymar, the Brazilian soccer great, telling him how to compete in the World Cup. We see athletes performing all kinds of rituals in preparation for the games—washing socks, writing words on socks—while spectators and fans alike around the world undertake similar rituals. Meanwhile, various nationalistic images are paraded before the screen, and one gets the sense that the entire world is gathering together, unified around a singular event. The commercial flaunts sexuality, toys with superstition, and paints a deeply textured image of spirituality. Yet even as religion occupies center stage, the lyrics of the song paradoxically proclaim, "There ain't no god on the streets." At the end of the video, we return to the father talking with Neymar. He tells his son to wear "the armor of God" (Eph. 6) and says, "God bless you; I love you."

The commercial narrates a compelling message through the medium of mixing. We not only experience the blending of domains (such that sports, celebrity culture, religion, nationalism, and technology overlap) but also experience the mixing of spirituality ("God bless you") with what appears to be anti-religion ("ain't no god on the streets").

We speak of the public sphere in the singular to refer to a common space open to all people.[55] But in reality this one public is made up of a plurality of interpenetrating publics. This is especially the case in the context of globalization, where various texts flow into each other in a spirited dance.

However, mixing is not our normal image of publics. Ever since Max Weber, we've thought of public life through the lenses of discrete value spheres, such as religion, politics, economics, aesthetics, the erotic, and intellectualism. Each of these spheres functions independently of the others. According to Weber, the spheres operate according to their own rationality, and thus boast a measure of independence from the others.

Talcott Parsons expands on Weber's ideas, offering his own theory of social action, arguing that Western societies gave rise to four systems: political,

54. "The Game before the Game: Film Presented by Beats by Dre," YouTube video, 5:03, posted by Beats by Dre, June 5, 2014, https://www.youtube.com/watch?v=v_i3Lcjli84.

55. In reality, the public sphere of the eighteenth century represented a restricted public, accessible only to the bourgeoisie, much in the way that ancient Greece was only open to free men.

economic, social, and cultural.[56] Parsons contends that in highly complex societies, each of these four becomes "differentiated" from the others through processes of self-regulation and boundary maintenance. While Parsons does not mention religion as one of these four systems, Terry Muck takes "differentiation" a step further to show how religion becomes "radically differentiated." Radical differentiation, for Muck, means that religion moves "beyond the compartmentalized, often privatized, differentiated phenomena observed by modern sociologists."[57] Religion is not just a specialized field but can be found within all the other domains.

Let's watch the Beats commercial again. Religion mixes with sports, nationalism, technology, and celebrity culture—while doing so to sell more headphones (economics). The commercial is a good example of the kinds of mixing we experience every day. Scholars will continue to talk about publics as "spheres,"[58] but this should not imply that humans experience any of the domains separately from the others.

Stackhouse likewise argues that we cannot think of any sphere as a closed system. He says that each sphere requires the resources of the others. For as much as politics or economics wants to operate as a totalizing influence in the world, each of the spheres involves the others.[59] For example, Stackhouse says that economic life is shaped not just by politics or new developments in technology but also by "the fact that people fall in love at the factory or office, which alters work habits, and sometimes leads to marriage and families, which further alters both earning and spending patterns."[60] This highlights another reality. We don't just reason publics but embody them. Birgit Meyer explains this as a distinct shift: from understanding publics as cognitive categories to viewing them as embodied entities made up of "shared sentiments and tastes, based on appeals made to senses and emotions."[61] World Christianity has

56. Talcott Parsons, *The Evolution of Societies* (New York: Prentice Hall, 1977).

57. Terry C. Muck, *Why Study Religion? Understanding Humanity's Pursuit of the Divine* (Grand Rapids: Baker Academic, 2016), 67.

58. The language of spheres has been central to the burgeoning field of public theology. Scholars use this terminology to refer to a multitude of publics. In 1981 David Tracy famously postulated three publics, referring to them as church, academy, and society. Others have since added to this number, including economics, media, and politics (and many others).

59. Stackhouse explains, "Each sphere must draw from what is around it; the permeability of each sphere means that each is always influenced by powers beyond itself." "General Introduction," 40.

60. Stackhouse, "General Introduction," 40.

61. Meyer, "Going and Making Public," 156. Meyer argues that publics in Africa are messier than those in the West and that we need to ask of Habermas's model new analytical questions to help flesh out the nature of public life on the continent. Andrew Walls says something similar about the nature of politics (and economics) in Africa: "Our existing theologies of church

known this for a long time. Indeed, it is how I first experienced thick publics in Tanzania. Publics are not just thought of; they are felt.[62]

Our minds alone cannot handle the complexity of the public realm—which is why we don't reason the public realm but navigate it holistically. Some of this happens quite naturally as various domains occupy a common space. But it can also occur with sinister intent. I have already talked about the dangers of religion in society. We also run the risk of economics or politics totalizing everything, where "instead of the political realm being seen as one part of public life, all of public life tends to be reduced to the political,"[63] or where "political life is now the subsystem of a greater economic system."[64] When publics move with totalizing influence into other realms, "they overstep their proper boundaries and cease to function appropriately for the good of society as a whole to the degree that they are made a surrogate for other essential spheres of social life."[65]

While the mixing of domains is a troubling feature in the landscape, let me end on a positive note: to the extent that publics interpenetrate with each other, there is the possibility that they themselves can be interpenetrated with the lordship of Jesus Christ as embodied by a community of believers located in a specific place.

Order and Center

Let me say one final thing about publics. All this talk of publics tugging and pushing in different directions suggests that public life is nothing but a free-for-all. And that is sometimes how the public realm feels. We daily live

---

and state were carved out of the experience of Western Christendom, and were never meant to deal with anything as complicated as networks of political and economic structures that will characterize the twenty-first century." *The Cross-Cultural Process in Christian History* (Maryknoll, NY: Orbis, 2002), 113.

62. Birgit Meyer says, "Looking at how the public sphere operates in practice, it appears as a site of negotiation and struggle, in which different publics claim presence and power, making themselves visible and audible to others through specific aesthetic styles. The point is to explore actual processes and power structures in which publics are formed, so as to find out why and how certain publics become more present and powerful than others, generating tensions between dominant and counterpublics." "Going and Making Public," 157. We find a similar kind of statement from Warner: "When people address publics, they engage in struggles—at varying levels of salience to consciousness, from calculated tactic to mute cognitive noise—over the conditions that bring them together as a public." *Publics and Counterpublics*, 12.

63. Hunter, *To Change the World*, 105.

64. Jürgen Moltmann, "Political Theology in Germany," in Storrar and Morton, *Public Theology*, 37–43, here 41.

65. Deirdre King Hainsworth and Scott R. Paeth, eds., *Public Theology for a Global Society: Essays in Honor of Max L. Stackhouse* (Grand Rapids: Eerdmans, 2010), xii.

amid these realities. They sometimes crash around us like waves of the sea, and other times lull us to sleep like the gentle rains. How do we make sense of it all?

First, overlap and mixing is a natural part of all cultures. It's important to interpret public life as an integrated system made up of many parts rather than as isolated spheres. Mike Rynkiewich defines culture as "a *more or less integrated system* of knowledge, values and feelings that people use to define their reality (worldview), interpret their experiences, and generate appropriate strategies for living; a system that people learn from other people around them and share with other people in a social setting; a system that people use to adapt to their spiritual, social, and physical environments; and a system that people use to innovate in order to change themselves as their environments change." He later explains, "Culture provides for mixing and matching ideas and goods into new configurations that can lead to change in society."[66] Hence, people take in what is available to them (economics, politics, and cultural systems they inherit) and appropriate these resources for themselves, sometimes into "new configurations." For example, humans have long undertaken agricultural development, but through the introduction of new technologies enabling people to harvest and thresh wheat, societies experience changes to economics and dietary practices as well as politics (take, for example, the farm lobby). Changes to one part of a system produce changes throughout. This is how human societies grow.

However, not only do cultures mix, but they insert an "order" into the "integrated system." Let me describe the order of contemporary publics in three distinct ways: as a rhythm, by means of rules, and through an ideology.

RHYTHM

I used to live in Machakos, Kenya. We would travel into Nairobi once or twice a month to purchase supplies we could not get in our city. Machakos is only fifty miles from Nairobi, but to get there one has to drive past countless lories (trucks) heading inland from the port city of Mombasa, and then navigate Nairobi's traffic flows, roundabouts, side lanes (when there are traffic jams), flooded roads after the rains, random police checks, public vehicle strikes, accidents, broken down cars, and other unexpected happenings. One day I was talking with a young Nairobite woman who had grown up in the city. We exchanged pleasantries, and then I asked her, "How do you do it? How do you manage all the chaos, the disorder of Nairobi?" She responded

---

66. Rynkiewich, *Soul, Self, and Society*, 19, 23 (italics added).

with one of the best cultural statements I have ever heard: "I love the order within all of the seeming disorder."

All publics possess an order. That order looks different in different contexts, much like the order of Nairobi appears different from, say, that of Chicago. And, of course, the order of a public can possess a sinister side, much like Nazi Germany or South African apartheid promoted an order that abused certain people. At this point, I am not making any moral ascriptions about the order. I am merely highlighting a fundamental reality of public life. All publics operate with an order, and they mix according to certain principles.

When I asked this young woman about living in Nairobi, the order she referred to was one she learned intuitively from growing up there. She knew where to get vehicles, what to do when the unexpected happened, and who to talk to when there was a problem. Her body had acquired certain rhythms. When I entered the same space, I only saw (and felt) disorder. My actions were not in step with the rhythms around me, and hence I interpreted things as I experienced them, which felt like disorder. But this young woman was in tune with the deeper cadence of public life. Everything made perfect sense to her, even though she admitted it often seemed chaotic. This does not mean she was not frustrated from time to time, even as we in the West get upset when there is an accident causing a traffic jam, or when people step out of the cadences of daily life. And it does not mean that public life always benefited her. I am only highlighting that she indwelt the rhythms of the city.

RULES

We can also think of the order of publics in terms of certain rules that govern their operation. Stackhouse explains, "Each sphere is regulated by customary or legislated rules, and each is defined by its own specification of ends and means, as these accord with the nature of the activity and its place in the whole society."[67] This sounds very rational, and certainly publics function with a sensibility (they are not irrational). But as I explained above, we need to interpret these rules in a broader sense to include what happens through the imagination and the use of the body.

Let me describe this in a specific location. The public of a coffee shop, for example, operates very differently from that of a church. In the latter, we expect to get free coffee and participate in worship and sacrament. While in the former, payment for coffee is required and people come to the location expecting to surf the internet or do schoolwork. If you show up to a coffee shop and see people worshiping, it will undoubtedly create a visceral reaction;

---

67. Stackhouse, "General Introduction," 39.

alternatively, if you come to church and see people undertaking financial transactions, it will likely create a similar response. Publics operate according to certain rules, even if they are not officially codified.

IDEOLOGY

Finally, publics become attached to ideologies to such an extent that the ideology becomes the established "order." At one level, an ideology is a way of organizing human life. However, ideologies can easily become hegemonic.[68] And hegemonic ideologies want to be uncritically accepted. Speaking of this kind of ideology, Alistair Kee says, "An ideology is a shy creature: it does not want to be seen, to be identified, to be named. It would rather that its view of reality were simply taken for granted, without further thought. It rests content if its values and prejudices are simply assumed as too obvious to be contested."[69]

Ideologies lie behind "large" publics such as politics and economics, but no less "small" publics such as sports and bodies. They can relate to topical publics such as a city transport, or notional publics such as a national identity. When people accept an ideology, they interpret the entire world through that ideology. It's not just that we think of economics through capitalism, politics through democratic liberalism, or soccer through Manchester United—but we interpret life outside of those domains through the same ideology. People vote on the basis of their economic ideology or purchase a brand on the basis of their political associations. Ideologies do not just order domains; they want a broader scope of influence. The deeper the ideology, the more virulent its force; the thicker the ideology, the more it interpenetrates all of life. By "thickness" I am referring to the ways the ideologies "are embedded within narratives that often have overlapping themes and within various myths that often reinforce common ideals."[70]

68. Jean and John Comaroff write, "Hegemony, we suggest, exists in reciprocal interdependence with ideology: it is that part of a dominant worldview which has been naturalized and, having hidden itself in orthodoxy, no more appears as an ideology at all." *Of Revelation and Revolution*, vol. 1 (Chicago: University of Chicago Press, 1991), 25. Kevin Vanhoozer describes ideologies as "systems of meaning in the service of power." "What Is Everyday Theology?," in *Everyday Theology: How to Read Cultural Texts and Interpret Trends*, ed. Kevin J. Vanhoozer, Charles A. Anderson, and Michael J. Sleasman (Grand Rapids: Baker Academic, 2007), 54.

69. Alistair Kee, "Blessed Are the Excluded," in Storrar and Morton, *Public Theology*, 351–64, here 352. Later he develops this further: "Ideologies are by definition idealist systems. They generate pictures and images which, far from reflecting social reality, seek to create and maintain illusions which further the interests of those who benefit from the ideology" (359).

70. Hunter, *To Change the World*, 33. In fact, Hunter says this is precisely the way you change culture: "Cultural change is most enduring when it penetrates the structure of our imagination, frameworks of knowledge and discussion, the perception of everyday reality" (42).

One way of knowing of the existence of an ideology is when it bumps up against other ideologies. So, if you are with a group of white men and mention "black lives matter"—what is the response? If there is a visceral reaction, it probably indicates the presence of a deeper ideology within the group. Or post something on Facebook about socialism or capitalism. If people respond emotionally against one of those two words, then it probably indicates they are guided by an alternative ideology. This does not mean that publics are reducible to ideologies. But there is always more happening under the surface. Publics (inclusive of their ideologies) function like a looking glass, revealing the nature of the people. They are not just human products but arise from deeper "powers." We take them wherever we go!

Publics mix on the basis of a certain ordering. I have suggested three possible ways of thinking about their order: as a rhythm, rule, or ideology. One reason for devoting so much time to this is that while all publics possess an order, they long for a center.[71] They are like the Tin Man from *The Wizard of Oz* in a never-ending search for a heart. And that is precisely where local congregations come into play. I will argue that the church is a different kind of public in and for the world. They function with their own rhythms and order based upon the reign of Jesus Christ through the power of the Holy Spirit. The next three chapters will take us deeper into the narrative of Scripture (chap. 3) for understanding what public missiology is (chap. 4), and what this means for how local congregations can witness to public life (chap. 5).

Conclusion

I have defined publics as a common space of togetherness where people participate with one another in life and form opinions through the circulation of different texts. I have drawn on the language of "audiences" to expand this definition, such that publics can be proximate (in a certain location) or meta-topical (stretching out across time and space). My primary point in this chapter is to highlight the thickness of contemporary publics. We like to think of publics in certain ways: as anything nonprivate or associated with one particular domain (such as politics); however, publics are everywhere, and people experience them thickly.

How do we witness to publics? We don't have good answers for that. When I teach on this, I show students the Beats commercial and ask them, "How

---

71. Terry Muck makes this point: "Fragmentation of the social system leads to the loss of an integrating center, which in turn leads to a potential loss of meaning and results in growing existential anxiety." *Why Study Religion?*, 71.

would you witness to the publics of this commercial?" I usually get blank stares. We have been trained to witness to people (and we should never lose that passion!), but we have not been trained to witness to publics, and certainly not to the mixing of publics we experience in everyday life.

Here is my point. Even as publics interpenetrate each other, they can be interpenetrated by the lordship of Jesus Christ embodied within a community of believers located in a place. Even as they operate according to an order, they long for a center. And that is precisely what congregations possess through the different movements of the Trinity.

3

The *Missio Dei*—
a Thick, Public Story

We have faith in the God of paradoxes who, on the jumbled landscape of our broken world, draws straight with crooked lines.

—John Stackhouse, *Making the Best of It*[1]

The Bible does, in some sense, tell an overall story that encompasses
all its other contents, but this story is not a sort of straitjacket that
reduces all else to a narrowly defined uniformity.

—Richard Bauckham, *Bible and Mission*[2]

We live in a complex world. That fact is indisputable from everything
we have seen in the previous chapter. I have referred to that complexity through the imagery of thickness to illustrate how the public realm
arises from the movement of different parts into new wholes. We experience
publics thickly.

1. John G. Stackhouse Jr., *Making the Best of It: Following Christ in the Real World* (New
York: Oxford University Press, 2008), 291.
2. Richard Bauckham, *Bible and Mission: Christian Witness in a Postmodern World* (Grand
Rapids: Baker Academic, 2003), 93.

Here is the problem that lies at the heart of this book. In the face of this complexity, Christians too often counter by retreating into simplistic solutions. The complexity of the public realm, I believe, is one of the primary reasons we fail to witness to publics. Perhaps it is because we focus too much on the individual or believe sin in public places is far too great.[3] Our reticence to witness to publics could also be due to the desire to reduce the swirling complexity of the public realm down to a single domain (such as politics or economics) or else leverage that domain for change to the public realm (e.g., focusing solely on political advocacy or marketplace ministries). Perhaps we fail to witness to the public realm as a result of lingering cartographies of our post-Enlightenment world where we separate everything into simplistic binaries of public-private, secular-sacred. There are many reasons for our hesitation, especially when sin worms its way into publics, resulting in something akin to what Wesley calls "complicated wickedness."

However, I believe the fundamental problem is much deeper than even these reasons suggest. We don't witness to something as thick as the public realm because we possess thin understandings of the mission of God. We have taken something complex (and filled with abundant movement) and made it far too simple (e.g., attempting to keep the pieces static). When this happens, our Christian identity runs the risk of being dangerously thin, influencing how we think about the church and how we participate in God's mission.

In this chapter, I will argue that God's mission offers a thick, public narrative by which to witness to the complexity of the public world. Of course, in talking about complexity I do not mean to imply that God's mission cannot be told simply; or in referring to it as a public story, I do not want to suggest we flee from all things "private." It seems to me that many who are currently championing the outward direction of God's mission do so at the expense of any inward focus. Even though such people challenge the separation of private and public, or sacred and secular, they implicitly reinforce such dichotomies by reacting against the privatization of religion in order to make Christianity become utterly public.

That's not how I read God's mission. I will narrate the story of God's mission through the lenses of movement and how movement results in a thickness of identity. God's mission is thus a complex, public narrative that local congregations inhabit thickly.

---

3. Some of these issues are dealt with in a book I coauthored; see Stephen Offutt, F. David Bronkema, Krisanne Vaillancourt Murphy, Robb Davis, and Gregg Okesson, *Advocating for Justice: An Evangelical Vision for Transforming Systems and Structures* (Grand Rapids: Baker Academic, 2016).

A Public Story "Thickly" Told

Let's begin with stories. Stories are critical for shaping human existence. In the last chapter I explained how the public realm feeds off of different narratives at play within the world. Thus we can only answer the question, What am I to do? if we ask the prior question, Of what story or stories do I find myself a part?[4] We know this to be true in everyday life, even if we struggle to name the stories that define human existence, such as progress, freedom, materialism, and so forth. Many of the most powerful stories that shape public life come laden with invisible ideologies and social imaginaries that privilege some people (or publics) over against others and thus run counter to human flourishing. Stories are not value neutral in the world. They offer us a rendering of truth, but not the whole.

God's mission offers us a different kind of narrative. Lesslie Newbigin contends that "the Bible tells a story that is *the* story, the story of which our human life is a part."[5] Similarly, N. T. Wright explains the Bible as "the story of the whole world. It is public truth."[6] How then does God's story of mission inform all the others?

To begin with, God's mission is public truth. We don't have to make it public, as if needing to tug it forcibly by the arm out into the open. C. S. Lewis says, "Christianity is not merely what a man does with his solitude. It is not even what God does with His solitude. It tells of God descending into the coarse publicity of history and there enacting what can—and must—be talked about."[7] As we shall soon see, God's mission begins with the Trinity and from there moves into creation, including an affirmation of bodies, land, work, power, family, and social relations, and thus subsequently into fields of health, agriculture, economics, politics, and kinship. God's mission thus plunges headfirst into what Lewis calls "the coarse publicity of history."

If God's mission is public truth, it requires humans to share that story as public truth, doing so *in and through our publics*. We cannot privatize it, sacralize it, or relativize it for special places, people, or "just for me." We must believe it, as Newbigin explains, "with universal intent."[8] Which means

---

4. Alasdair C. MacIntyre, *After Virtue: A Study in Moral Theory* (Notre Dame, IN: University of Notre Dame Press, 1984), 216.

5. Lesslie Newbigin, *The Open Secret: An Introduction to the Theology of Mission*, rev. ed. (Grand Rapids: Eerdmans, 1995), 82.

6. N. T. Wright, *The New Testament and the People of God* (Minneapolis: Fortress, 1992), 41–42.

7. C. S. Lewis, "The Founding of the Oxford Socratic Club," in *God in the Dock: Essays on Theology and Ethics*, ed. Walter Hooper (Grand Rapids: Eerdmans, 1970), 128.

8. Building on the work of Michael Polanyi, Newbigin says that nobody believes something really important just for themselves; the nature of belief is always for others as well, or "with

that we believe it for all people, in all places, and for all aspects of public life. Elsewhere Newbigin says, "We have a gospel to proclaim. We have to proclaim it not merely to individuals in their personal and domestic lives. We do certainly have to do that. But we have to proclaim it as part of the continuing conversation that shapes public doctrine. It must be heard in the conversation of economists, psychiatrists, educators, scientists, and politicians. We have to proclaim it not as a package of estimable values, but as the truth about what is the case, about what every human being and every human society will have to reckon with."[9] This also means we must proclaim the gospel through the totality of what it means to be a human in God's world, which implies that if we are publishing it as public truth to science, we do so as people who are part of God's creation; or if to politics, then as political beings. And if we experience publics thickly, owing to the mixing and interpenetration of domains (as we saw in the last chapter), then witness must occur through *being a different kind of public in and for the world*—which invariably means through a thick community.

By all of this, I mean that this public story needs to be thickly told. We cannot reduce it to a few simple principles, like the Four Spiritual Laws; rather, we must narrate it through the fullness of the *missio Dei*. We also must embody it through the whole of our lives. God's mission is not just a philosophical argument we reason with our minds but a story we inhabit with our bodies. Let me say it another way. If Jesus Christ "sums up" this public story and does so through the fullness of his life (such that the apostle Paul says we are "saved through his life" [Rom. 5:10]), then we must witness to Christ through the fullness of what it means to be human in and for God's world. Christ functions as a "new starting point"[10] in human history, which means he reorients all the things arising out of creation, including the use of power, social relationships, economics, and even structures within society "to bring unity to all things in heaven and on earth under Christ" (Eph. 1:10; cf. 3:10).

However, in describing the *missio Dei* as a public story, thickly told, I do not mean to repudiate anything interior to humans, as if in correcting one wrong we inadvertently inflict another. I see subtle (and sometimes not-so-subtle) hints of this among some public theologians, along with contemporary discourses in social justice. People argue for "all things public" at the expense

universal intent." Lesslie Newbigin, *The Gospel in a Pluralist Society* (Grand Rapids: Eerdmans, 1989), 35.

9. Lesslie Newbigin, *Truth to Tell: The Gospel as Public Truth* (Grand Rapids: Eerdmans, 1991), 64.

10. Newbigin, *Truth to Tell*, 37.

of a secret, inward faith.[11] However, for Israel, fidelity to God (described as "circumcision of the heart") was always to be lived in public, external ways. Likewise, the internal confession of faith for the early church gave rise to external realities, such as how they cared for widows and orphans.[12] Now, one could argue that the internal life God intends is but a far cry from the privatized faith of Western individualism, and that would certainly be true. But it's hardly helpful to argue for public engagement by means of movement away from interiority. God's mission does not ask us to do that.

As I explained in the previous chapter, I want to argue that private and public represent less fixed, binary poles and more "moveable slots" that people use to give agency to the world. Hence, God's mission lies less in demarcating public from private, inward, domestic, or secret (whatever word we choose— and biblical writers draw on a variety of words) and more in cultivating fluid, back-and-forth movement across all the spaces of the cosmos.

Movement and Thickness

Movement results in a thicker narrative. And that's what we have in the *missio Dei*. It would be nice if we could wrap up this public story into a nice little box, tied with a bow on top, enabling us to take it wherever we go. But there is a problem with simple stories: they tend to be *thin* stories, and thus become easy prey to dominant narratives in the world, such as nationalism, tribalism, global capitalism, and progress.[13] To be fair, most people do not intentionally set out to tell God's mission thinly. It happens whenever we reduce all the twists and turns of Scripture to one dominant theme (such as forgiveness of sins) or force the text around a prevailing cultural assumption (say, individual freedom). Indeed, forgiveness of sins and personal freedom are critical story lines within God's mission, but a thin reading of Scripture reduces God's mission to static story lines, rather than cultivating a thickness through movement. Simple stories tend to be thin stories, and thin stories struggle to interpenetrate the thickness of the world.

11. For a good treatment of this, see Jonathan Malesic, *Secret Faith in the Public Square: An Argument for the Concealment of Christian Identity* (Grand Rapids: Brazos, 2009).

12. It might be preferable to use the language of personal-social rather than private-public to avoid some of the cultural associations with these words, but somehow "public" proves more helpful than "social," as it implies a much bigger entity, filled with overlapping elements inclusive of imaginative import.

13. Richard Bauckham notes the danger of assimilating either global capitalism and/or Western views of "progress" into the story of God's mission; see *Bible and Mission: Christian Witness in a Postmodern World* (Grand Rapids: Baker Academic, 2003), 90–91.

By way of contrast, Richard Bauckham narrates God's mission through a complex assortment of movements.[14] One might say it's the thickest story of all. To unpack this complexity, Bauckham narrates the *missio Dei* as a movement from particularity to universality, but without ever leaving particularity behind.[15]

According to Bauckham, the mission of God begins with particularity (seen in Adam then Abraham, Israel, and ultimately Jesus) in order to include the gentiles and thus people all around the world.[16] He outlines three specific dimensions of that movement. The first is *temporal*, in which God's mission moves from past to present by constantly rehearsing the past and translating it into the present. Bauckham shows how Israel, exile, and Pentecost are not aspects of God's mission we leave behind, but neither are we bound to the past as if by some preconditioned destiny.[17] We "remember!"—as Scripture constantly admonishes—but in a way constantly open to God's future. Second, Bauckham discusses the *spatial* dimension as a movement from "the centre to the periphery, or from Jerusalem to the ends of the earth."[18] God's mission thus begins in a garden, moves to a specific city (Jerusalem), and eventually makes its way around the world, leading to a universal, eschatological kingdom. The kingdom of God is constantly retranslated into new locations.[19] Finally, Bauckham talks about the movement of the *people* themselves: "Mission is a movement that is always being joined by others, the movement, therefore, of an ever-new people."[20]

14. Bauckham, *Bible and Mission*, esp. 90–94.

15. Bauckham, *Bible and Mission*, 15–16.

16. Bauckham says, "The Bible is a kind of project aimed at the kingdom of God, that is, towards the achievement of God's purposes for good in the whole of God's creation. This is a universal direction that takes the particular with the utmost seriousness. Christian communities or individuals are always setting off from the particular as both the Bible and our own situation defines it and following the biblical direction towards the universal that is to be found not apart from but within other particulars. This is mission." *Bible and Mission*, 11.

17. Bauckham explains temporal movement as going backward to the past in order to interpret the present: "We are always figuratively starting again from Jerusalem on our way to the ends of the earth. We are always starting again from Jesus who is the one human for all others, and we are always starting again from Pentecost, the event that gives birth to the new community on its way to the new future." *Bible and Mission*, 21.

18. Bauckham, *Bible and Mission*, 14. What might appear as a linear movement from one specific location to the global church might be further nuanced if we consider recent developments with world Christianity, such that we are now seeing previous centers (places such as Antioch, Rome, and even London) becoming the margins while the margins (such as those in the global South) are becoming the new centers of Christianity.

19. In contrast to Islam, "Christianity . . . has throughout its history spread outwards, across cultural frontiers, so that each new point on the Christian circumference is a new potential Christian centre." Andrew F. Walls, *The Missionary Movement in Christian History: Studies in the Transmission of Faith* (Maryknoll, NY: Orbis, 1996), 22.

20. Bauckham, *Bible and Mission*, 15.

Because God's mission is about movement, it weaves a thick narrative in the world. Bauckham identifies the goal of movement in God's mission as "the gathering of all particulars into the one kingdom of the one God."[21] Hence, he speaks of it as a unified story told through multiple threads, doing so from a diversity of angles. "The plurality of angles on the same subject matter," he explains, "disrupts any expectations of a single perspective for the reader to adopt unproblematically. Rather we are encouraged to view the same events from varying perspectives."[22] In talking about the complexity, Bauckham does not suggest God's mission is a free-for-all in interpretation. Rather, he says, "The Bible does, in some sense, tell an overall story that encompasses all its other contents, but this story is not a sort of straitjacket that reduces all else to a narrowly defined uniformity."[23] In a similar manner, I would argue that particularity unsettles the pretensions of universality, while universality draws particularity into a thicker whole.

What does this mean for public witness? First, I will show how the movement of the different parts within the *missio Dei* cultivates a thick narrative. Second, I will explain how God uses that thickness to witness to all of God's world.

Public Missiology and the *Missio Dei*

Through the remainder of the chapter, I will narrate some of this thick, public story. I don't do it as a biblical scholar, and the lenses I will be using will be more theological than biblical, similar to how Kevin Vanhoozer utilizes doctrines to provide "theatrical direction" for God's theodrama.[24] I want to show that God's mission utilizes movement: within the Trinity, into creation and humanity, and ultimately through the back-and-forth movement of pieces being woven together into a thicker whole—for the redemption of the entire world and the flourishing of all things under God's reign.

The Trinity and the Missio Dei

God's mission begins with the Trinity. The God of mission is no thin, singular divinity, but a thick oneness revealing himself through movement.

21. Bauckham, *Bible and Mission*, 16.
22. Bauckham, *Bible and Mission*, 92.
23. Bauckham, *Bible and Mission*, 93.
24. Kevin Vanhoozer highlights the dramatic performance of Scripture, with God as the playwright and director, the Bible as script, doctrines as theatrical directions, and humans as the actors/actresses on their unique stages all around the world; see *The Drama of Doctrine: A Canonical-Linguistic Approach to Christian Doctrine* (Louisville: Westminster John Knox, 2005).

Within this thick oneness, we find an openness that makes room for the diversity of others. Hence, it might be possible to describe the Trinity in terms I have been using in this book, as a togetherness but with large spaces in it, or as integrated persons who, through eternal back-and-forth movement of sending-receiving, represent a thick divine community of love. This entire book revolves around such a point. Movement of the divine persons leads to a thickness of community, and in that thickness, others are invited to participate through love. Everything else builds on such a foundation.

A trinitarian God calls the world into existence. The world is public because God chose to allow the "interiority" of Father, Son, and Holy Spirit to be made known publicly in the world.[25] Hence, the starting point for talking about the public realm must begin with God.

THE PUBLIC SIGNIFICANCE OF THE TRINITY

Speaking of the Trinity as public truth is a tall order in this day. For those of us living on this side of the Enlightenment, it is hard to grasp the public significance of any aspect of theology, let alone when dealing with the Trinity. We have not been trained that way. We think of the Trinity as a private, theoretical doctrine—not as public truth, embodied within society.[26]

However, that is not the way it should be. All of creation bears the characteristics of God's triune nature. We see the fingerprints of the divine community throughout the entire world, and God fashions humans, the pinnacle of creation, as image-bearers, whose very identity relates to imaging God in and for the flourishing of the world. Any talk of public witness must begin with faithfulness to imaging God through the Trinity. "If that is true," Jürgen Moltmann explains, "then we [as humans] correspond to God not through domination and subjugation but through community and relationships, which further life. It is not the solitary human subject who is God's image on earth; it is the true human community."[27] Here we find the theological basis for local congregations, who witness to the public realm through the movements of Father, Son, and Holy Spirit.

25. Miroslav Volf speaks of the perichoresis as "the reciprocal *interiority* of the trinitarian persons." *After Our Likeness: The Church as the Image of the Trinity* (Grand Rapids: Eerdmans, 1998), 209.

26. For a good treatment of the public significance of the Trinity, see Lesslie Newbigin, "The Trinity as Public Truth," in *The Trinity in a Pluralistic Age: Theological Essays on Culture and Religion*, ed. Kevin J. Vanhoozer (Grand Rapids: Eerdmans, 1997), 1–8.

27. Jürgen Moltmann, "The Destruction and Healing of the Earth," in *God and Globalization*, ed. Max L. Stackhouse, vol. 2, *The Spirit and the Modern Authorities*, ed. Max L. Stackhouse and Don S. Browning (New York: T&T Clark, 2001), 166–90, here 175.

However, rather than faithfully imaging God's trinitarian nature, humans make God in their own image. For Western societies, this means endorsing *thin* forms of divine unity to support individualism, or *static* notions of hierarchy to sanction monarchial authority. We project our cultural predispositions back onto God. For example, by stressing God's thin singularity, we authorize Western forms of individualism. The unitarian God thinks of itself as the only reality in the world. Or as Newbigin explains, "In this way of thinking, the autonomy of the individual self is the highest value, and the business of politics is to safeguard and extend this individual freedom against the pressures of the collective."[28] Alternatively, static forms of difference also envision community, but arranged in a hierarchy. According to Moltmann, this configuration represents the heritage bestowed on Western Christianity.[29] When the Trinity is arranged as a hierarchy, it sanctions authoritarian forms of leadership.[30] This allows us to rationalize human governance on the basis of God's monarchial nature, endorsing singular rulers: whether males over females, kings over servants, one-party politics, patron-client relationships, or the ubiquitous "senior pastor" syndrome found in many of our churches.

The doctrine of the Trinity confronts both individualism and authoritarianism at their core. Neither thin singularity nor static hierarchy faithfully represents the God of mission. Both aberrations feed on half-truths by neglecting any movement between the divine persons, and thus implicitly or explicitly sanctioning public ills meted out on the world.

Movement within the Trinity

To counter these errors, we need to examine movement within the Trinity. I will argue it is hard to maintain thin forms of unitarianism or static forms of monarchial hierarchy while stressing movement between the divine persons. The former (unitarianism) rejects all movement (viewing God as a singular monad), while the latter (monarchial hierarchy) only considers movement downward (from a lofty authoritarian figure to the rest of society). What then does movement look like within the Trinity? Let me offer a few examples. My purpose is to show *how* congregations witness to the publics, and to do so, we need to start with the theological basis for congregations: the Trinity.

28. Newbigin, "Trinity as Public Truth," 5.

29. See Jürgen Moltmann, *The Trinity and the Kingdom: The Doctrine of God* (Minneapolis: Fortress, 1993), 191–222.

30. Moltmann says, "The fusing of biblical and cosmological monarchism gave rise to the notion of the single, universal pyramid: the one God is creator, Lord and possessor of his world." *Trinity and the Kingdom*, 193.

Radical Differentiation

First of all, movement within the Trinity involves something taking place *between* the persons. This is similar to what Terry Muck refers to as "radical differentiation" (where religion is seen within all the other domains).[31] To draw on this analogy, we could refer to the Trinity as "radical differentiation": the persons interpenetrate each other, but without losing their distinct identities. Volf says, "All [persons] mutually permeate one another, though in so doing they do not cease to be distinct persons."[32] The Father does nothing independently of the Son and the Holy Spirit. Each of the persons is *radically present* with the others and *radically differentiated* from the others. We may refer to this as "differentiated unity," or even triunity. Steve Seamands says, "Triunity means that divine unity is not absolutely undifferentiated unity but differentiated unity, not simplistic unity of mathematical integers but the complex unity of divine persons."[33] In the language of this book, I am calling it "thick oneness."

Internally and Externally

Another way of conceptualizing movement within the Trinity is by integrating the *immanent* and *economic* Trinity. *Immanence* refers to what the Trinity is like internally with the community of persons, while the word *economic* explains how the divine community acts externally in human history. While these notions are helpful for noting internal and external differences, we cannot separate one from the other. Movement internally within the divine community goes out externally into the entire world.[34] "Publicness" arises fundamentally from the internality of the persons of the Trinity. And to the extent this is true, it provides local congregations with the theological basis for a robust public missiology.

Giving and Receiving

A more organic way of exploring movement involves delving into the dynamics of giving and receiving within the divine community. This way of looking at things takes us deeper into the dynamic nature of divine love. The

31. Terry C. Muck, *Why Study Religion? Understanding Humanity's Pursuit of the Divine* (Grand Rapids: Baker Academic, 2016), 69.

32. Volf, *After Our Likeness*, 209.

33. Steve Seamands, *Ministry in the Image of God: The Trinitarian Shape of Christian Service* (Downers Grove, IL: InterVarsity, 2005), 112.

34. Scholars use the language of processions to refer to what happens internally and the language of missions to speak of that external to the Trinity. Rather than thinking of them as separate, we need to understand them as belonging together.

Greek word *perichōrēsis*, as noted earlier, relates to the "reciprocal interiority of the Trinitarian persons,"[35] where Father, Son, and Holy Spirit indwell each other through active movement. Some scholars interpret *perichōrēsis* as "making room for" the other persons. In other words, the persons do not overlap or bump up against each other but give and receive through eternal movement. There is an "open weave" within the divine community that makes room for others.

Giving and receiving is critical in these discussions, as it involves a different economy of power. As I explained earlier, Moltmann contrasts static hierarchical predispositions, found within Western societies, with more organic, communal understandings of the Trinity.[36] The persons relate to one another through constant giving and receiving. Douglas Meeks says, "There can be no simple notion of self-possession because God is a community in which persons find their distinct identities in mutual relationships of self-giving."[37] Or as David Cunningham explains it, "It is of the very nature of God's power to be in a constant state of donation, always turned out from itself, always giving and forgiving, always *producing* the world."[38] This is a helpful insight for the remainder of this chapter. Movements between the persons of the Trinity result in the creation of the world. And if this is true for the Trinity, we must later reflect on how the church reflects the inner life of the Trinity through its public witness, sowing seeds of new creation into the present.

Sender, Being Sent, and Sending Power

We find in the Trinity not only giving and receiving but also sending. As Timothy Tennent explains, "From the opening chapters of Genesis, . . . we are confronted with a personal God who is *not silent*, a God who *acts*, and a God who *sends*."[39] Sending is intrinsic to the divine community. The Father is the sender, the Son the one sent, and the Holy Spirit the sending power. Internal sending among the persons of the Trinity gets played out externally in the world. We see this most notably in the New Testament, as the Father sends the Son (John 3:17; 5:36; 6:57; Gal. 4:6); the Father and Son send the Holy Spirit (John 14:26; 15:26; Acts 2:33); and the Father, Son, and Holy Spirit

35. Volf, *After Our Likeness*, 209.
36. Moltmann, *Trinity and the Kingdom*, 197.
37. M. Douglas Meeks, *God the Economist: The Doctrine of God and Political Economy* (Minneapolis: Fortress, 1989), 111.
38. David S. Cunningham, *These Three Are One: The Practice of Trinitarian Theology* (Malden, MA: Blackwell, 1998), 144 (italics added).
39. Timothy C. Tennent, *Invitation to World Mission: A Trinitarian Missiology for the Twenty-First Century* (Grand Rapids: Kregel, 2010), 105.

send the church into the world (Matt. 28:19–20; John 17:18; 20:21; Acts 1:8; 13:2–3).[40] It is for such reasons that Moltmann says, "It is not the church that has a mission of salvation to fulfill in the world; it is the mission of the Son and the Spirit through the Father that includes the church, creating a church as it goes on its way."[41]

Thickness within the Trinity

If each of these snapshots of movement within the persons of the Trinity is faithful to what we know of God's nature, then we may probe the extent to which the movements of the persons thicken the divine community. The Puritans used to say, "God is, within Himself, a sweet society."[42] Meanwhile, David Cunningham describes the Trinity as "a complex network of relations."[43] In fact, one may refer to the Trinity as the first institution in the world, if by an institution we mean "stable structures of social interaction."[44] Who God is relates to what God creates and, further, how God accomplishes his mission in the world.

Theologians draw on a range of imagery to express *how* movement within the divine community thickens identity, from freedom (Moltmann) to participation (Cunningham) to communion (Zizioulas) to love (Wesley). I will not take the time to analyze the differences, except to point out that each of these represents an attempt to capture something of dynamic complexity: the persons of the Trinity relate to each other thickly, with the result of accomplishing God's mission in and for the world.

Throughout the remainder of this section, I will show how movements found within the Trinity (and its ensuing thickening) play out in the grand unfolding of the *missio Dei*.

Movement within and around Creation

Let's begin with creation. The internality of God spills out into the created world. He is the author of the public realm.[45] Thus we need to stop and listen to the rhythms of God's mission as evidenced within the creation account in

---

40. Seamands, *Ministry in the Image of God*, 161.

41. Jürgen Moltmann, *The Church in the Power of the Spirit: A Contribution to Messianic Ecclesiology* (London: SCM, 1977), 64.

42. Tennent, *Invitation to World Mission*, 78–79.

43. Cunningham, *These Three Are One*, 20.

44. Volf, *After Our Likeness*, 235.

45. Tennent says it this way: "The Trinity is not merely a metaphysical puzzle that concerns a few erudite theologians; it is the lens through which reality is finally understood and exposed." *Invitation to World Mission*, 175.

order to properly witness to the public realm. In the last chapter, I described something of the "rhythm" and "order" of publics. We can speak in such ways because of how God created the world. Publics thrive on rhythm and order. The rhythm and order found in creation correspond with how God uses movement. Let me explore three dimensions of this movement within the creation account: (1) bringing together and keeping apart, (2) diversity-in-unity, and (3) fruitfulness.

BRINGING TOGETHER AND KEEPING APART

God creates the world through simultaneous movements of "bringing together" and "keeping apart."[46] The cosmos does not fuse together into some amorphous whole but bears the characteristics of God's shalom. Cornelius Plantinga says, "In a shalomic state each entity would have its own integrity or structured wholeness, and each also possess many edifying relations to other entities."[47] Everything exists in relation to the other parts of creation, but without infringing on the integrity of the parts. We might say there is an open weave within creation. God creates certain things to come together (e.g., fish require water; plants need sunlight; humans depend on oxygen). Meanwhile, other things are kept separate, lest we end up with confusion (sun and earth require optimal distance from each other; too much water in relation to land causes flooding; too much land in relation to water leads to drought). Ephraim Radner explains it this way: "God separates, or literally 'divides' light and darkness, waters and earth (firmament), day and night (stars) (Gen. 1:4, 6, 14) and *through this division he creates what is 'good.'*"[48]

Biblical writers describe the bringing together and keeping apart through the language of "drawing lines" or "establishing boundaries" (e.g., Job 38:10). And God accomplishes it through the persons of the Trinity. Or as Moltmann explains, "The Word specifies and differentiates. The Spirit joins and forms the harmony."[49]

---

46. Cornelius Plantinga explains, "So God begins to do some creative separating: he separates light from darkness, day from night, water from land, the sea creatures from the land cruisers. God orders things into place by sorting and separating them." He continues, "At the same time God binds things together: he binds humans to the rest of creation as stewards and caretakers of it, to himself as bearers of his image, and to each other as perfect complements—a matched pair of male and female persons who fit together and whose fitting harmony itself images God." *Not the Way It's Supposed to Be: A Breviary of Sin* (Grand Rapids: Eerdmans, 1995), 29.

47. Plantinga, *Not the Way It's Supposed to Be*, 10.

48. Ephraim Radner, *A Brutal Unity: The Spiritual Politics of the Christian Church* (Waco: Baylor University Press, 2012), 428 (italics added).

49. Moltmann, "Destruction and Healing," 177.

Diversity-in-Unity

A similar way of looking at movement is to understand how God's shalom requires differentiation and harmony. The Trinity is a triunity, or "differentiated unity." As I have explained, who God *is* results in *what* God creates and, as I hope to show later, *how* God redeems. "Thick oneness" within the triunity is shared with the created world; hence, we should not be surprised to see complexity within creation (and later within publics). In fact, the greater the diversity within creation, the stronger the ecological frame. God creates "each according to its own kind" (Gen. 1:11, 12, 21, 24, 25), allowing the particularities of individual organisms to nourish a thick order we call the planet Earth. As organisms become extinct or biodiversity wanes, the entire earth suffers. For "nature abhors monoculture. It thrives on diversity."[50]

Diversity within creation is perfectly ordered by God. Before the entrance of sin in the world, there was no domination, competition, or disintegration in the ways the different parts of creation fit together. Organisms gave and received within a dynamic, integrated ecosystem. Complexity is thus part of God's created design. God's diversity-in-unity in the Trinity is shared liberally with creation's diversity-in-unity. As the different parts come together into a thicker whole, all of creation prospers.

Fruitfulness

This leads to the final aspect of movement, which happens to be the part we enjoy the most: fruitfulness. God does not just create but allows the various parts of creation to create more life. Waters teem with fish. Animals proliferate. Andy Crouch explains that when God declares "let there be" in Genesis 1, he "makes room for more being, for more agents who can utter their own 'let there be.'"[51] God unleashes fruitfulness and delight into the created world.[52]

Fruitfulness emanates from the movements we find in the Trinity, and subsequently from similar movements seen in the created world. Dynamic giving and receiving sows seeds for fruitfulness in the world. Crouch continues, "The

50. Howard A. Snyder with Joel Scandrett, *Salvation Means Creation Healed: The Ecology of Sin and Grace* (Eugene, OR: Cascade, 2011), 223.

51. Andy Crouch, *Playing God: Redeeming the Gift of Power* (Downers Grove, IL: IVP Books, 2013), 32.

52. Cornelius Plantinga defines shalom as "*universal flourishing, wholeness, and delight*—a rich state of affairs in which natural needs are satisfied and natural gifts fruitfully employed, a state of affairs that inspires joyful wonder as its Creator and Savior opens doors and welcomes the creatures in whom he delights." *Not the Way It's Supposed to Be*, 10. Plantinga acknowledges borrowing this definition from Nicholas Wolterstorff, *Until Justice and Peace Embrace* (Grand Rapids: Eerdmans,1983), 69–72.

Creator is not seeking a world full of pets, individually domesticated animals bred to be attentive to their human masters. He delights in wildness. Swarming and teeming are part of what makes the world good—the overflow and excess of life."[53] God blesses creation. We might interpret God's blessing as generative power entrusted to creation that causes all life to flourish.[54] And when he blesses everything, God declares everything "good."

Movement within and around Humanity

Movement is not just shared with creation but overflows to humanity. Bringing together and keeping apart, diversity-in-unity, and fruitfulness all help inform what it means to be human, in the image of God (Gen. 1:26–27). As with creation, it is imperative to listen to the deeper rhythms of what God is doing in and around humans, in order to help us understand what it means for human communities to witness to and for the public realm.

Why is this so? The public realm arises from the agency of humans *with* creation, *under* God. Humans nurture their powers (received from God) into the open weave of creation, giving rise to work, family, economics, politics, technology, and many other public domains. Hence, if publics arise from God's image, then it is imperative to understand how human imaging relates to the flourishing of all things under God's rule.

BRINGING TOGETHER AND KEEPING APART

First, God creates humans by bringing together as well as keeping apart. What is true in creation is also true of humanity. Adam and Eve belong together, and they belong together with the rest of creation. God gifts creation to humans (e.g., Gen. 1:29) and tells man it is not good for him to be alone (2:18). Bringing together thus lies at the heart of God's mission, which is why we use words such as *integration* and *holism* to describe God's mission. However, humans do not just belong together but are ontologically distinct from the rest of creation, with each person being discrete from the others. Particularities need to be celebrated (and protected) lest they become ignored, dominated by others, or amalgamated into one amorphous whole.[55] Without

---

53. Crouch, *Playing God*, 33.

54. Richard Bauckham says, "Blessing in the Bible refers to God's characteristically generous and abundant giving of all good to his creatures, and his continual renewal of the abundance of created life." *Bible and Mission*, 34.

55. Cornelius Plantinga explains, "The image of pollution suggests bringing together what ought to be kept apart. To pollute soil, air, or water is to blend into them foreign materials—machine oil, for example—so that these natural resources no longer nourish or delight very

the twin actions of bringing together and keeping apart, we "become split selves, not differentiated souls, attacking within ourselves and in other people the very dignity God bestowed with the *imago*."[56]

To guard against this, Miroslav Volf shows what the simultaneous actions of "separating-and-binding" mean for human identity: "The human self is formed not through a simple rejection of the other—through a binary logic of opposition and negations—but through a complex process of 'taking in' *and* 'keeping out.' We are who we are not because we are separate from others who are next to us, but because we are *both* separate *and* connected, *both* distinct *and* related; the boundaries that make our identities are both barriers and bridges."[57] Public witness must uphold the dignity and rights of each person while bringing all the particularities of persons together into a thicker whole.[58] And if this is true for how people relate to each other (and creation), it is likewise true for how we interact with publics, and further how we witness within and for the public realm.[59]

POWER AND FRUITFULNESS

Throughout this section, I have intimated at power language within the image of God. Now, let me be explicit. Biblical writers borrow the "image of God" from the ancient Near Eastern practice of a king erecting an image of a deity within a particular land. They then draw on this cultural practice, creating parallels between what kings in the ancient Near East do and what God accomplishes through human vice-regents.[60] The image of God is un-

---

well. Similarly, the introduction of a third lover into a marriage or an idol into the natural human relation to God adds a foreign agent to them; it corrupts those entities by addition." *Not the Way It's Supposed to Be*, 45.

56. *God and Globalization*, ed. Max L. Stackhouse, vol. 4, *Globalization and Grace*, by Max L. Stackhouse (New York: Continuum, 2007), 151.

57. Miroslav Volf, *Exclusion and Embrace: A Theological Exploration of Identity, Otherness, and Reconciliation* (Nashville: Abingdon, 1996), 66.

58. Speaking of this, John G. Stackhouse Jr. says, "Let us not be romantic but realistic and acknowledge that cultivation of diversity is inefficient, or at least more costly in time, effort, and attention. . . . God has so arranged the world, that is, that we actually need a certain amount of diversity just to avoid going wrong, let alone to help us go more and more right." *Making the Best of It: Following Christ in the Real World* (New York: Oxford University Press, 2008), 327.

59. Max Stackhouse explains, "But in a complex, differentiated civilization, religion becomes a crowning synthesis of meaning, an ordered reminder in the midst of many spheres of existence that they are all under an ultimately unifying reality that can be named." *God and Globalization*, 4:154.

60. D. J. A. Clines says it this way: "In Genesis, therefore, humanity takes the place of God on earth, a point that becomes clearer if we adopt the suggestion that Genesis 1:26 should not be translated 'in our image,' but 'as our image, to be our image' (understanding the preposition *beth* as the *beth* of essence)." "Image of God," in *Dictionary of Paul and His Letters*, ed.

doubtedly a dignity entrusted to all humans. But it's also a responsibility, and thus a power![61] Humans do not passively represent God's image but actively *image* God back into the open weave of creation. By doing so, they orient everything back to God; or as Gerhard von Rad says, "Thus man's creation has a retroactive significance for all nonhuman creatures; it gives them a new relation to God."[62]

If this is true for the natural world (land, trees, and animals), then it is likewise the case for the publics arising from human imaging: such as work, family, and culture, along with domains such as politics and economics, and thus also for the overlapping "togetherness" of contemporary publics. Humans are gardeners, not only with regard to the land but also with regard to the public realm; our "powers" orient all of creation back to God.

Why talk about power? I was teaching on this subject several years ago and asked my class if power is redeemable. Most of the students nodded, but one young woman shook her head. She approached me after the class session to explain how she had suffered miserably under the authority of oppressive leaders and thus found it hard, if not impossible, to see any redemptive use of power. We see many such instances in our world today. When dealing with the public realm, however, we don't need less emphasis on power but more—but of a certain kind. As I will explain later, God's kingship (evidenced primarily in the ordering of power within the Trinity) is the only thing powerful enough to hold publics together. The greater the diversity of the parts, the greater the strength required to maintain cohesion. If the public realm is, as I explained in the last chapter, formed by the interpenetration of publics, such that it feels as if everything were splintering into a million pieces, then God's mission calls us to be gardeners not only of creation but of everything arising from creation. And that requires a different kind of power.

Humans, made in the image of God, are entrusted with derivational powers. These powers flow from the inner life of the Trinity. God blesses male and female, commands them to be fruitful and to rule, and instructs them to name the animals (Gen. 2:20). As Walter Brueggemann says, "The image of God in the human person is a mandate of power and responsibility. But it is power exercised as God exercises power. The image images the creative use

---

Gerald F. Hawthorne, Ralph P. Martin, and Daniel G. Reid (Downers Grove, IL: InterVarsity, 1993), 426–28, here 427.

61. Crouch says, "And image bearing is for power—for it is the Creator's desire to fill the earth with representatives who will have the same kind of delighted dominion over the teeming creatures as their Maker." *Playing God*, 35.

62. Gerhard von Rad, *Genesis* (Philadelphia: Westminster, 1961), 60. We see this later in Romans, where Paul talks about how "creation waits in eager expectation for the children of God to be revealed" (8:19).

of power which invites, evokes, and permits."[63] As indicated above, power in the image of God can best be expressed through the imagery of gardening. Humans function as gardeners within the world of creation (and publics),[64] doing so in a manner that "is spacious, open, and deeply participatory, in which identities are interdependent and mutual."[65]

BLESSINGS

A final way of looking at movement is through the imagery of blessings. I have learned more about blessings living in Africa than any other place. The cosmology of the entire continent operates on an "economy of affection" positioned for the flourishing of life. Whether walking through a field, visiting someone in the hospital, or exchanging greetings while traveling along a path, all of life relates to blessings. And blessings are for life!

We see blessings throughout the creation account. In chapter 1 the text reads, "God blessed them [Adam and Eve] and said to them, 'Be fruitful and increase in number; fill the earth and subdue it. Rule over the fish in the sea and the birds in the sky and over every living creature that moves on the ground'" (Gen. 1:28). Blessing relates to fruitfulness, not just for humans but for the interconnectedness of life (shalom). Then, after the flood, God once again blesses humans, commanding them, "Be fruitful and increase in number and fill the earth" (Gen. 9:1). Blessings move *from* God *into* human life and *for* the fruitfulness of the entire earth.

No passage captures the essence of blessings quite like Genesis 12. God calls Abraham and Sarah from a distant country and settles them at the crossroads of the nations. There he blesses them and makes them a blessing to the surrounding nations. Let's examine three brief submovements within this passage. First, blessings involve a movement into Yahweh, where Abram trusts God and it is credited to him as righteousness (Gen. 15:6). Second, God tells them to physically move. Blessings are dependent on Abraham and Sarah departing from their land, extended family group, and ethnic belonging—in other words,

---

63. Walter Brueggemann, *Genesis*, Interpretation (Louisville: Westminster John Knox, 1986), 32.

64. John Stackhouse, speaking of publics, uses the imagery of gardening to show what this looks like: "Each sector of society, and the groups and individuals within those sectors— whether education, health care, government, business, or the arts—maintains a central concern to improve the earth, to garden the world, to increase shalom—and will therefore welcome and cooperate with others who have the same concern." *Making the Best of It*, 231.

65. Dwight Zscheile, "Forming and Restoring Community in a Nomadic World: A Next Generation Perspective on the Future of the Discipline of Missiology," *Missiology* 42, no. 1 (January 2015): 26–38, here 29. He cites Jürgen Moltmann, "Perichoresis: An Old Magic Word for a New Trinitarian Theology," in *Trinity, Community, and Power: Mapping Trajectories in Wesleyan Theology*, ed. M. Douglas Meeks (Nashville: Kingswood, 2000), 111–25.

from all the building blocks of social identity. Finally, blessings involve Israel being inserted into the open weave of the nations around them. Election, the law, and the covenants were given to Israel from God in order to be shared freely with the other nations. Christopher Wright depicts Genesis 12 as the reversal of Babel. In Genesis 11 the builders of the city gathered and sought to make a great name for themselves; in Genesis 12 God says to Abram: "I will make your name great" (v. 2) and "all peoples on earth will be blessed through you" (v. 3).[66]

In the Old Testament, blessings proceed from God to humanity, and if into humanity, then to all the things that arise from human agency, such as culture, institutions, systems, and other societal elements. When God forms the nation of Israel, he blesses them, nurturing them into a thick community and locating them on a land bridge in order to bless the nations. Hence, as we will soon see, Israel's thickness, inclusive of family systems, public laws, and social institutions, but no less private mores, codes of conduct, and domestic arrangements, was the very means to witness to the nations.[67]

Back-and-Forth Movement within the *Missio Dei*

Let me show how movement plays out in the remainder of the *missio Dei*. This is to say, who God is and how God creates provide the very basis for how we, the people of God, participate in God's mission. Eventually, all of this gives birth to the church: a diverse, thick community that witnesses to the fullness of the world through faithfulness to the movements of the persons of the Trinity.

To make this claim, we first need to break down many of the rigid dichotomies of the Enlightenment. The mission of God can be told through back-and-forth movement. However, unlike other kinds of back-and-forth movement that remain fixed in one place (such as with a seesaw or a game of ping-pong), God's mission moves outward into the world through back-and-forth movement.

Back-and-Forth Movement between Internals and Externals

To narrate movement, let me begin with internals and externals. As I explained earlier, the internality of the persons of the Trinity gives rise to the externality of the world, and thereafter to the redemption of the entire cosmos,

---

66. Christopher J. H. Wright, *The Mission of God: Unlocking the Bible's Grand Narrative* (Downers Grove, IL: IVP Academic, 2006), 202.

67. Walter Brueggemann says, "Yahweh is not some universal idea floating above Israel. Yahweh is a concrete practice in the embodied life of Israel." *Theology of the Old Testament: Testimony, Dispute, Advocacy* (Minneapolis: Fortress, 1997), 701.

helping us interpret how human communities should witness to the publics of this world.

All throughout God's mission, internal things go external (public), and external things move internal. This back-and-forth movement opposes all efforts to privatize the faith, while critiquing contemporary tendencies to make the Christian faith utterly public (lacking any internality). We need to interpret God's mission in more dynamic ways than simplistic binaries allow. God's mission is complex because of the movements of the persons of the Trinity, and this movement gets played out in the pages of Scripture.

What does such movement between internals and externals look like in the *missio Dei*? At the conclusion of his *Theology of the Old Testament*, Walter Brueggemann argues for a fluid relationship between internality and externality in relation to Yahweh. He says, "The testimony of Israel concerning Yahweh is always of two kinds, one to reorder *the internal life* of the community in ways faithful to Yahweh, the other to invite *the world out beyond* this community to reorder its life with reference to Yahweh. Both enterprises are preoccupied with the recognition that the acknowledgment of Yahweh at the center of life (the life of Israel or the life of the world) requires a reordering of everything else."[68] This lies at the heart of a public missiology. Yahweh orients Israel's internal life (often referred to as circumcision of the heart), which subsequently shapes external realities, such as how Israel governs, practices justice, cares for the land, and treats strangers, widows, orphans, and the poor; and these external expressions function as a means for Israel to "invite the world beyond this community to reorder its life with reference to Yahweh," resulting in a thicker internal ordering (inclusive of the nations), and the cycle continues.

It is common for us today to think of witness in terms of a private faith shared with individuals in a private setting. But for Israel witness was always an external (public) reality, drawing on the resources of how Yahweh reorients "the internal life of the community."[69]

Yahweh informs *every aspect of life*. In Deuteronomy 6, God reveals how back-and-forth movement between different aspects of life orients Israel to God, and thus to the world. The passage begins with Yahweh telling Israel

---

68. Brueggemann, *Theology of the Old Testament*, 747.

69. Chris Wright explains how the law was never meant as "a compendium of moral teaching to enable the individuals to lead privately upright lives before God. . . . For God's purpose . . . was not to invent a production line for righteous individuals, but to create a new community of people who in their social life would embody those qualities of righteousness, peace, justice and love that reflect God's own character and were God's original purposes for humanity." Christopher J. H. Wright, *Old Testament Ethics for the People of God* (Downers Grove, IL: InterVarsity, 2004), 51.

how the love of God is to permeate all aspects of Israel's humanity: heart, soul, and strength (v. 5). From there, God's love was to enter internal (or domestic or private) and external (or public) places in the world. Yahweh tells the Israelites, "Impress them [these teachings] on your children. Talk about them when you sit at home and when you walk along the road, when you lie down and when you get up. Tie them as symbols on your hands and bind them on your foreheads. Write them on the doorframes of your houses and on your gates" (vv. 7–9). It is notable that the passage ends with the mention of gates, where people in the ancient Near East governed, made laws, tried people in courts of law, and undertook financial transactions. God's love moves back and forth between all aspects of life.

We see a similar movement elsewhere in the Old Testament. In the book of Proverbs, Lady Wisdom calls out in the public square. She shouts from the top of the wall, speaks to the people from the gates, and climbs to the highest point in the city—all public places (Prov. 1:20–21; 8:3; 9:3). What is her message? She says, "Let all who are simple come to my house" (Prov. 9:4). In this instance, public witness is about welcoming people to the internality of Lady Wisdom's home.[70] We see similar back-and-forth movement later as the Israelites are marched off to Babylon (Jer. 29:4–7). Jeremiah tells them to settle down, build houses, plant gardens, and have children (all activities revolving around domestic spaces), and then pray for the city, seek its peace and prosperity (all things with public significance). In the case of Proverbs, public witness invites people to the "privacy" of Lady Wisdom's home, while in Jeremiah domestic activities intermingle with public witness.

At the beginning of the New Testament, God does the unthinkable. He enters into the internality of human existence, through a single Jewish family, in order to redeem everything from the inside out. However, what begins in relative secret goes public in the most remarkable ways. Angels herald Jesus's birth. Wise men come to worship him. Herod attempts to kill Jesus. It's not just highly visible, public personalities who change the world, but, perhaps more so, those who arise in secret, quiet places. Jesus calls together a community of disciples and, with them, recapitulates everything in the world: taking what is already there and turning it inside out to reveal the really real. The incarnation is not just the story of a singular human but involves turning everything in the world to God. Andrew Walls refers to this as "conversion." He explains that the incarnation does not add to or take away from

---

70. It is interesting to note that Lady Folly also sits atop the highest point of the city and bids travelers to come into her home (Prov. 9:14–15).

humanity, but "conversion is the turning, the re-orientation, of every aspect of humanity—culture-specific humanity—to God."[71]

The incarnation lies at the heart of the redemption of publics. It is not the intrusion of something from the outside (like a colonial imposition) but the weaving of the inner life of the Trinity into all human spaces.[72] It is the essence of what I am calling "thick humanity." And if God himself enters into the open weave of human life through the incarnation, he redeems not only internal, spiritual aspects of existence but also public, material parts.

We see this in Jesus's life. He begins (in what we call his *public* ministry) by announcing, "The kingdom of God has come near!" In the West, we have spiritualized (and privatized) our interpretation of the kingdom of God, but for Jews living in first-century Palestine, "kingdom" carried explicit connotations of living under the occupancy of the Roman Empire.[73] The term *kingdom* has overt sociopolitical meaning.[74] With Jesus there is a new King in the land.[75] However, Jesus was never content to allow the kingdom to serve just external sociopolitical meanings but calls people back to internal realities, such as how they think (Matt. 5:22, 28) and what they treasure in their hearts (Matt. 6:21). We need back-and-forth movement between internality and externality. The language of kingdom pertains to all "spaces" within the cosmos. It points us to where all of life is heading: "to bring unity to all things in heaven and on earth under Christ" (Eph. 1:10).

Jesus moves fluidly between internality and externality. On the one hand, he condemns the public ways the Pharisees give, pray, and fast, telling the disciples, "Be careful not to practice your righteousness in front of others to be seen by them" (Matt. 6:1). When Jesus cautions them not to "be seen" by others, he uses the Greek word *theathēnai*, which is where we get our English

71. Walls, *Missionary Movement*, 28. Walls goes on to say, "Conversion is not the substitution of something new for something old (in the great act of translation into humanity, Christ took nothing away from humanity made in God's image); nor the addition of something new to something old (in the great act of translation, Christ added nothing *to* humanity as made in God's image)."

72. This is especially the case if we interpret Jesus's life through the Holy Spirit. See Gerald Hawthorne, *The Presence and the Power: The Significance of the Holy Spirit in the Life and Ministry of Jesus* (Eugene, OR: Wipf & Stock, 2003).

73. Despite these political considerations, it would be a mistake to interpret the kingdom of God solely as a political construct. It is political, but more broadly relates to the lordship of Jesus Christ within all aspects of life.

74. Richard Mouw says, "The New Testament's use of the political term 'kingdom' to describe the sum of God's redemptive purposes indicated that the total transformation of all things which he intends for his creation includes a transformation of the political realm as well as other realms." *Political Evangelism* (Grand Rapids: Eerdmans, 1973), 24.

75. See N. T. Wright, *How God Became King: The Forgotten Story of the Gospels* (New York: HarperOne, 2012), for a great treatment of this oft-neglected reading of the Gospels.

word *theater*. Jesus is telling the disciples not to dramatize their religiosity out in the open for public praise. Instead, he commands them to practice their righteousness in secret (Matt. 6:4, 6, 18). On the surface, this sounds like a "private" faith, except that in the previous chapter Jesus tells them to "let your light shine before others, that they may see your good deeds and glorify your Father in heaven" (Matt. 5:16). Later in the Sermon on the Mount, he says, "Thus, by their fruit you will recognize them" (Matt. 7:20). On the one hand, Jesus teaches the disciples, "It is what comes out of a person that defiles them" (Mark 7:15). On the other hand, he teaches that external actions matter. He says, for example, "Now that you know these things, you will be blessed if you do them" (John 13:17).

There is no internality that does not go public and no public truth that does not require inward reordering. It is not a matter of choosing between the two but a matter of how the two serve each other. Secret faith guards people from flaunting their religiosity for public praise, while public faith pushes people out into the open, where the kingdom of God orients all aspects of life.

Why is this important? Enlightenment interpretations of private and public largely color how we interpret Christ's life. If we think of the public realm as dirty, we will retreat into a private faith, interpreting Christ's salvation in such a way to fit this privatized existence: focused on his deity, cross (to cleanse sins), and resurrection (as a means of escaping the "world"). If our concern lies with the public realm, we will prioritize Jesus's humanity, along with the political or economic significance of his salvation. People who read the Gospels accordingly will move into societal issues, yet at the expense of internal realities, avoiding things like individual salvation or holiness.[76] Both means of interpreting private-public read Enlightenment dichotomies back onto the text. The former spiritualizes Jesus, lifting him out of the context of first-century Palestine like some Gnostic vapor and thus applying salvation only to the future. The latter focuses on Jesus's earthly life and thus reads the Gospels through contemporary economic or political ideologies, giving them a decidedly "this-wordly perspective."[77] Neither of these approaches faithfully images the salvation offered by Christ. The former turns a public

---

76. Scot McKnight chronicles a similar distinction of "camps"; for him the difference lies in how Christians interpret the reign or rule of God. See *Kingdom Conspiracy: Returning to the Radical Mission of the Local Church* (Grand Rapids: Brazos, 2014). It is also critical to see the public significance of holiness. For a good treatment of this, see Morna Hooker and Frances Young, *Holiness and Mission: Learning from the Early Church about Mission in the City* (London: SCM, 2010).

77. For a good, healthy critique of those who would interpret New Testament "empire" language to fight modern-day ideological battles, see Scot McKnight, ed., *Jesus Is Lord, Caesar Is Not: Evaluating Empire in New Testament Studies* (Downers Grove, IL: IVP Academic, 2013).

truth into a private reality, while the latter hijacks public truth to fight modern ideological battles.[78] We need not choose between internal or external faith. The gospel moves readily between them.

Ultimately, Jesus dies a public death. He stands before all earthly and cosmic rulers and defeats all their hatred and jealousy with a love that is sourced from the internality of the Trinity. Jesus then commissions the church through the sending of the Holy Spirit. As we saw earlier with Israel, the church orders its internal life around the nature of God (through the Holy Spirit) and witnesses to the rest of the cosmos by inviting the entire world (inclusive of publics) to likewise order its life around God's nature. This is the theological basis for a public missiology of the local congregation.

Back-and-Forth Movement between Scattering and Gathering

However, movement does not just take place internally and externally but proceeds, as Bauckham explains, from particularity to universality, but without ever leaving particularity behind. Biblical writers refer to this movement from particularity to thick universality through the language of scattering and gathering.

We see this in the creation account. God creates the entire cosmos through bringing together (gathering) and keeping apart (scattering). He pulls everything into a thicker whole while blessing everything for growth and fruitfulness within a never-ending cycle of gathering and scattering.

Yet there are dangers. Too much gathering and we have the Tower of Babel, where the nations join together in their arrogance and independence from God's rule to "make a name for [themselves]" (Gen. 11:4). As a result of those attempts to gather outside of God's kingship, "the nations are made to receive 'scattering,' exposed displacement, just as Israel's worst negation is the scattering from which it is always being gathered."[79] Similarly, too much scattering and we have "everyone [doing] as they saw fit" (Judg. 17:6). People frantically clutch at anything that provides them the slightest hints of a durable, eternal center—whether ethnicity, religion, wealth, or military strength.

How does God redeem the world? In a manner similar to how he creates: through gathering and scattering.

---

78. N. T. Wright says something similar; see *How God Became King*, 167. We are all guilty of reading our own cultural assumptions into the text. It is impossible to look at anything without some kind of cultural distortion. I only highlight this here because it shows a danger (befalling both camps) when we talk about the publicness of the gospel. "Public" can easily become a way of interpreting Christ that gives warrant to our own reading of Enlightenment cartographies.

79. Brueggemann, *Theology of the Old Testament*, 494.

For example, after scattering Adam and Eve after they sinned, God blesses Noah and his family. He tells them to scatter in a different manner: to "be fruitful and increase in number and fill the earth" (Gen 9:1). Later, after God scatters the nations after the Tower of Babel, he gathers them together into a new community. God calls Abram and Sarai from the farthest corners of the world and tells them to move to Canaan, where he blesses them for the blessing of the surrounding nations. God's mission thus is not linear, told from one location to another as if in a straight line, but zigzags across the entire landscape, expanding as it moves. Or, as John Stackhouse explains, "We have faith in the God of paradoxes who, on the jumbled landscape of our broken world, draws straight with crooked lines."[80]

Scattering unsettles the pretensions of idolatrous forms of gathering: God is not just for the Israelites but for all families on the earth; meanwhile, gathering (inclusive of the nations) nurtures a thicker form of scattering: as public witness within the fullness of our world.

We see this all throughout the Old Testament. The law was not just for Israel but for the nations (Deut. 4:6), while the law oriented all aspects of life around Yahweh: inclusive of economics, politics, land, social codes, and treatment of the poor, widows, orphan, and stranger in your midst.

Later in the New Testament we see the scope of gathering and scattering expanding further, where the Holy Spirit descends on Jew and gentile alike, and the new community witnesses as a new, public reality. The Holy Spirit descends on the disciples in Jerusalem, and they begin speaking the tongues of the surrounding nations (Acts 2:1–12). But rather than being divided or splintered by the languages, the Holy Spirit draws them together into a new, thicker whole, where "all the believers were together and had everything in common" (Acts 2:44), reorienting the ways they undertook economics, family, and social activities (Acts 2:45–47). Gathering is a good thing. It is not just physical gathering but includes all the publics associated with humanity, under Christ, and by the Holy Spirit. Cycles of gathering and scattering would continue to thicken the early church's witness for many years as a result of persecution, and Luke poignantly explains, "Those who had been scattered preached the word wherever they went" (Acts 8:4).

Whenever we choose one over the other, we encounter dangers. When it's gathering (as we are prone to do), we risk universalizing our own cultural forms of gathering as exclusionary—just for ourselves. When we privilege scattering, however, we risk becoming utterly public—relativizing the faith and losing Christ as the center. When this happens, we attach ourselves to

80. Stackhouse, *Making the Best of It*, 291.

other centers, such as ideologies of nationalism or economics. Back-and-forth movement unsettles the pretensions of exclusivist forms of gathering, while cultivating thicker forms of gathering within and for the redemption of the entire world.

Back-and-Forth Movement between Heaven and Earth

One last type of movement we find in the mission of God integrates heaven and earth. All throughout Scripture, God heals the divide that sin has ruptured between God and humans. In the Old Testament, the tabernacle and temple are the places where heaven and earth are brought together. With the incarnation, Jesus unites them in his person. He commands us to pray, "Your kingdom come, your will be done, on earth as it is in heaven" (Matt. 6:10). Ultimately, the resurrection is a sign of a new heavenly reality with this world, and the church of Jesus Christ is a foretaste of that new reality in the present.

It is because of this new reality that Paul says to "set your hearts on things above, where Christ is, seated at the right hand of God" (Col. 3:1). Similarly, the writer of Hebrews explains the great faith of men and women of old by virtue of their "longing for a better country—a heavenly one" (Heb. 11:16). Public missiology is profoundly eschatological: we are constantly living the in-breaking of the kingdom in the present. As N. T. Wright explains, "Easter is about the wild delight of God's creative power."[81] All of life changes with Christ's resurrection. It enables us to move fluidly between the realms: we carry the future kingdom of God into the present, while living the present in a way that will last for all eternity. Public missiology is constantly moving back and forth between the realms. Wright describes it this way: "What you *do* in the present—by painting, preaching, singing, sewing, praying, teaching, building hospitals, digging wells, campaigning for justice, writing poems, caring for the needy, loving your neighbor as yourself—*will last into God's future*."[82] The church witnesses to the public realm through back-and-forth movement. The more movement between the realms, the greater the thickness.

From Thick Humanity to Public Witness

Let me conclude this chapter by briefly reflecting on how God is using thickness as told through the *missio Dei* to lead to public witness.

---

81. N. T. Wright, *Surprised by Hope: Rethinking Heaven, the Resurrection, and the Mission of the Church* (New York: HarperOne, 2008), 255.
82. Wright, *Surprised by Hope*, 193 (italics original).

Trinitarian Witness

I began this narrative by explaining various aspects of movement within the divine community. I made the argument that who God is helps us understand what God is accomplishing in the world. Movement between the persons of the Trinity (understood in terms of giving and receiving or dynamic love or Sender, the One Sent, Sending Power) enables us to know how to image God in and for the world. I also explained how this movement allows us to speak of the Trinity as "a complex network of relations," or a thick divine community.

Thickness within the Trinity has an open weave that invites others and indeed leads to the creation of the entire world. "The trinitarian circle of Father, Son and Holy Spirit is therefore an open, not a closed, circle."[83] It always makes room for others and is world-producing.

If this is who God is, and how he is redeeming the entirety of the world, then it stands to reason that the same should orient our ecclesiology.

Witness through the Church

What does this mean for the church? First, congregations receive their identity and mission from the divine community, which means they image the movement of the divine persons in and for the world. Local congregations are thus the image of the Trinity.[84] This means that the church must faithfully image God's self-giving love within the internal life of the community.

Second, the internality of the local congregation needs to be shared openly with the public world. In the same way that movement within the persons of the Trinity leads to the creation of the world, the church is a different kind of public inserted into the world for the purposes of world construction. We are gardeners of God's creation, which must include publics.

Witness in and for the Coming Kingdom

We like to play with Enlightenment dichotomies as if they were fixed categories, but back-and-forth movement breaks down the binaries of the small,

---

83. Seamands, *Ministry in the Image of God*, 12.

84. Lesslie Newbigin says, "The salvation of which the Gospel speaks and which is determinative of the nature and function of the Church is—as the very word itself should teach us—a making whole, a healing. It is the summing-up of all things in Christ. It embraces within its scope the restoration of the harmony between man and God, between man and man and between man and nature for which all things were at the first created. It is the restoration to the whole creation of the perfect unity whose creative source and pattern is the unity of perfect love within the being of the triune God. It is in its very essence, universal and cosmic." *The Household of God: Lectures on the Nature of the Church* (1953; repr., Eugene, OR: Wipf & Stock, 2008), 140.

insecure Enlightenment cosmos and introduces us to a much larger cosmology, filled with movement (as we are seeing presently from all the tremendous gifts received from world Christianity). All around the world we are discovering new insights into God's mission from congregations that move fluidly between what Western Christians interpret as fixed binary poles. They move back and forth between heavenly and earthly realms, between internal and external realities, and they nurture greater thickness of identity through the means of movement.

Jesus teaches us to pray with fluid movement between heaven and earth, telling his disciples to say to God, "Your kingdom come, your will be done, on earth as it is in heaven" (Matt. 6:10). He announces the in-breaking of the eschatological kingdom of God and applies it to all facets of life, reorienting economics, ethnic identity, and family relations, while speaking to Pilate regarding the true nature of power (John 19:11). He then forms a community whose very identity is to witness to the in-breaking of the kingdom of God in the here and now, and through all parts of its humanity, and for all aspects of God's created world: as a "servant, witness, and sign of the kingdom."[85]

Scripture ends with a vision of "a new heaven and a new earth" (Rev. 21), intimating the eternal durability of the public realm. A city descends from heaven laden with public imagery: gold, jewels, gates, and streets. The eschatological city includes a garden, with direct implications for our eternal connectedness with the publics of creation. Central to this new heaven and new earth is the proclamation early in the passage, where a voice from the throne declares, "Look! God's dwelling place is now among the people, and he will dwell with them. They will be his people, and God himself will be with them and be their God" (v. 3).

Conclusion

In this chapter I have offered a retelling of the *missio Dei* through the lenses of movement and thickness of witness. It is not an all-inclusive hermeneutic. God's mission resists any efforts to be packaged into a convenient whole. Nevertheless, what I have described here provides a faithful representation of what God is accomplishing through the pages of Scripture.

Why is this important? Public missiology is birthed from God's mission as described in the narrative of Scripture. It is not a private, spiritual message

---

85. Lesslie Newbigin, *Foolishness to the Greeks* (Grand Rapids: Eerdmans, 1986), 117.

but a thick, public story that local congregations inhabit through the entirety of our humanity.

We encounter so much complexity in the world, or "complicated wickedness," and erroneously think the problem is with the complexity. Meanwhile, God is weaving his own thickness into the world through local congregations who embody God's own thick triune community.

In the next chapter I will explain what I mean by public missiology, and then in the following chapter I will describe how movement within and around local congregations enables them to witness to the public realm. So let's first define public missiology.

4

What Is Public Missiology?

It is surely a fact of inexhaustible significance that what our Lord left behind Him was not a book, nor a creed, nor a system of thought, nor a rule of life, but a visible community.

—Lesslie Newbigin, *The Household of God*[1]

The church exists always as an integral part of human life in the world; it is interwoven always with public life in society and community; it should be aware of and interested in the resulting impact in both directions—the impact of public life on the church, its place, social form and self-understanding and also the impact of the church on public life and the many spheres that together constitute life in the world.

—Dirkie Smit, "Notions of the Public and Doing Theology"[2]

What is a public missiology,[3] and why does it matter for living within all the overlapping complexity of public life? I define public missiology as *congregational witness that moves back and forth across all "spaces"*

1. Lesslie Newbigin, *The Household of God: Lectures on the Nature of the Church* (1953; repr., Eugene, OR: Wipf & Stock, 2008), 27.
2. Dirkie Smit, "Notions of the Public and Doing Theology," *International Journal of Public Theology* 1, no. 1 (2007): 431–54, here 441.
3. I should state up front that there is no agreed-upon definition of public missiology. Our public missiology working group is developing its own framework, which you can see in the appendix. My work is narrower in scope and focused primarily upon a public missiology of the local congregation.

of public life in order to weave a thickness of the persons of the Trinity for the flourishing of all of life. Hopefully by now a few of these themes will be familiar to the reader.

I began this book by walking the reader through a complex assortment of reasons why we need a public missiology. I highlighted the separation of theology from public life during the Enlightenment. I then explained how theology separated from mission. I described the thickness of overlap found within contemporary publics and how this thickness is sourced by an implicit spirituality. Finally, I sought to show how our current diet of individualistic, technological problem-solving strategies struggles to interpenetrate the swirling complexity of public life.

I will now propose a better way. Let me briefly contrast different kinds of complexity we experience in the world: good forms and bad forms. I will then explain how public theology arose and how it relates to public missiology. I will then offer a proposal for a public missiology of the local congregation to show how we can leverage thickness for public witness.

Good and Bad Forms of Thickness

Thickness is not a "good" or "bad" thing—as if we could simply assign a moral value to it and either embrace it as a friend or fear it as a villain. Thickness arises from movement, and movement has always been a primary feature of human experience within the world.

I do, however, see the good in some forms of thickness. Take, for example, my children. Both of them are biracial. They have lived in four countries on three continents. They are United States citizens, but they self-identify through a unique mixture of the elements composing their narrative. They would be the first to tell you they're not sure what this means. At times they identify by the color of their skin (such as when I heard my daughter talking to a "mixed" friend about how "white girls go to Starbucks"); other times they self-identify through their global citizenry, such as when questioning the ways things are done in America. In some instances they bring a particular aspect of their history into the foreground, such as my daughter using British English, or my son asking if he can get a tattoo of a Kenyan flag. In other cases they reveal characteristics of living in Kentucky. All of these various elements, and the flows between them, make it hard for my kids to say who they are, which is perfectly understandable given the diversity of pieces. What my children experience is increasingly the reality for people around the world.

Several years ago, a student asked if she could have lunch with me. She shared with me her story. This young woman, South Korean by birth, had lived extended periods in five countries covering three continents. It was a long, beautiful narrative with many twists and turns. At the end of her self-disclosure, she paused and asked, "Who am I?" I must admit I was caught off guard by her question and immediately thought of my kids and how they might ask a similar question. I didn't have good answers for her. Who could? But I remember telling her that once she figured it out, the result was going to be profoundly thick and incredibly beautiful.

This is the good side. Movement produces a thickness of identity. And that thickness, such as we saw in the last chapter, possesses the ability to generate incredible fruitfulness in the world. What God is accomplishing through movement in the *missio Dei*, we are presently seeing all around us. Kwame Appiah refers to it as "cosmopolitanism," which he explains as "universality plus difference."[4] The world is thickening. And such thickening has the ability to generate incredible fruitfulness within all of life.

However, there is another side of thickness. Not all thickness is dense and beautiful. It also can be deceitful and alluring, and this gives rise to what Wesley refers to as "complicated wickedness."

We swim within a sea of publics hitting us from every direction. Just open your favorite social media site. Messages tug and pull from all sides. Or walk through a mall during Christmastime, and you are tossed and turned within a sea of advertisements. The interpenetration of different domains thickens the appeal. Images define beauty according to some airbrushed ideal, while multinational companies court our constant allegiance, and a host of digital friendships stoke our ego by their constant "likes." There are no neutral spaces in the world. Publics communicate through a mixture of cognition and affection, while doing so through images, symbols, and myths. As they thicken movement, so they entice. We navigate the thickness every day of our lives. It's like walking into a colorful, open-air market with vendors pulling us toward them from all sides. Publics constantly evangelize us.

Hence, thickness in contemporary life is an enormous power struggle. Birgit Meyer explains, "Looking at how the public sphere operates in practice, it appears as a site of negotiation and struggle, in which different publics claim presence and power, making themselves visible and audible to others through specific aesthetic styles."[5]

4. Kwame Anthony Appiah, *Cosmopolitanism: Ethics in a World of Strangers* (New York: Norton, 2006), 151.
5. Birgit Meyer, "Going and Making Public: Pentecostalism as Public Religion in Ghana," in *Christianity and Public Culture in Africa*, ed. Harri Englund (Athens: Ohio University

We experience this all around us. "Complicated wickedness" is not a puzzle to be solved but something we need to witness to through the fullness of the gospel. And we need to do so through different kinds of movement in the world, or what I have described as thick witness.

Public Theologizing within and for Public Spaces

Let me suggest a better way. I propose we need to move beyond a focus on solutions and strategies to deep-seated theologizing taking place *within* and *for* public spaces. This shifts any focus from the actions of individuals to community, from "secular" strategies to a trinitarian back-and-forth movement across all spaces of the cosmos (refusing to polarize sacred from secular), and thus from thinness to thickness of witness. Let me highlight how public theology helps us find a better way, and then use that foundation to unpack my definition of public missiology.

What Is Public Theology?

Theology has always been related to public realities. As we saw in the last chapter, the love of God (Deut. 6:4–9) was to be located in public spaces (such as the gates of the city). While for the early church, theology was tightly connected with wisdom and thus inseparable from public life.

The Enlightenment changed all of that. I will not take the time to rehearse how the arrival of the Enlightenment severed theology from the public realm, except to acknowledge it did. Public theology has since arisen as a discipline within heavily secularized contexts as a means of overcoming the old dichotomies that separated theology from animating public life.

Martin Marty is widely recognized as the first person to coin the term *public theology*. He used it in the context of civil religion in the mid-1960s. Since that time, many other theologians have found in public theology a return to theological engagement within and for public life.[6] David Tracy would be the first to map out different public audiences, which he refers to

Press, 2011), 157. She goes on to explain, "The point is to explore actual processes and power structures in which publics are formed, so as to find out why and how certain publics become more present and powerful than others, generating tension between dominant and counterpublics."

6. For a helpful historical development of the term, see H. Harold Breitenberg Jr., "What Is Public Theology?," in *Public Theology for a Global Society: Essays in Honor of Max L. Stackhouse*, ed. Deirdre King Hainsworth and Scott R. Paeth (Grand Rapids: Eerdmans, 2010), 3–17.

as academy, society, and the church.[7] Others have subsequently named other publics, including specific public domains, such as politics, economics, and media. No authoritative definition of public theology exists. However, most public theologians would at least find some affinity with describing it as "theologically informed descriptive and normative public discourse about public issues, institutions, and interactions, addressed to the church or other religious body as well as the larger public or publics, and argued in ways that can be evaluated and judged by publicly available warrants and criteria."[8]

Public theology, I propose, helps in those areas where individual solutions-driven responses are weakest. Public theology begins with a theological reading of the cosmos, critiquing the ways publics become unfettered from God's shalom, while doing so *within* specific communities and especially *by* and *for* the people most affected by sin in public spaces. Hence, public theology is not a technique or strategy; it is rather "an apologetics of presence,"[9] or a way of living with "soft difference" in the world.[10]

Scholars attempt to map out the different types of public theologies: those focusing on the writings of key theologians; those offering a descriptive account of the theological activity arising out of a particular context; and those constructing a normative guide for how theology should function within public life.[11] All three types share common concerns: they are rooted in specific contexts; they are sensitive to justice issues (with a bias toward action), with a desire to critique society; and they want to speak in language accessible to the public realm. Let me briefly explain each of these characteristics.

CONTEXTUALITY

First, public theology is deeply rooted in specific contexts. Martin Marty understands public theology as located within the everydayness of life, shifting the focus away from any preoccupation with speculative concerns.[12] Max

7. David Tracy, *The Analogical Imagination: Christian Theology and the Culture of Pluralism* (New York: Crossroad, 1981), 3, 5.

8. Breitenberg, "What Is Public Theology?," 5.

9. Elaine Graham, *Between a Rock and a Hard Place: Public Theology in a Post-secular Age* (London: SCM, 2013), chap. 7.

10. Miroslav Volf, *A Public Faith: How Followers of Christ Should Serve the Common Good* (Grand Rapids: Brazos, 2011), 93. He describes *difference* as "to divert without leaving." Elsewhere he refers to it as "soft difference." Volf, "Soft Difference: Theological Reflections on the Relation between Church and Culture in 1 Peter," *Ex Auditu* 10 (1994): 1–29.

11. This is similar to the three types of public theology proposed by Breitenberg, "What Is Public Theology?," 11–12.

12. Martin Marty, *Public Church: Mainline, Evangelical, Catholic* (New York: Crossroad, 1981), 98–99.

Stackhouse describes the fundamental nature of public theology as "descriptive, empirical, and indicative," as opposed to "prescriptive, speculative, or imperative."[13] Public theology's embrace of contextuality can be attributed to a range of factors, but especially liberation theology's long, hard pull toward praxis, along with postmodernity's embrace of social location, or what Elaine Graham describes as the "impossibility of a neutral, disembodied and detached subject."[14]

Until recently, public theologies have focused on confronting the lingering effects of modernity in the world.[15] Hence, the publics that scholars engage arise out of a context in which religiosity is branded as private or even toxic to public life. By emphasizing social location, public theologians provide a timely response, moving from theology's previous preoccupation with private belief to one of public truth located within the vicissitudes of life; or, as Graham says, "from a world-view premised on objective, pure reason to one of reflexivity and contextuality."[16]

Public theologians thus focus on the local, while attempting to marry it with the universal. Max Stackhouse combines these, bringing together the universals associated with globalization and a robust focus on the contextual nature of theology. This allows him to speak of "common" values found within all contexts around the world, while embracing "highly sophisticated contextualisms."[17] Likewise, Dirkie Smit reveals three distinct strands of public theology, one addressing the "normative vision underlying contemporary democratic life,"[18] the second focused more generally upon serving humanity (i.e., justice efforts),[19] while the third narrows the emphasis to specific issues within discrete publics.[20]

With the rise of world Christianity, public theologians are becoming more diverse than ever, broadening the scope of contextual issues to include those arising from within global publics. What began with Western scholars challenging the privatization of religion has grown to global voices doing theology

13. Max L. Stackhouse, *Apologia: Contextualization, Globalization, and Mission in Theological Education* (Grand Rapids: Eerdmans, 1988), 35.
14. Graham, *Between a Rock and a Hard Place*, 106.
15. As I will explain later, we have recently witnessed the rise of public theologies from the majority world, expanding the scope of contextual matters—helping us focus not just on secularity, or modernity, but on other issues of relevance to global scholars, such as the environment, poverty, ethnicity, and engagement with world religions.
16. Graham, *Between a Rock and a Hard Place*, 106.
17. See esp. Stackhouse, *Apologia*, 158.
18. Smit, "Notions of the Public," 443–45.
19. Smit, "Notions of the Public," 445–46.
20. Smit, "Notions of the Public," 446.

within and for their own contexts.[21] Some of the most exciting developments within public theology are currently taking place in global locations, with recent articles in the *International Journal of Public Theology* dealing with pertinent issues arising from South Africa, Brazil, Indonesia, and the Caribbean (to name just a few).[22] Hence, global public theologies offer insightful perspectives into new relationships between private-public, sacred-secular, along with highlighting important theological categories often neglected in the West, such as power dynamics, suffering, and human relationship with land and the rest of creation.

JUSTICE AND SOCIETAL CRITIQUE

Second, from its concern for context, public theology reveals a strong orientation to issues of justice, especially as experienced by vulnerable communities, such as women, the poor, and minority populations. Sebastian Kim defines public theology as "critical, reflective and reasoned engagement of theology in society to bring the kingdom of God, which is *for the sake of the poor and marginalized*, by engaging [the] academy, the church, and society."[23] However, public theologians are not just concerned that people around the world experience justice. They further want to promote the agency of people within grassroots communities to bring about justice for their own contexts.[24] Hence, we see a marked shift from the theology taking place under modernity, where individuals reasoned their faith in and for private places, to what we are currently seeing, where local communities do theology for public life within specific locales.[25]

---

21. Of course, theology always is and has been undertaken in specific contexts. The rise of public theology merely foregrounds what has always been the case and strengthens the voices of global public theologians in the process.

22. For more on public theology in global contexts, see Sebastian Kim, *Theology in the Public Sphere: Public Theology as a Catalyst for Open Debate* (London: SCM, 2011), along with Paul Chung, *Public Theology in an Age of World Christianity* (New York: Palgrave Macmillan, 2010). See also Felix Wilfred, *Asian Public Theology: Critical Concerns in Challenging Times* (Delhi: India Society for Promoting Christian Knowledge, 2010). The *International Journal of Public Theology* offers one of the best resources for highlighting the voices of global public scholars available today.

23. Sebastian Kim, "Mission's Public Engagement: The Conversation of Missiology and Public Theology," *Missiology* 45, no. 1 (2017): 8 (italics added).

24. Elaine Graham makes this point by asking the question of "whose voices, whose perspectives are incorporated into theology; and by implication, whose voices and experiences are absent." "Power, Knowledge, and Authority in Public Theology," *International Journal of Public Theology* 1, no. 1 (2007): 42–62, here 44.

25. Alison Elliot explains, "Public theology is, above all, theology that is meant to lead to action. It is the meeting point between the perspective and the resources of faith and the detail of a world that is broken and hurting, and in that encounter there is a momentum towards

To address justice, public theologians often speak of the common good,[26] human flourishing,[27] and God's shalom. The language of the common good arises from Greek philosophy, while finding a more recent home in Roman Catholic social teaching. It focuses more on interpersonal relationships and praxis. Public theologians move readily between the language of the common good, human flourishing, and God's shalom to orient public life back to God's original intent. They do so with a bent toward action, applying them to such diverse topics as eco-theology, political advocacy, women's rights, and poverty alleviation.[28]

Public theologians believe that we love society best by critiquing it, calling it back to God's created purposes. Because of their strong concern to invest society with theological resources for the common good, public theologians seek to harness theology for these ends. For some scholars, the goal of public theology is to explore "moral, metaphysical and theological dimensions of a society's economic, cultural and intellectual milieu."[29] Other scholars will draw on overt biblical language, such as wisdom, to address how theology should breathe life into the public realm.[30] No part of public life can escape the gaze of theology, especially if by theology we mean the knowledge of God within and for the flourishing of the entire world.[31]

Critique takes many forms. Max Stackhouse says that under globalization contemporary public life has lost sight of its theological moorings and been co-opted by ideological powers in a way "that flatten[s] life's potential meanings," while in some instances "becoming ends or idols in themselves."[32]

---

changing the world." "Doing Theology: Engaging the Public," *International Journal of Public Theology* 1, no. 3 (2007): 290–305, here 304.

26. Graham, *Between a Rock and a Hard Place*, 70.

27. Miroslav Volf, *Flourishing: Why We Need Religion in a Globalized World* (New Haven: Yale University Press, 2015).

28. Public theology focuses on specific issues of theological concern, or as John de Gruchy says, "There is no universal 'public theology,' but only theologies that seek to engage the political realm within particular locations." "From Political to Public Theologies: The Role of Theology in Public Life in South Africa," in *Public Theology for the 21st Century*, ed. William F. Storrar and Andrew R. Morton (New York: T&T Clark, 2004), 45.

29. Graham, *Between a Rock and a Hard Place*, 82.

30. Volf defines biblical wisdom as "an integrated *way of life* that enables the flourishing of persons, communities, and all creation." Or later, "to reject wisdom as a way of life, or Christ as the embodiment of wisdom, is not like leaving the dessert untouched after a good meal; rather, it is like refusing the very nourishment without which human beings cannot truly flourish." *Public Faith*, 101, 102.

31. Sebastian Kim explains it this way: "The key aims of theological engagement are to challenge any kind of monopoly in public life and seek for a fairer and more open society by employing advocacy, critical dialogue, and debate" and to do so by reforming these areas so that they function as agents of life in the world. "Mission's Public Engagement," 7.

32. *God and Globalization*, ed. Max L. Stackhouse, vol. 4, *Globalization and Grace*, by Max L. Stackhouse (New York: Continuum, 2007), 38, 43.

When this happens, public theology must reenergize, correct, challenge, and generate new forms of public life, calling everything back to God. There is not any singular way Christians should do this, but a myriad of simultaneous movements, which is why I liken it to weaving—where the various threads move back and forth across the surface of the fabric or, in the case of public theology, across the whole of public life. Volf explains public faith this way: "Christian identity in a culture is always a complex and flexible network of small and large refusals, divergencies, subversions, and more or less radical and encompassing alternative proposals and enactments, surrounded by the acceptance of many cultural givens."[33] Public theology thus critiques public life through a multifaceted process I describe as thick witness.

ACCESSIBILITY OF FAITH

Finally, the primary goal of public theology is not just to engage public life but to do so in language and means that are accessible and open to the public sphere.[34] Given its primary concern for issues open to all people, public theology does not want to rely on overtly Christian terminology.[35] In heavily secularized contexts, such language would not just be unintelligible but might also be repugnant to people. Public theologians thus draw on a wide range of language and metaphors to capture this, including bilinguality,[36] middle axioms,[37] fragments,[38] and apologetics,[39] in order to move Christian theology into the public sphere. They also differ in where they place the emphasis, with some saying that every aspect of theology needs to be translated into the language of the public sphere, and others maintaining

33. Volf, *Public Faith*, 93.

34. Kim, *Theology in the Public Sphere*, 10. He defines publicness with openness, not in contrast with the private realm. "Being public means that theology is open to engage in public issues wider than religious matters, and also open to be engaged in receiving critique from outside the church circles." "Mission's Public Engagement," 12–13.

35. Or as Philip Zeigler explains, "This is not to say that theology must or even can be intelligible to everyone, the way a public park is accessible to everyone. Yet it must aim to communicate to an audience which, while informed and educated, is not limited to the professional guild." "God and Some Recent Public Theologies," *International Journal of Public Theology* 4, no. 2 (2002): 137–55, here 144.

36. Graham, *Between a Rock and a Hard Place*, 99.

37. E.g., see John Howard Yoder, *The Christian Witness to the State* (Scottdale, PA: Herald, 2002), 32–35.

38. In a world where Christian values have been lost, fragments are part-truths that emanate from the lingering memory of a Christian past that may be used to help in public discourse. Elaine Graham says, "Fragments are parts of a whole that has been shattered." *Between a Rock and a Hard Place*, 101.

39. Graham, *Between a Rock and a Hard Place*, 99–102.

that theology should remain deeply rooted to its own particular traditions.[40] At heart, public theologians want to "defend the right both of theology to speak about and into public issues, and to advance the conviction that theology must do its reflection in public as a transparent and generally accessible form of discourse."[41]

From Public Theology to Public Missiology

I would like to suggest that public missiology builds on the foundations of public theology and fills in some of the critical gaps.[42]

Like public theologians, missiologists appeal to the Scriptures to argue for the intrinsically public nature of theology. The *missio Dei* is the story of God's reign over the entire cosmos, which naturally includes the public realm. As I explained in the last chapter, it's a public story, told thickly. The word *public* reminds missiology of what has always been the case and makes explicit our need to broaden the scope of our missiological energies to include the publics within the world. This is especially critical in light of changing dynamics in contemporary publics described in chapter 2.

For years, public theology has danced around missiological issues. Max Stackhouse actively courted one of my colleagues, Kima Pachuau, years ago and told him that public theology required the resources of mission.[43] One hears the language of witness in such scholars as Duncan Forrester, who declares, "It [public theology] has a gospel to share, good news to proclaim."[44] Likewise, Dirkie Smit says, "The crucial question, therefore, always is whether and how their [believers'] lives actually correspond to the message of the gospel and how the life of the church is founded and motivated by the gospel."[45] Public theologians will speak about witness, gospel, and church on occasion but are less explicit in what they mean by these terms. Some of this reticence

40. Stanley Hauerwas is an example of those who argue that Christian witness must remain deeply rooted in its own distinctive character (see Stanley Hauerwas and William H. Willimon, *Resident Aliens: Life in the Christian Colony* (Nashville: Abingdon, 1989). Jonathan Malesic is another example. See *Secret Faith in the Public Square: An Argument for the Concealment of Christian Identity* (Grand Rapids: Brazos, 2009).

41. Graham, *Between a Rock and a Hard Place*, 102–3.

42. In what follows, I highlight specific gifts that missiologists offer public theologians. I do not mean to suggest, however, that public theologians don't acknowledge these areas, only that they are more pronounced within the writings of public missiologists.

43. I share this story that Kima Pachuau related to me. Max Stackhouse has been ardent in his use of the language of mission, whether in his book *Apologia* or at the very end of his four-volume work on God and globalization; see *God and Globalization*, 4:246–50.

44. Duncan B. Forrester, *Truthful Action* (Edinburgh: T&T Clark, 2000), 128.

45. Smit, "Notions of the Public," 452.

might be due to subtle associations between missions and colonialism that continue to influence how people think of missiology, and some of it might be colored by the desire for public theologians to speak in language accessible to the public realm.

Meanwhile, public missiology has recently emerged as a subdiscipline in the field of missiology. Those of us calling ourselves public missiologists would appeal to Lesslie Newbigin as the father of public missiology. More recently (and building on Newbigin's foundation), George Hunsberger brought the topic to the American Society of Missiology (ASM) annual meeting in 2005 with his presidential address "The Mission of Public Theology." Hunsberger would later publish that paper under the title "The Missional Voice and Posture of Public Theologizing."[46] Years later, Gregory Leffel brought the theme to the 2016 ASM annual conference. He called together a few of us scholars who had been writing on "public" areas of missiology, and we organized ourselves into a separate track of paper presentations in 2015. We then met regularly leading up to the 2016 ASM meetings, where the annual theme, perhaps for the very first time, was explicitly stated as "public missiology."

Since then, our public missiology working group has been hosting paper presentations at annual ASM meetings and collaborating during short retreats during the rest of the year to spell out precisely what we mean by public missiology.[47] The appendix includes a recent statement that attempts to define what the working group means by public missiology. It is much broader in scope than what I offer here since my focus is on congregational witness.

A Public Missiology of the Local Congregation

Let me show how public missiology offers unique gifts to public theology. In some cases the gifts highlighted below are shared by public theologians though not as pronounced; in other instances, public missiology provides unique offerings. My intent is to strengthen the relationship between the two disciplines, while exploring the agency of local congregations.

Public Missiology as Trinitarian

First of all, public missiology revolves around the Trinity. It locates itself within the inward life of the divine community in order to embody the

46. George Hunsberger, "The Missional Voice and Posture of Public Theologizing," *Missiology* 34, no. 1 (2006): 15–28.

47. The working group is composed of George Hunsberger, Gregory Leffel, Charles Fensham, Robert Hunt, Bill Kenney, Hendrik Pieterse, and me.

outward manifestation of the Trinity within and for the world. For this reason we need to explore the role of the local congregation for public witness as the embodiment of the divine community in the world.

The *missio Dei* begins within the inner life of the divine community. Hence, before we get to the common good or human flourishing, or shalom, or even the church, we start with the Trinity. David Bosch explains how, prior to the sixteenth century, the term *mission* "was used exclusively with reference to the doctrine of the Trinity, that is, of the sending of the Son by the Father and of the Holy Spirit by the Father and the Son."[48] Later, the term began to take on human-centric meanings. To speak of a public missiology requires that we begin with a trinitarian perspective. The Trinity is public truth.

It is not that public theologians neglect the subject of God or fail to speak of the Trinity, but they are less explicit on these matters. For example, Max Stackhouse offers an extended treatment on the meanings of theology in one of his books but places less emphasis on the topic of God.[49] Others similarly bypass any treatment of God's nature, moving quickly into matters of public engagement, but without asking *who* it is we image. There are exceptions. Charles Mathewes develops his Augustinian theology of public life on the basis of what it means for Christians to live "before God, during the world."[50] Meanwhile, Kevin Vanhoozer, a systematic theologian turned public theologian, readily names the subject of God.[51] And Dirkie Smit argues that we need all three persons of the Trinity for any public theology.[52] Despite these exceptions, though, public theologians as a whole are relatively silent on the subject of God, and especially any overt mention of the Trinity.[53]

Public missiologists, meanwhile, begin with the Trinity. For example, Newbigin explains, "We should insist that Christian doctrine, with its prime model

48. David Bosch, *Transforming Mission: Paradigm Shifts in Theology of Mission* (Maryknoll, NY: Orbis, 1991), 1.

49. Max L. Stackhouse, "The Meanings of 'Theology,'" in Stackhouse, *God and Globalization*, 4:105–14. To be fair, Stackhouse does mention God in other places. In one instance he says that public theology "is made fuller by the knowledge of the God, who comes to us through Jesus Christ and the power of the Holy Spirit." But this does not occupy his primary interest. See Max Stackhouse, "Reflections on How and Why We Go Public," *International Journal of Public Theology* 1, no. 3 (2007): 421–30, here 428–29.

50. Charles Mathewes, *A Theology of Public Life* (Cambridge: Cambridge University Press, 2007), 44–47.

51. Kevin J. Vanhoozer, "What Is Everyday Theology?," in *Everyday Theology: How to Read Cultural Texts and Interpret Trends*, ed. Kevin J. Vanhoozer, Charles A. Anderson, and Michael J. Sleasman (Grand Rapids: Baker Academic, 2007), 15–62.

52. Smit, "Notions of the Public," 451.

53. Later in this book I will highlight two other theologians, Jürgen Moltmann and Miroslav Volf, who build heavily upon the doctrine of the Trinity.

in the doctrine of the Trinity, ought to be playing an explicit and vigorous part in the public debate that makes up the life of the public square."[54] By focusing on local congregations, we will explore in the sections below how the different movements of Father, Son, and Holy Spirit contribute to a thickening of the church's public witness within and for the world.

Public Missiology as Congregational

Inasmuch as public missiology begins with the Trinity, we discover the theological foundations for a public missiology *of the local congregation.* The church is a diverse community called to announce in word and action the redemptive presence of the inner life of the Trinity within the world. The church is thus an image of the Trinity. Newbigin says, "The most important contribution which the church can make to a new social order is to be itself a new social order."[55] And Moltmann reminds us, "It is the mission of the Son and the Spirit through the Father that includes the church, creating a church as it goes on its way."[56]

Public theologians are less explicit about the role of the church in the public realm. Some of this reticence is understandable. The church possesses a sordid history of relationship with the public realm, sometimes complicit in abuses under Christendom and colonialism, and other times separatistic as if huddling far away from any dangers associated with publics.

However, every church is situated within its own delicate ecosystem. People come to church *carrying with them* their participation in the public realm in the form of ideologies and social imaginaries sourced deep down in their collective humanity. Inside the gathered body, congregants are exposed to another way of being human through sacraments, liturgy, and preaching. Parishioners are then *sent out* as representations of the Trinity in the world through the totality of their lives, as "a new social order." Dirkie Smit seems to acknowledge this back-and-forth movement when he says, "The church exists always as an integral part of human life in the world; it is interwoven always with public life in society and community; it should be aware of and interested in the resulting impact in both directions—the impact of public life on the church, its place, social form and self-understanding and also the impact of the church on public life and the many spheres that together

---

54. Lesslie Newbigin, "The Trinity as Public Truth," in *The Trinity in a Pluralistic Age: Theological Essays on Culture and Religion*, ed. Kevin J. Vanhoozer (Grand Rapids: Eerdmans, 1997), 1.

55. Newbigin, "Trinity as Public Truth," 1.

56. Jürgen Moltmann, *The Church in the Power of the Spirit: A Contribution to Messianic Ecclesiology* (London: SCM, 1977), 64.

constitute life in the world."[57] To mention "the impact of public life on the church" is to examine how publics enter into congregations. Meanwhile, to study "the impact of the church on public life" is to explore how churches have contributed to the public realm—in healthy and unhealthy ways. Smit even uses the language of weaving to describe what this looks like, suggestive of a thickness of witness.

Religion, for example, always goes public. We can decry, critique, and challenge the ways it goes public in the world. But we cannot return to the days when we divided the world into simplistic dichotomies of private and public (locating the church as a subset of the former). Sociologists Peter Berger and Harvey Cox have helped us appreciate the publicness of faith. Public theologians have similarly joined the chorus. Max Stackhouse explains how religion "forms an organized space to express its assumptions and convictions."[58] This "space" is not just physical but is also notional, carried by people wherever they go. By gathering together, people practice their faith in tangible, relational, and embodied ways, which then allows their faith to enter into the space around the church. Or as Stackhouse seems to suggest, "A revised public is ever under construction."[59]

Let me briefly consider three characteristics of churches that highlight their public nature: their particularity, their incarnational nature, and their ubiquitous presence.

First, why *particularity*? For one, God begins with the particular. He does not create generic humans, or fashion a generic nation, or send a generic redeemer into the world. Rather, God creates specific humans, giving them names. He then fashions a distinct nation whose identity directly relates to Yahweh. Then God enters our world as a Jewish man in first-century Palestine. As we saw in the last chapter, particularity is never an end in itself. Particularity unsettles the pretensions of universality, while universality draws the different threads of particularity into a thicker whole. By focusing on particularity, we see the visibility of the kingdom of God in Jesus Christ. "The first divine act of translation into humanity thus gives rise to a constant succession of new translations."[60] And these new acts of translation always take place in communal form. Newbigin explains, "It is surely a fact

57. Smit, "Notions of the Public," 441. Earlier he says, "The church exists always in the world and as part of the world, whether or not it wants to, and thereby impacts public life in varied and complex ways, regardless of whether it is aware of this" (439).

58. Stackhouse, "Reflections," 423. Of course, this does not mean the revised public is healthy but that religion is always involved in creating a revised public.

59. Stackhouse, "Reflections," 424.

60. Andrew F. Walls, *The Missionary Movement in Christian History: Studies in the Transmission of Faith* (Maryknoll, NY: Orbis, 1996), 27.

of inexhaustible significance that what our Lord left behind Him was not a book, nor a creed, nor a system of thought, nor a rule of life, but a visible community."[61] Particularity leads to increased visibility, and visibility through the local congregation serves as a primary means of public witness within and for the public realm.[62]

Second, if congregations are particular, they are *incarnational*. Particularities arise in the world from collective human imaging and relate to all the things that make us human, such as ethnicity, place, and language, as well as cultural values, norms, and institutions. I find it regrettable how common (and indeed fashionable) it has become to promote missional ecclesiology through the means of vilifying the church's institutions and structures. Indeed, there are plenty of valid reasons for faulting the institutional nature of the church. But such a reaction neglects how these structures arise from our collective humanity (as a gift to us), while failing to see how they can be a form of its witness (as a gift back to the public realm).[63]

Incarnation further accentuates the beauty of humanity. It is tempting in our contemporary world to treat publics as suprahuman, elevating the ideologies attached to publics as more than human. Many publics want us to think of them in precisely such ways. Economics aspires after visions of immortality;[64] politics demands omnipotence; technology functions as a secular eschatology. Meanwhile, media circulates everywhere, yearning for omnipresence. Then there are the little publics, such as sports teams, the neighborhood pub, social media sites, and video gaming communities that quietly make claims on human identity. Each of these publics demands our total allegiance.

When the ideologies attached to contemporary publics become unfettered from human origins, they become modern-day idols. Christians become entranced by the sonorous song of the sirens, lulled into believing in the immortality of economics or the omnipotence of the state. We see too many examples of baptized forms of Christian nationalism, or sectarian ideologies vigorously championed through the misguided use of Scripture, to be blind to the ways congregations fall captive to the divinizing lure of contemporary publics.

61. Newbigin, *Household of God*, 27.
62. George Hunsberger explains, "To embrace a self-conscious sense of the particular of our witness challenges the dynamics of discourse that we will find present in many places." "Missional Voice," 24.
63. Gregg Okesson, "Christian Witness to Institutions: Public Missiology and Power," *Missiology* 44, no. 2 (2016): 142–54.
64. In commenting on Jesus's teachings about mammon (Matt. 6:24; Luke 16:13), Jacques Ellul says, "He is speaking of a power which tries to be like God, which makes itself our master and which has specific goals." See *Money and Power* (Eugene, OR: Wipf & Stock, 1984), 76.

Unlike public theology, where the focus lies solely on what happens outside the church, public missiology initially engages publics in a unique way: by gathering. Within the local congregation, all the particularities of public life are gathered up into liturgy, worship, and sacrament and there are opened up to the resources of the Trinity. Inside the church, publics are reminded of their own humanity, which sets them free to be a blessing to others. Thus, when the people of God scatter, they do so within and for their surrounding publics. In other words, local congregations show contemporary publics that there is a different way of being human in the world.

Finally, local congregations are *ubiquitous*. They are like little seeds blowing in the morning breeze. Wherever the seed lands, it finds fertile soil and puts down roots, eventually covering the earth with a thick carpet of green. Wherever one travels in this world, one finds local congregations. They stand tall like majestic old cathedrals outlining the horizon of historic cities such as Montreal and are located in new malls throughout the Philippines. One finds churches in storefronts in São Paulo, Brazil, and dotted across the rural landscape of East Africa. The ubiquitous nature of local congregations accentuates both aspects already mentioned: their particularity (while nurturing a thicker universality) as well as their incarnational presence (showing the public world there is a different way of being human). To the extent that congregations link up with other congregations in their local area (or around the world), they nurture networks of relationship that further thicken their public witness.

Public Missiology as Robustly Soteriological

Public missiology likewise possesses a robust soteriology. While public theologians occasionally draw on the language of witness, they are less explicit about what they mean by it. Public missiology, meanwhile, builds on what David Bosch calls "total comprehensive salvation," which actively solicits the totality of Christ through the Holy Spirit for the redemption of the entirety of the world.[65]

While public missiologists retain a strong belief that salvation is always deeply personal, we do not limit the scope of salvation to what happens with individuals but include the entire cosmos within the arc of God's salvific work. The entire world needs to experience God's salvation. Bosch explains what this means:

65. Bosch, *Transforming*, 399–400. He says, "We stand in need of an interpretation of salvation which operates within a *comprehensive* christological framework, which makes the *totus Christus*—his incarnation, earthly life, death, resurrection, and parousia—indispensable for church and theology" (399).

In a world in which people are dependent on each other and every individual exists within a web of inter-human relationships, it is totally untenable to limit salvation to the individual and his or her personal relationship with God. Hatred, injustice, oppression, war, and other forms of violence are manifestations of *evil*; concern for humaneness, for the conquering of famine, illness, and meaninglessness is part of the *salvation* for which we hope and labor. Christians pray that the reign of God should come and God's will be done *on earth* as it is in heaven (Mt 6:10); it follows from this that the *earth* is the locus of the Christian's calling and sanctification.

To expand the reach of God's salvation, we need to foreground the actions of the entire Trinity as they relate to accomplishing God's mission. Only through the Father, Son, and Holy Spirit can the church be the church *within* and *for* the entirety of the world. Only through the actions of the entire Trinity can salvation be woven into public spaces for the redemption of all things.

Public Missiology as Movement

Finally, congregations witness through movement. Throughout this book I have argued that movement is a good thing. As we saw in the last chapter, it is what we find in the persons of the Trinity, and it is how God creates and redeems the world. Movement can be likened to weaving, or dance, or drama, or dialogue. Public missiology uses movement in and around the local congregation for public witness.

We can understand movement in different ways. Think of the sound waves of a tuning fork (the kind people use when testing the quality of a piano). As the sound waves vibrate between the two forks, air pressure gets applied to the particles with the result being perfect pitch. Similarly, the greater the movement back and forth, the better the "sound" a local congregation makes in and for its local community.

Movement and Salvation

Let me pull all of these elements together. I have spoken of public missiology as trinitarian, as congregational, as possessing a robust soteriology including the entirety of the cosmos, and as nurtured through a thickening movement.

We like to think of local congregations simply. They are where people meet, chat while drinking a cup of coffee, worship by singing a few songs, listen to a sermon, participate in the Eucharist at the end of the service, and then depart back into public life. We assume that's the extent of it. However, more is happening within a local congregation through movement.

We also love to criticize churches for how they gather. It is easy to bemoan the ways that ideologies of race, economic status, nationalism, and political affiliation make their way inside a church and get baptized with sacred resources, such as through sermons or prayers. Unfortunately, this is all regrettably true. Thus we lash out at the ways the church gathers (while placing all our emphasis on the scattering, which we call by various names: public theology, social entrepreneurship, social change, or any number of other "public" possibilities).

But what if gathering is central to witness? What if local congregations are not as simple as we assume? What if the movements internal to the church eventually go public, much as nutrients seep out of semipermeable membranes within an entire ecosystem?

Without gathering, the local congregation would have nothing to offer its surroundings except its own cultural identity (which it already shares with the public realm). It would be utterly open. However, by gathering into, around, and through the persons of the Trinity (for, indeed, there are many ways a local congregation moves around the Trinity, and even more ways the persons of the Trinity move in and around a church) a local congregation nurtures its life in God and thus weaves difference into the world.[66] Darrell Guder explains that the gathering of a local congregation is always for witness outside the church.[67] He says, "The inward life of the church does, in fact, become a major form of witness to the world."[68] Focusing on "inward dimensions of doing the witness," Guder refers to the ways Christ orients every part of the local congregation. This involves how we undertake liturgy, treat those different from us, practice power dynamics, and even organize the structures within the local congregation. "The Christian church does the witness as it seeks to unfold all the concrete and tangible outworkings of this radically new order of life in Christ."[69]

Guder then relates inward witness to outward witness. Whatever takes place within the congregation must eventually go public; or in his words, "It has been said that the Christian must experience at least two conversions, one to Christ, and then one to the world."[70] Inward witness opens the local congregation to *more of God's salvation*, which then enables the church to

---

66. In the last chapter, I explored different aspects of movement within the narrative of God's mission. I looked at internal and external, gathering and scattering, as well as movements between heaven and earth. These are but a few of the movements evident in Scripture.

67. Darrell L. Guder, *Be My Witnesses: The Church's Mission, Message, and Messengers* (Grand Rapids: Eerdmans, 1985), 124–32.

68. Guder, *Be My Witnesses*, 124.

69. Guder, *Be My Witnesses*, 127.

70. Guder, *Be My Witnesses*, 129.

enter *more aspects of life* outside the congregation. What do these "two conversions" look like for a local congregation?[71]

More of God's Salvation

More salvation arises from the movement of persons of the Trinity in and around a local congregation. It is larger than anything an individual can handle, which is why we need the entire congregation as a "new social reality" to embody this salvation for the world. Local congregations do so through song, dance, prayer, liturgy, or participation in the sacraments. Salvation thus is not something we experience once and leave behind, such as with a pleasant but lingering memory. Nor is it a commodity we give and receive, like exchanging money for services rendered. It is participation in the entire life of the Trinity within all the spaces of human existence—and this lies at the core of what it means to be the church.[72]

What does this look like? We need to study how the different persons of the Trinity are incorporated into the songs, liturgy, sermons, and sacraments of the church. Think of each congregation as telling a story through movement. As a congregation focuses in its worship on the persons of the Trinity, it thickens its witness. This carries direct implications for how the community relates to the rest of society.

More Aspects of Life

Not only do we need more salvation, but that salvation needs to be located in more aspects of life. We cannot partition the gospel from the publics surrounding the church but need to actively nurture meaningful contact. Some of this happens within the gathered church, as parishioners carry with them their internalized publics, in the form of ideologies and social imaginaries, into liturgy, sacrament, and doxology. We need to spend more time pondering how the persons of the Trinity help us address public life. For example, the cross and resurrection of Jesus Christ are not just spiritual topics for the salvation of souls but critical resources for the salvation of publics. Or as Newbigin explains, "A society which accepts the crucifixion and resurrection of Jesus as its ultimate standards of reference will have to be a society whose

71. What I describe below is a heuristic to show the different movements within a congregation. I do not mean to suggest that all congregations do so thickly. Indeed, one of the major problems is that congregations try to witness out of the thinness of their faith.

72. Craig Van Gelder and Dwight J. Zscheile offer this critique of the missional church, arguing that it requires a more robust trinitarian framework. See *The Missional Church in Perspective: Mapping Trends and Shaping the Conversation* (Grand Rapids: Baker Academic, 2011), 52–55.

whole style of life, and not only its words, conveys something of that radical dissent from the world which is manifest in the Cross, and at the same time something of that affirmation of the world which is made possible by the resurrection."[73] By moving back and forth between "the edges of Jesus's life"[74] we constantly declare God's definitive yes to humanity, creation, and the public realm (by the incarnation), while saying no to any distortion of God's shalom that would dehumanize and perpetrate injustice (through the cross), and then once again affirming God's yes to creation (by means of the resurrection). Witness involves movement across the full expanse of Christ's life.

Movement within the gathered congregation is always for collective movement outward into the public realm. If all of creation itself arises from the inner life of the Trinity, then a congregation that nurtures that inner life will be life-giving in all its ways when scattered in the public realm. For example, if a church participates in God's self-giving love, then it will be a collective of agents of that love in public spaces. If a congregation organizes its powers around the inner life of the Trinity, it will be a different kind of public in the world. Likewise, to the extent a congregation mirrors the unity in diversity of the persons of the Trinity, then it will weave that thickness of identity in and for the world.

Conclusion

Weaving brings together a variety of threads into a new whole, which is what Jesus Christ is accomplishing in the world (Eph. 1:10) through the church, "the fullness of him who fills everything in every way" (Eph. 1:23).

Weaving is not a practice I know well, except that I have strung many traditional lacrosse pockets over the years. I grew up playing lacrosse in the 1970s in Syracuse, New York, when most of the pockets were made up of leather, crosslace, sidewall, and shooting strings. You could purchase a premade pocket in the store, or you could learn to string one yourself. I chose the latter, and it is a hobby I continue to this day.

To weave, one has to move a variety of pieces, placing them alternately on top of and then under other pieces (and sometimes anchored with a knot). The more pieces involved, the thicker the weave. The greater the movement

73. Lesslie Newbigin, "Stewardship, Mission, and Development," (address, Annual Stewardship Conference of the British Council of Churches, Stanwick, UK, 1970), 6.

74. Bosch, *Transforming*, 399. Bosch critiques our fascination with "the edges" of Jesus's life, with some Christian traditions more focused on the incarnation and others devoting more time to his death and resurrection. Ultimately, I am arguing, we need to foster movement back and forth between these to nurture a thickening of Christology.

of the pieces, the tighter the whole. The better placement of any strategic knots into the weave, the stronger the cohesiveness.

Weaving is a helpful analogy because it attends to the parts and the whole. It uses movement to create thickness. I think the same is true for congregational witness. As Lesslie Newbigin explains, "Salvation is a making whole and therefore it concerns the whole."[75] Local congregations nurture a form of thickness, which they use for the purposes of weaving into their surroundings. The greater the movement across the persons of the Trinity, the thicker the congregation's identity. The thicker the church's identity, the better positioned the church is to witness in and for publics.

In this chapter, I have outlined what I mean by a public missiology of local congregations. I will now proceed in the next chapter to show precisely what it looks like for the church.

---

75. Lesslie Newbigin, *The Open Secret: An Introduction to the Theology of Mission*, rev. ed. (Grand Rapids: Eerdmans, 1995), 80.

5

Thick Congregational Witness

The revolution of the cross sets us free to be in-between people, caught up in the rhythm of worship and mission.

—N. T. Wright, *The Day the Revolution Began*[1]

The only hermeneutic of the gospel . . . is a congregation of men and women who believe it and live by it.

—Lesslie Newbigin, *The Gospel in a Pluralist Society*[2]

I began this book by asking the question, Why don't we witness to the public realm? I then suggested one of the reasons we hesitate is that the thinness of our faith struggles to interpenetrate the thickness of our surrounding publics. The thickness of publics is not just seen, like a heavy fog wafting across the coastline, but is felt by our bodies. The public realm serves "as a site of negotiation and struggle, in which different publics claim presence and power."[3] At its best, the public realm invigorates us with a sense of unlimited

---

1. N. T. Wright, *The Day the Revolution Began: Reconsidering the Meaning of the Jesus's Crucifixion* (New York: HarperOne, 2016), 363.
2. Lesslie Newbigin, *The Gospel in a Pluralist Society* (Grand Rapids: Eerdmans, 1989), 227.
3. Birgit Meyer, "Going and Making Public: Pentecostalism as Public Religion in Ghana," in *Christianity and Public Culture in Africa*, ed. Harri Englund (Athens: Ohio University Press, 2011), 157.

possibilities, like walking down an urban street during the holidays. At its worst, the public realm entangles us in a multifaceted web of negotiation and struggle, best described by Wesley's "complicated wickedness."

Meanwhile, our Christian faith too often possesses thinness, like a powdery coating of snow covering the ground early on a brisk, wintry morning. It gives the entire world a sense of freshness and purity but lacks any depth or substance. Try as we might, thin forms of faith accomplish little to interpenetrate the thickness of the public realm. And so we don't try. We have been trained to witness to individuals (primarily), with a gospel sized to fit for easy delivery (emphasizing strategy), focused on "private" aspects of human life (inwardly), applied only to the future (like a get-out-of-jail-free card), argued on the basis of one part of our humanity (usually the soul) and through a simple, static reading of the Trinity (often hierarchical).

Thin views of salvation struggle to make any sense of thickness. Can a piece of paper grasp the magnificence of a library? Or a tiny sapling survey all the twists and contours of a majestic oak tree? Thinness looks at the world one-dimensionally and fails to comprehend, let alone enter into and witness to, the interiority of complex, interpenetrating publics.

What then do we do with publics? In the absence of any robust Christian witness to the public realm, we have sought to engage publics in other ways. Whether it is public theology, engagement in the marketplace, undertaking political advocacy, or championing social justice, we have reacted to our historical legacy of the privatization of the Christian faith by stepping out boldly into the public realm. I only wonder whether any of these alternatives is thick enough to enter the open weave and witness to the public realm from within, whether through "total comprehensive salvation"[4] or through the dynamic movements of the persons in the Trinity.

In this chapter, I want us to hold two truths together. First, the church is a different kind of public in the world. Second, as a public, the church exists in and for all the surrounding publics, to witness to them from within.

Thick Local Congregations

To argue these truths, we, like Newbigin before us, cannot allow the church to function as some partitioned reality in the world, nor can we limit its witness to individuals. The problems we experience in the world are social and thick, and thus the answers to those problems must also be social and thick.

4. David Bosch, *Transforming Mission: Paradigm Shifts in Theology of Mission* (Maryknoll, NY: Orbis, 1991), 399–400.

Newbigin makes the bold statement, "I have come to feel that the primary reality of which we have to take account in seeking for a Christian impact on public life is the Christian congregation," which he later calls "the only hermeneutic of the gospel."[5]

A local congregation fits all of the criteria I previously defined for a public. It is *a common space of togetherness where people participate with one another in life and form opinions through the circulation of different texts*. Of course, a local congregation is a very different kind of public. It is formed by the movements of the triune God and thus exists to share those resources with the world around it. Its "texts" comprise liturgical and doxological elements that make up worship, such as how people rehearse God's Word, participate in the sacraments, and dramatize their faith in God in corporate, embodied ways.

Local congregations share their public nature with the people and publics surrounding the community. Or as Newbigin explains, "A salvation whose very essence is that it is corporate and cosmic, the restoration of the broken harmony between all men and between man and God and man and nature, must be communicated in a different way. It must be communicated in and by the actual development of a community which embodies—if only in foretaste—the restored harmony of which it speaks."[6] Hence, each local congregation is a sent community into the fullness of the world. The church is public witness.

Of course, I am not suggesting that churches always go public in healthy ways. Yet, if we go back to its origins, the church was called as a public assembly and witnesses to God's truth through the aggregate actions of its members. George Hunsberger explains how the Greek word *ekklēsia* arose from the notion of a civic meeting and thus can be defined as a community "called into public assembly," or a "gathered public."[7] Hunsberger goes on to illustrate how every aspect of the church should be understood in relation to its public identity, whether public proclamation (*kerygma*), public worship (*doxologia*), or public liturgy (*leitourgia*).[8] By privatizing the faith, not only do we squeeze the church into Enlightenment categories it was never meant to fit, but we neglect its identity as a witness to the person of Christ, as "the fullness of him who fills everything in every way" (Eph. 1:23).

---

5. Lesslie Newbigin, *The Gospel in a Pluralist Society* (Grand Rapids: Eerdmans, 1989), 227.

6. Lesslie Newbigin, *The Household of God: Lectures on the Nature of the Church* (1953; repr., Eugene, OR: Wipf & Stock, 2008), 141.

7. George Hunsberger, *The Story That Chooses Us: A Tapestry of Missional Vision* (Grand Rapids: Eerdmans, 2015), 135. The last quote Hunsberger borrows from a chapter he cowrote with Linford Stutzman, "The Public Witness of Worship," in *Treasure in Clay Jars: Patterns in Missional Faithfulness*, ed. Lois Y. Barrett (Grand Rapids: Eerdmans, 2004), 100–116, here 109.

8. Hunsberger, *Story That Chooses Us*, 136.

How then does the church witness *in* and *for* the public? We have tended to have two knee-jerk reactions. Either we retreat from publics or we step out with self-confident swagger. Neither option does much good. The former does not make any attempt to witness to the public realm but interprets life outside the church as the enemy of the gospel. The latter sees public life as the pathway to relevancy, much like exchanging a pair of outdated polyester pants for chic skinny jeans. Martin Marty suggests another option. He says the church must combine "special interiority" with "specific openness."[9] The joining of these two phrases requires deft maneuvering. "Special interiority" takes seriously what the church does in its gathering. It is "special" in the sense that the congregation gets its identity from the divine community. Meanwhile, "specific openness" is not utter openness. "The church does not merely sprawl and spill itself until all its substance is gone."[10]

Every congregation exists in intimate relationship with its surroundings. This should also be a matter of analysis. We like to paint with broad strokes and refer to congregations as either private or public, drawing on a limited two-color palette afforded us by our Enlightenment heritage, but all congregations paint into their publics through an assortment of colors, hues, and textured brushstrokes.

Local Congregations and Movement

I am arguing there is another kind of public in the world, and that is the local congregation. Local congregations nurture different kinds of movement, and through such movement they thicken their identity. That thickness overlaps into the surrounding publics to provide the basis for its witness. To explain what this means, I will draw on three primary images: weaving, an organism, and a narrative. Each of these metaphors helps us explore *how* a local congregation interacts with its surroundings.

To make the argument for the church as a different kind of public, we first need to rethink the boundaries around the local congregation. I ask us to consider them less as fortified walls with a gate policed by ecclesiastical elites and more as semipermeable membranes where back-and-forth movement is constantly taking place. I find the imageries of weaving, an organism, and a narrative helpful in this regard. All three images take seriously

---

9. Martin E. Marty, *The Public Church: Mainline, Evangelical, Catholic* (1981; repr., Eugene, OR: Wipf & Stock, 2012), 4. Marty acknowledges borrowing these words from Karol Cardinal Wojtyla of Cracow, who went on to become Pope John Paul II.

10. Marty, *Public Church*, 4.

the importance of gathering. What would a tapestry look like if its threads were unraveled and spread across the ground, or an organism if it were open to everything in the entire ecosystem, or a narrative if it did not go any-where? Each of these images also accomplishes something through movement outward. Weaving moves outward, and then back inward again, through continuous movements of the different threads. An organism exists in its ecosystem through symbiotic relationships. And a narrative moves back and forth through complex story lines in order to move forward into the story's climax and resolution.

The Enlightenment project accomplished many things, but one of them was to create maps of the cosmos through carefully articulated binary lines. We see this in the drawing of national boundaries during the colonial era, or the delineation of highly specialized disciplines after the scientific revolu-tion. Cartography by solid lines has become the primary way we interpret the world, and it carries over into how we view local congregations. Hence, we speak of *inside* the church to refer to private, spiritual realities, and *outside* to refer to public, secular domains. Whenever we diagnose a problem as stem-ming from one of these two (e.g., the privatization of our faith), we push in the other direction because it is the only way we know how.

What if we saw the boundary markers less as lines that separate and more as threads of a cloth (weaving), semipermeable membranes (organisms), or story lines found within a classic novel (narrative)? Such images propel us deeper into movement and thickness. They help us see the church as a differ-ent kind of public: in the world, and for the world.

Our fear with such images is that they risk syncretism, where we become utterly open to our surroundings. That is a valid concern. I only want to suggest that we guard the faith best not by huddling together behind mas-sive walls, guarded by ecclesiastical elites, but more by movement: deeper inward into the sacraments, liturgy, and doxology, and more fully outward into public proclamation. Miroslav Volf similarly argues that Christians need both movement into the divine (what he calls "ascent") and move-ment further into the public world (what he calls "return"). He explains, "Without the 'receptive ascent,' there is no transforming message from God; without the 'creative return,' there is no engagement in the transformation of the world."[11]

We can refer to the movement in and around a local congregation by many different names (whether Marty's "special interiority" and "specific openness,"

11. Miroslav Volf, *A Public Faith: How Followers of Christ Should Serve the Common Good* (Grand Rapids: Brazos, 2011), 8–9.

or Volf's "receptive ascent" and "creative return"), but what these have in common is the desire to nurture intimate relationship between inward and outward. Of course, in talking about movement, or the boundary markers around the church, I risk inadvertently endorsing the private-public dichotomy I so ardently want to dismantle. But this is a risk we need to take if we want to focus on movement. Every congregation exists in its surrounding publics much like an organism thrives within an ecosystem, and those surrounding publics desperately need its nutrients.

Newbigin likewise stresses movement in and around the local church: "If the gospel is to challenge the public life of our society, . . . it will only be by movements that begin with the local congregation in which the reality of the new creation is present, known, and experienced, and from which men and women will go into every sector of public life to claim it for Christ, to unmask the illusions which have remained hidden and to expose all areas of public life to the illumination of the gospel."[12] Newbigin is surely right. What we do when gathered together is *for* witness when scattered. However, what if we expanded his thoughts to consider movement in the other direction? Parishioners are not just sent into the public realm from their gathering, but they come into their gathering *from* their scattering. Thus, when they enter into the place of worship, they bring their publics with them, especially in the form of social imaginaries. I want to argue that what takes place in the context of gathering is as much a part of public witness as what happens on the outside. We need to see the boundaries around the church less as a one-way street moving from church to the public and more as a multilane highway with traffic streaming in both directions. The local congregation is a different public in the world through the movements taking place in and around the community.

Let me explain what bidirectional movement looked like for the early church and then unpack what it means for us today.

The Early Church and Movement

Back-and-forth movement has long served as the means by which the church witnesses to its surrounding publics. In chapter 3, I narrated the *missio Dei* through movement across all the spaces of the cosmos, arguing that God is cultivating a thicker form of humanity in the world through movements mirroring the persons of the Trinity. Let me now build on that to show what back-and-forth movement looked like in the early church.

---

12. Newbigin, *Gospel in a Pluralist Society*, 232–33.

Movement and Networks

Scholars such as Rodney Stark, Alan Kreider, Morna Hooker, and Frances Young all explore the meteoric growth of Christianity during the first few centuries.[13] Each contends the early church expanded rapidly through the movement of people and especially via what Young refers to as "open and overlapping networks."[14] Each of these scholars further highlights the role that artisans and traders played in Christianity's expansion throughout the Roman Empire, along with the movement of slaves and migrants. What becomes clear through their research is that early Christians traveled, and wherever they were, they took advantage of existing networks, such as those found within Jewish diaspora communities, or created new ones, as with house churches.[15] These networks were "open" in the sense of allowing believers to move in and out of them whenever they traveled. They were "overlapping" to the extent that many of the networks were intimately connected with each other, as evidenced in the use of letters to communicate from one house church to another.[16] As people moved in and out of networks, the early church thickened its witness throughout the Roman Empire.

What began as a small, marginalized religion soon morphed in size and scope to the point where, by the time of Constantine's conversion, scholars estimate between 8 and 12 percent of people living in the Roman Empire were Christian.[17] However, sociological evidence alone cannot explain the growth of these faith communities. We find a different kind of movement happening below the surface, which Kreider describes as "patient ferment."[18] These communities were founded on the persons of the Trinity in their midst. On the surface, they lived like people in their regions; they were Carthaginians,

---

13. Rodney Stark, *The Rise of Christianity: How the Obscure, Marginal Jesus Movement Became the Dominant Religious Force in the Western World in a Few Centuries* (San Francisco: HarperSanFrancisco, 1997); Alan Kreider, *The Patient Ferment of the Early Church: The Improbable Rise of Christianity in the Roman Empire* (Grand Rapids: Baker Academic, 2016); Morna Hooker and Frances Young, *Holiness and Mission: Learning from the Early Church about Mission in the City* (London: SCM, 2010).

14. Frances Young, "Being Holy in the Cities of the Roman Empire," in Hooker and Young, *Holiness and Mission*, 47.

15. Alan Kreider explains, "Christians followed their business opportunities or the imperatives of their jobs by moving from their home areas to new areas as merchants, artisans, doctors, prisoners, slaves, and (by the third century) soldiers. As they traveled, they often moved in existing networks of family, profession, and faith (not least communities of Jews). Taking their faith with them, in new places they founded Christian cells." *Patient Ferment*, 75.

16. Kreider, *Patient Ferment*, 75.

17. See, e.g., Stark, *Rise of Christianity*, 6; Kreider, *Patient Ferment*, 7–8.

18. Kreider, *Patient Ferment*, 12.

or Romans, and dressed and acted as such. But under the surface they lived with difference. Gathering together in house churches altered their identity, which allowed them to reconfigure public domains, such as wealth, sex, and power.[19] The early churches had a different center, defined by Jesus Christ through the Holy Spirit. Kreider explains, "The worship and common life of local Christian communities shaped the believers and gave them distinctive habitual approaches to issues that faced everyone in society."[20] In the Christians' gathering together as a community, publics were carried into the worship, liturgy, and practices of the early church and were there "converted" to Jesus Christ. The language of ferment implies a bubbling up from under the surface, which is hardly noticeable at first but "has the cumulative power that creates and transforms."[21]

Diffused Witness

This "cumulative power" to which Kreider refers can be likened to diffused witness. Early Christians worshiped in small communities throughout the Roman Empire. They were like ubiquitous little dots on parchment paper that combine to display an artistic masterpiece. In one particularly telling observation, a second-century person describes some of the characteristics found within these early Christians:

> The difference between Christians and the rest of humankind is not a matter of nationality, or language or customs. Christians do not live apart in separate cities of their own, speak a special dialect, nor practice any eccentric way of life. . . . They pass their lives in whatever township—Greek or foreign—each person's lot has determined; and conform to ordinary local usage in their clothing, diet, and other habits. . . . To put it briefly, the relation of Christians to the world is that of a soul to the body. As the soul is diffused through every part of the body so are Christians, throughout all the cities of the world.[22]

The last sentence captures the essence of diffused witness. Early Christians looked and acted like other persons, but they were people of difference; they were diffused witnesses inserted into all aspects of their public worlds.

19. Kreider, *Patient Ferment*, 100–107.
20. Kreider, *Patient Ferment*, 101.
21. Kreider uses the language of fermentation to describe a slow, gradual process: "Except for a stray bubble that emerges now and then, nothing seems to be happening. Until late in the operation, it is unimpressive. And yet it has a cumulative power that creates and transforms." *Patient Ferment*, 73.
22. *Epistle to Diognetus* 5–6, quoted in Young, "Being Holy," 46.

Hybridity and Habitus

Early Christians moved fluidly between home, work, and worshiping with other believers. In some cases, house churches gathered multiple times a week, when persecution from the outside demanded a more frequent rhythm of gathering.[23]

Gathering produces difference. Scholars describe the difference of these Christian communities in terms of wisdom,[24] practices,[25] or "soft difference,"[26] but what all these have in common is the fundamental conviction that belief gets played out in corporate, embodied ways, and especially through small, repeated practices that shape the local community. Hooker and Young describe the early church through the language of holiness and show how holiness gets applied to public life.[27]

Another way of referring to this is to speak of a habitus. A habitus is something constructed over time by repeated embodied practices within a community.[28] For the early church, these practices included memorization of Scripture, prayer, fasting, and worship. Kreider says, "The worship of the Christian community, repeated week by week, shaped the worshipers' habitus by giving them kinesthetic as well as verbal habits."[29] Kreider thus explains the growth of the early church not by evangelistic campaigns or church growth strategies but by patient ferment in and through its habitus.

We all know that internal difference goes public. I suppose it might be conceptually possible to keep a very privatized, heavily spiritualized kind

23. I have observed around the world that the greater the external threat around the church, the more frequently cycles of gathering are needed.

24. Daniel J. Treier, *Virtue and the Voice of God: Toward Theology as Wisdom* (Grand Rapids: Eerdmans, 2006).

25. See, e.g., Dorothy C. Bass, ed., *Practicing Our Faith: A Guide for Conversation* (San Francisco: Jossey-Bass, 1997); Miroslav Volf and Dorothy C. Bass, eds., *Practicing Theology: Beliefs and Practices in Christian Life* (San Francisco: Jossey-Bass, 2001).

26. Miroslav Volf, "Soft Difference: Theological Reflections on the Relation between Church and Culture in 1 Peter," *Ex Auditu* 10 (1994): 1–29.

27. Young explains, "Loving God and one's neighbour would remain the essence of Christian holiness, and, as we have seen, however underground the Church seems to be have been, it was the practical out-workings of those commandments which would prove to be the fundamental way in which Christianity spread." Hooker and Young, *Holiness and Mission*, 58. Hooker says, "Holiness is about transforming *this* world" (25).

28. Pierre Bourdieu is recognized as the leading scholar in discussions about habitus, which he defines as "systems of durable, transposable dispositions, structured structures predisposed to function as structuring structures, that is, as principles which generate and organize practices and representations that can be objectively adapted to their outcomes without presupposing conscious aiming at ends or an express mastery of the operations necessary to attain them." *The Logic of Practice*, trans. Richard Nice (Stanford, CA: Stanford University Press, 2000), 53.

29. Kreider, *Patient Ferment*, 51.

of internality hidden (but even then I am not entirely convinced). The early church's habitus was formed by publics being reshaped *within* the context of worship. What happened when the early church met in secret was not visible to the surrounding culture, but its results were highly visible.[30] That is why Kreider calls it kinesthetic, suggesting that the practices of gathering together trained the early church for society. They brought an alternative to the status quo, challenging the prevailing way of doing things. They practiced hospitality[31] and reoriented economics.[32] Early Christians embodied alternative ways of using power. Love ruled their activities. They took in orphans abandoned in the streets. They cared for widows. Wherever they traveled (and travel they did), they carried seeds of the kingdom of God into all aspects of life. Indeed, at various times persecution forced them into self-protective postures. But their interiority was always open to others.[33] Kreider refers to the early Christians as "hybrid people."[34]

Hybridity results from different kinds of movement. Early Christians "moved" internally around the persons of the Trinity, and they moved externally into all facets of public life. Each of these movements nurtured a habitus in these small communities, which subsequently allowed them to witness to their surrounding publics.

Congregational Witness

I have explained how movement trains a local congregation for public life. We gather to scatter, and in scattering we pull the different publics we in-

30. Kreider explains, "Christians maintained that if they were attractive, it was not because they were born that way. It was because they had been reborn—changed, converted—to be attractive. Outsiders could see the results of the formation but not the formation itself, which happened privately, secretly, out of the public eye." *Patient Ferment*, 134.

31. Christine Pohl, *Making Room: Recovering Hospitality as a Christian Tradition* (Grand Rapids: Eerdmans, 1999).

32. Kreider, *Patient Ferment*, 100–101.

33. Referring to the same community, Kreider says that the community responded to persecution in two ways, "small acts of cunning resistance, and a bold gesture of martyrdom." *Patient Ferment*, 248.

34. Kreider, *Patient Ferment*, 99. Kreider goes on to explain that they are both "and" and "but" people. "They do some things that their neighbors do, *and* at times they do local things with greater intensity and energy than their non-Christian neighbors. *But* the Christians are also inconvenient: they view some local behaviors—that most people view as normal—to be dehumanizing and destructive. These behaviors are contrary to the Christians' own habituated values, and Christians simply cannot do them and be true to themselves. So they will marry like everyone else and have children *but* they will not expose unwanted infants on the local landfill. They will share food *but* they will not share sexual partners."

habit outside the congregation into a new form of gathering. This process of gathering-scattering continues through a never-ending cycle. It's like the waves of the seashore or the weaving of a great tapestry. The more we nurture bidirectional movement, the thicker the congregation becomes, and that thickness of identity directly relates to public witness.

Congregational Rhythms

N. T. Wright hints at bidirectional movement when he says, "The revolution of the cross sets us free to be in-between people, caught up in the rhythm of worship and mission."[35] The words "in-between people" could suggest a static state of living in tension between two poles. However, the rest of Wright's statement shows he actually means back-and-forth movement. Rhythm demands movement. Rhythmic music or rhythmic dance involves back-and-forth flows between different melodies or embodied actions. We often treat worship and mission as separate activities, or as polar opposites. Worship, we assume, takes place when a people of God gather, while mission only happens when they scatter. The goal of worship is inward, private movement, while the objective of mission is outward, public activity. By contrasting these, we decrease the likelihood that they will come into contact with each other. By separating them, we divorce the habitus of a congregation (formed through worship) with how that habitus functions in the surrounding public realm.

Congregations develop rhythms, and it is in and through these rhythms that they witness to their surrounding publics. I explained in chapter 2 that publics also possess certain rhythms. Congregational witness takes seriously how the rhythms of the church come into contact with the rhythms of public life. Alan and Eleanor Kreider refer to this as breathing in, breathing out.[36] I have been describing it similarly through the imagery of weaving.

Models of Congregational Rhythms

Let me briefly highlight different models of the church that nurture this back-and-forth movement. In the same way that breathing takes on different rhythms depending on what a person is doing at a given moment (e.g., an individual will breathe more rapidly during strenuous exercise than during periods of rest), or similar to how artisans adopt different rhythms of weaving,

---

35. N. T. Wright, *The Day the Revolution Began: Reconsidering the Meaning of the Jesus's Crucifixion* (New York: HarperOne, 2016), 363.

36. Alan Kreider and Eleanor Kreider, *Worship and Mission after Christendom* (Harrisburg, VA: Herald, 2011), 256–57.

depending on culture, tools, or the object being made, so congregations reveal different rhythms, depending on their surroundings.

Avery Dulles's classic text, *Models of the Church*, provides a helpful typology for considering six models of the church: as institution, mystical communion, sacrament, herald, servant, and eschatology.[37] While this typology is still relevant, most of Dulles's models imply one particular kind of movement: into systems (institution), toward each other (mystical communion), into Christ (sacrament), outside the church (herald), for each other (servant), and more deeply into the fulfillment of all things (eschatology).

I would like to highlight other "models" or typologies that nurture multi-directional movement (or rhythms).[38] There is good precedent for this, since scholars have increasingly framed the church around the different movements of the persons of the Trinity, which has the potential to thicken our understanding of power dynamics within the community of believers, along with expanding the soteriology of the church to include everything in the world. Each of these models I am highlighting below builds on these assumptions.

Some scholars highlight *ecological* imagery to describe the church. Howard Snyder offers a good example.[39] He combines traditional marks of the church (unity, holiness, catholicity, and apostolicity) with other marks that strengthen the ecological cohesion of the church (which he cites as diversity, charisma, contextuality, and prophecy). Rather than keeping these separate from each other, Snyder sees them coming together in service of each other, much like organisms within a broader ecology promote holistic flourishing of the whole.[40] All through Scripture, biblical writers frequently draw on organic language for the church (e.g., the bride of Christ in Rev. 21:9, a living temple of the Holy Spirit in Eph. 2:21–22, a new humanity in Eph. 2:15, or the flock of God in 1 Pet. 5:2). One of the reasons organic language is helpful is that organisms are alive; they breathe, move, and relate to each other in intimate ways. Organisms require nutrients outside themselves in order to grow, and give of themselves to others within the ecosystem. Or as Snyder explains, "Creation healed means seeing the *connections*—because of who the Trinity is. The best mark of the church is a community of disciples that discovers and lives the interconnected strands which together weave the intricate tapestry of creation healed."[41]

---

37. Avery Dulles, *Models of the Church* (New York: Doubleday, 1974).

38. These are not models in the strict sense of the word but are more working typologies to help us think of the church with greater movement and its ensuing thickness.

39. See Howard A. Snyder with Joel Scandrett, *Salvation Means Creation Healed: The Ecology of Sin and Grace* (Eugene, OR: Cascade, 2011), 190–205.

40. Snyder, *Salvation Means Creation Healed*, 193–94.

41. Snyder, *Salvation Means Creation Healed*, 205.

Other scholars use images of *existing in hostile territory* to explain the nature of the church. This way of looking at things represents a departure from older Christendom models that interpreted the church through cultural assimilation to its surroundings. Though not presenting them as fully operational models, Sandra Richter refers to the church as the "outpost of the kingdom in Adam's world,"[42] while Emmanuel Katongole describes the church as a "field hospital."[43]

The idea of an outpost implies a place of refuge *within* a hostile land,[44] while a field hospital suggests a location of healing *for* people *while* living in the midst of violence. Being surrounded by danger shapes both of these images. However, Richter describes this outpost as being located within Adam's world (creation), implying that the territory surrounding the church is intimately involved in God's mission. Salvation, for her, is not about removing humans from creation but redeeming humans precisely in relation to it. The image of a field hospital focuses less on *safety from* and more on *succor for*. The church, Katongole contends, exists to offer holistic healing to those ravaged by violence (which he illustrates through a case study in the Democratic Republic of the Congo).

In both of these examples, the publics surrounding the church (those involving creation and violence) are intimately involved in God's salvation. The church exists to help not only individuals be saved but also the entire community be saved with and for their publics.

Still others focus on the *complexity of the church*. Darrell Guder offers an example through what he calls "a multicultural and transnational approach," where he begins with apostolicity (the church as sent) in order to move toward catholicity (bringing together diverse representations of the church into a broader form of unity across cultural boundaries). He explains the mandate of the church as a "vastly complex process by which the witness of the called and sent community is formed for particular cultural contexts so that the witness mandate is faithfully carried out from one cultural setting to the next."[45] Hence, the church is sent out into all the world and forms communities

---

42. Sandra L. Richter, *The Epic of Eden: A Christian Entry into the Old Testament* (Downers Grove, IL: IVP Academic, 2008), 128.

43. Emmanuel Katongole, "Field Hospital: HEAL Africa and the Politics of Compassion in Eastern Congo," *Missiology* 45, no. 2 (January 2017): 25–37. Katongole acknowledges borrowing this concept from Pope Francis.

44. I fully understand that an outpost can carry military or colonial connotations, which is very different from what Richter intends in using this provocative image.

45. Darrell L. Guder, "A Multicultural and Translational Approach," in *The Mission of the Church: Five Views in Conversation*, ed. Craig Ott (Grand Rapids: Baker Academic, 2016), 21–39, here 22.

everywhere it goes, nurturing a different kind of catholicity (what I am referring to as thick gathering). The church is constantly translating the gospel
from one cultural setting to another.[46] Guder does not use the language of
thickness to describe this model but hints at it by referring to complexity.

Steve Bevans also highlights the complex nature of the church, which he and
Robert Schroeder call *prophetic dialogue*. They describe prophetic dialogue
as involving both "dialogical openness and prophetic truthfulness."[47] The two
exist together as in a complex, beautiful dance: "'[It is] beautiful because it is
the rhythm of God's love moving throughout history' and 'complex because
it changes with time, place, creation's groaning and humanity's response.'"[48]
The language of dance and rhythm allows Bevans to nurture multidirectional
movement. Dance and rhythm also provide helpful imagery to allow for a
variety of music styles,[49] along with back-and-forth movement across the
dance floor. Bevans explains, "The dance is the dance of mission, the mission
of God; the rhythm is a combination of prophecy and dialogue; the kind of
dance depends on the particular context in which mission is being done."[50]

Finally, we can speak of *integral transformation* models. The Latin American
church has been among the most ardent voices calling for holistic (integral)
mission, inclusive of social, political, and economic realities surrounding the
church. Ruth Padilla DeBorst represents well those voices calling for the integral
transformation of society. She explains transformation as beginning with the
Trinity, highlighted in the kingdom of God, and moving with a robust Christology, through the work of the Holy Spirit, to influence all aspects of life in
the world. She says, "Reconciled relationships in the creation community are
at the heart of transformation. And this transformation affects all dimensions
of life, matters spiritual, social, political, economic, and ecological."[51] Of all
the models I am highlighting here, integral transformation takes most seriously
the gross realities of "complicated wickedness" in the world.[52] Padilla DeBorst

46. Guder, "Multicultural and Translational Approach," 24.

47. Steve Bevans, "A Prophetic Dialogue Approach," in Ott, *Mission of the Church*, 3–20,
here 5.

48. Bevans, "Prophetic Dialogue Approach," 9. Here he is quoting his previous work with
Roger Schroeder, *Prophetic Dialogue: Reflections on Christian Mission Today* (Maryknoll,
NY: Orbis, 2011), 156.

49. He says, "In some situations, the dance will take on the rhythm of salsa. In others it
will be a dance to the rhythm of African drums. Still others will require a Filipino tinikling."
Bevans, "Prophetic Dialogue Approach," 9.

50. Bevans, "Prophetic Dialogue Approach," 9.

51. Ruth Padilla DeBorst, "An Integral Transformational Approach," in Ott, *Mission of
the Church*, 41–67, here 42.

52. She writes, "The good news of God's reconciling purposes will reach into our world,
mired as it is in corruption, injustice, violence, poverty, and the plunder of creation, if and

describes integral transformation as a kind of movement, drawing on the Spanish word *integral* as "something complete, having all the parts that constitute the whole."[53] This movement is thus one of making new wholes out of diverse parts, for the purposes of human flourishing in specific locations.[54]

I present these models in order to highlight recent scholarship exploring with nuance the different kinds of movement taking place around the church. Each of these scholars draws heavily on the mission of God, the Trinity, creation, and an understanding of salvation that includes the entire world. The models show the need for congregations to relate intimately with their surroundings, as demonstrated by the language of creative tension or integral mission, and to employ sensitive agency, seen in the language of a posture, presence, transformation, translation, or prophetic dialogue. Through nurturing rhythms, all of these models intimate a thicker form of witness in the world, inclusive of the publics surrounding the church.

How Do Congregations Witness?

Now let's look at some of the ways congregations facilitate back-and-forth movements (or rhythms) to cultivate a thicker form of witness to the public world.

Witness in and for Location

To begin, congregations witness *in* and *for* their location. This means that a congregation in Lexington, Kentucky, for example, witnesses in and for the publics surrounding the church. These publics might include a sense of being marginalized because of the city's proximity to the Appalachia region, or the heightened role University of Kentucky basketball plays in unifying the entire state around a common identity. Meanwhile, a church in Machakos, Kenya, will witness in and for the public realities of people living in the region. Their witness will inevitably include elements of agriculture, regional politics, and poverty alleviation, and usually a combination of these three (as we will see in chap. 7).

---

when the followers of the wounded King allow the Spirit to weave them into a community of such radical discipleship that in all they are, and all they do, and all they say they witness to God's integral transformation until the kingdom comes in full." Padilla DeBorst, "Integral Transformational Approach," 64.

53. Padilla DeBorst, "Integral Transformational Approach," 42n1.

54. For another good treatment of this kind of model, see Al Tizon, *Whole and Reconciled: Gospel, Church, and Mission in a Fractured World* (Grand Rapids: Baker Academic, 2018).

Location is a gift of human identity. And if location is a gift, it plays a critical role in how a congregation witnesses to its surrounding publics. It is hard, if not impossible, to weave something from a distance. We might attempt to throw the strands far away in order to get them attached to some distant object, and then slowly pull them toward us like with a giant lasso. But weaving from a distance is not very effective and can create gaping holes in the fabric. Meanwhile, an organism cannot influence its ecology by lying in a Petri dish. And it's hard to dance alone. We might try, but it's always more enjoyable with another person. Proximity strengthens any public witness.

However, location can be a two-edged sword. Not only does nearness help us weave into the publics surrounding the church, but nearness comes with its own cultural blinders. For example, someone raised in Lexington might find it hard to see University of Kentucky basketball as an alternative form of religion, while a person from Machakos would undoubtedly struggle to find any problem with political systems favoring their own ethnic identity. Someone coming to a location from the outside can observe cultural blind spots or entanglements that a person on the inside cannot see. However, outsiders also possess fewer resources for interpreting the meanings given to those cultural forms. Hence, it might be easier for someone like myself to observe the dangers of Kentucky basketball, but I am less able to interpret why and how the sport plays such a significant role in the region and can therefore misinterpret publics through my own specific lenses. Intimacy with a location also elevates the risk that publics will co-opt a congregation's witness in the community. A congregation that meets in a mall, for example, might find it very difficult to speak prophetically against materialism. It is not that they cannot. Proximity to a location merely comes with strengths and weaknesses.

To undertake congregational witness, we need to exegete the publics surrounding the church. This involves taking location seriously as a subject of scholarly attention. I will explain how we can do some of this in the next chapter.

Witness through Overlapping Networks

Not only do churches witness to publics in and for their location, but local congregations witness through overlapping networks with other congregations. For example, I grew up in an independent Baptist church, which meant we were not associated with any larger denomination and thus functioned, for all intents and purposes, autonomously. We elected our own leaders, hired our own pastors, developed our own structures, and used our own liturgy (if you can call it that) every Sunday. But even this fiercely independent congregation associated loosely with other churches in the city and throughout the region. We planted several daughter churches, invited area pastors to share in pulpit exchanges, and collaborated with other congregations in evangelistic endeavors taking place in our city.

The image of overlapping networks expands the imagery of weaving, dance, and ecology to broaden public witness across a wider region (such as an entire city) or intensify witness within a specific area (such as a neighborhood). By linking together with other congregations, we weave in a different way. We saw the early church growing through overlapping networks, and we observe the same today throughout China. I recently returned from a theological conference where I heard presentations on the house church movement within mainland China. Leaders across the country explained how they arranged themselves through overlapping networks by sharing personnel and resources and strengthening social ties across the region. Overlapping networks can weave broadly or, if they exist within a smaller region, penetrate more deeply into local fabric.

Denominational affiliations can further broaden a church's witness throughout a country, or even across national boundaries. What if we viewed a denomination's institutional nature as a gift (or means of witness) to the institutions and structures of society? We might liken this to millions of microscopic organisms giving of themselves to nourish an entire ecosystem, such as with a coral reef. It has become fashionable to vilify a denomination's institutional nature, but it too can serve as a means of witness, especially to larger, thornier aspects of public life.

Witness Internal to the Congregation

If witness occurs through back-and-forth movement, then we need to probe more deeply the various kinds of movement occurring within the congregation and how they thicken for the formation of a habitus.

Let me say up front that many churches "thin out" their witness by the lack of movement. This happens when, for example, a church focuses on one primary person of the Trinity (say, the Son), one configuration of the persons of the Trinity (such as with a hierarchy), or one particular aspect of Jesus's life (such as the cross) and applies it to a specific aspect of humanity (cognition) or positions it for one compartment of life (to save souls). When churches do this, they lack a "special interiority" big enough to witness to larger, public aspects of life. This book is a call for the church to thicken its witness. Let me explore how this occurs.

Movement across the Persons of the Trinity

Congregations can thicken their witness by mirroring the movements of the persons of the Trinity. There is not one way this can happen, but many. High church traditions possess abundant resources for articulating the importance of each person of the Trinity and will dramatize congregants' participation in the Trinity using bodily actions of kneeling, crossing oneself, lying on the ground, and going up to the altar to participate in the Eucharist. Embodied actions (such as what we see in these liturgical traditions) train the congregation kinesthetically, and whenever a congregation is trained kinesthetically, the church takes those practices wherever it goes.[55] Or as James K. A. Smith says, "The postures of our bodies spill out beyond the sanctuary and become postures of existential comportment to the world."[56]

Worship trains our bodies to participate in the movements of the Trinity. "In worship we do not contemplate the three persons of the Trinity as if they were three supernatural beings, not even as an exercise in our minds. We do not observe God, but we participate in the divine fellowship as God opens up the divine life to make room for us to dwell."[57] Orthodox churches undertake liturgy in threes. For example, in the Litany of Fervent Supplication, the congregational response is to sing "Lord, have mercy" three times after each petition. At other times, the liturgy will begin with "Holy, Holy, Holy" and the congregants will repeat "Holy God, Holy Mighty, Holy Immortal, have mercy upon us!"[58] Or during the "feast of feasts" at the conclusion of the paschal matins, the choir sings, "To the Father, and to the Son, and to the Holy Spirit, now and ever, and unto ages of ages," after which the choir sings, "This is the day of resurrection. Let us be illumined by the feast. Let us embrace each other. Let us call 'Brothers' even those who hate us, and forgive all by the resurrection."[59]

In this example, liturgy trains the congregation for public witness (e.g., doxology of the Trinity teaches us to love and forgive those who hate us). The

55. Lower church traditions, such as Pentecostalism or charismaticism, also train the body, but in different ways. As we will see in chapter 7, Pentecostal and charismatic liturgy constitutes a major component of what we see within many varieties of African Christianity.

56. James K. A. Smith, *Imagining the Kingdom: How Worship Works* (Grand Rapids: Baker Academic, 2013), 167.

57. Paul S. Fiddes and Pete Ward, "Affirming Faith at a Service of Baptism in St. Aldates Church, Oxford," in *Explorations in Ecclesiology and Ethnography*, ed. Christian B. Scharen (Grand Rapids: Eerdmans, 2012), 51–70, here 61.

58. I am grateful to Kriss Whiteman for her help with these insights.

59. John Erickson and Paul Laraz, eds., *The Paschal Service* (Wayne, NJ: Orthodox Christian Publication Center, 1990), quoted in Miroslav Volf, *Exclusion and Embrace: A Theological Exploration of Identity, Otherness, and Reconciliation* (Nashville: Abingdon, 1996), 130.

movement between the divine persons trains us to love each other according to a different power in the world—not domineering but sacrificing, not exploiting but serving. Good liturgy nurtures a different habitus, informed by the movements of the persons of the Trinity. We become a different kind of public in and for the entirety of the world.

Movement across the Life of Christ

All Christian churches focus on the person of Christ, but they prioritize different aspects of his life. Congregations can thicken movement by increasing the scope of Christ's entire life.

To enter a church is to be drawn into the story of Christ, told through different parts of his life, whether incarnation, teachings, sufferings, death, resurrection, or ascension, while narrated through a variety of means, including song, prayer, liturgy, preaching, and sacrament. Congregations "tell" that story with attention to specific parts of Christ's life, expressed through particular doctrinal elements (which Kevin Vanhoozer refers to as "theatrical direction").[60] No two churches narrate the story in exactly the same way.

Why is this important? Publics come to us with their own kind of narrative, made up of many different texts. Most of the publics that directly affect human life possess a thickness to them that is not easily penetrated. Take, for example, ethnicity in Africa, or freedom in the United States, or justice in Latin America. Each of these requires thick description. We cannot describe any of these cultural themes thinly. This is especially true for how sin enters into the open weave of the public realm to create what Wesley calls "complicated wickedness." All of our well-meaning attempts to "solve" global poverty, racial discrimination, bigotry, or violent conflict will inevitably fail if we approach them with thin theological narratives. In some cases the thinness can actually be used to perpetrate violence against others.

Within congregations, we inhabit the thickest story of all. To narrate that story, we need the entirety of Christ's life located within the entirety of the world. Movement across the scope of Christ's life helps a congregation inhabit more of his life for more of the world. For example, if I am preaching on embodiment (as I have done on several occasions), I will draw on Christ's incarnation, affirming God's commitment to human bodies. However, to address certain idolatries in society attached to embodiment (such as altered body image, misguided importance given to sports, or hero worship), I will express our need for the cross of Jesus Christ. Then, after disarming the

---

60. See Kevin J. Vanhoozer, *The Drama of Doctrine: A Canonical-Linguistic Approach to Christian Doctrine* (Louisville: Westminster John Knox, 2005), 77–112.

ideologies that reign in the world, I will turn to the resurrection of Jesus Christ to once again affirm the eternality of our bodies. In such ways, movement back and forth across the scope of Christ's life provides local congregations with a thicker narrative.

To the extent that we dramatize the different parts of Christ's life through our bodies, it trains our witness in kinesthetic ways. We need more of Christ, woven into more of human life and positioned for greater parts of the world. James K. A. Smith defines a habitus as "the complex of inclinations and dispositions that make us lean into the world with a habituated movement in certain directions."[61] Smith's language of "leaning into the world" underscores how local congregations inevitably go public. We need the fullness of Christ's life, not simply what happens at "the edges" (incarnation and death).[62] N. T. Wright demonstrates how the Gospels narrate the story of how God became King over the entire world.[63] Or as Emmanuel Katongole explains, "All the realities of the Christian tradition—the Scriptures, prayer, doctrine, worship, Baptism, the Eucharist, the sacraments—point to and reenact a compelling story that should claim the whole of our lives."[64]

The Holy Spirit is the one who teaches us the fullness of Jesus Christ and is the very same power that raised Jesus from the dead. The Spirit is our greatest resource in thickening our witness. He goes before us into the world, and he sanctifies us through Christ's life and work. Congregations with a robust understanding of the Holy Spirit will already have an advantage.

Movement across the Scope of Publics

Finally, not only do we need the full resources of movement across the persons of the Trinity, and the comprehensive scope of Christ's life, but we need all of this in contact with publics. Some of this happens inside the gathered church, where liturgy, sacraments, and worship open their arms to surrounding publics.

Admittedly, this is the hardest part of all. Ideologies and social imaginaries attached to the public realm naturally make their way into a local congregation.

61. Smith, *Imagining the Kingdom*, 79. This is similar to Alan Kreider's explanation that the early church's habitus was formed "patiently, through careful catechesis as well as through the communities' reflexive behavior, and that it was renewed in the regular worship of the Christian assemblies." *Patient Ferment*, 134.

62. See Bosch, *Transforming Mission*, 399.

63. N. T. Wright, *How God Became King: The Forgotten Story of the Gospels* (New York: HarperOne, 2012).

64. Emmanuel Katongole, *The Sacrifice of Africa: A Political Theology for Africa* (Grand Rapids: Eerdmans, 2010), 61–62.

We wear sports clothing after a recent victory, or promote a program geared to help parishioners with their financial debt. We might even sing "God Bless America" on the Fourth of July or pray for our nation after a horrific tragedy. Other public narratives, though, are purposely kept out of congregations, such as our treatment of First Nation peoples, or the subject of immigration and national identity. In many global contexts, it is the subject of political corruption that no one talks about, especially to the extent that it involves key political patrons. We do anything we can to keep such topics outside the gathered church. Congregations everywhere intuitively know which publics to actively embrace and which to restrict.

However, I have been arguing throughout this book that publics always enter into worship. We cannot keep them locked inside our houses. They travel with us in the form of narratives, myths, social imaginaries, and ideologies. And that's a good thing. We want publics to enter the church. Once inside, they encounter a different narrative constructed by the persons of the Trinity or told through the parts of Jesus's life or through the power of the Holy Spirit. Of course, congregations will sometimes endorse prevailing public narratives. They might even privilege a certain economic ideology, promote ethnic privilege, or baptize a political party with sacred meaning. Publics can co-opt the habitus of a local congregation. We all know this to be the case. But the opposite is also true. The habitus of a congregation can reshape publics.

In the conclusion to this book, I help explain what this looks like. Let me offer just a couple of suggestions here. First, we need to identify the prevailing publics that shape the lives of parishioners. Lesslie Newbigin calls them "plausibility structures."[65] Most of what really matters to people operates at the invisible level. Worship needs to call these things to light. We need to name such things, exposing any implicit spiritualities associated with them. Next, congregations need to allow the habitus to come into contact with the publics. This involves a process I describe as weaving, dancing, or (in ecological language) grafting, where the liturgy, worship, or sacrament allows publics in, for the purposes of "converting" them with the gospel. Conversion, according to Andrew Walls, refers to "the opening up of the functioning system of personality, intellect, emotions, relationships to the new meaning, to the expression of Christ."[66] Through the process of worship, a congregation becomes a different public.

---

65. Newbigin, *Gospel in a Pluralist Society*, 8. Drawing on the work of Peter Berger, Newbigin defines plausibility structures as "patterns of belief and practice accepted within a given society, which determine which beliefs are plausible to its members and which are not."

66. Andrew F. Walls, *The Missionary Movement in Christian History: Studies in the Transmission of Faith* (Maryknoll, NY: Orbis, 1996), 28. Max Stackhouse even uses the language of

Here is where weaving is most delicate. Too much tugging on the threads, and they might break. Yet too general allusions to the publics, and some of the most pernicious ideologies will simply retreat beneath the surface. We need to bring them out into the open: to name the publics (and especially the ideologies behind them) in order to welcome them into the inner life of the persons of the Trinity. It is less a strategy and more wisdom; it requires storytellers brave enough to identify publics within the context of worship. There's no template for how to do this. Some congregations might show the words to a song about Jesus's lordship on a slide with Washington, DC, in the background (such as we will see in chap. 9). Other congregations will simply pray through the global news events of the week, such as I experienced when attending a church in England. We need the Trinity to come in contact with public realities, and we need to embody worship in such a way that trains us to inhabit life with difference. Or as Smith says, "The rites of worship—confession, offering, baptism, communion—carry a social imaginary that is an inescapably 'political' vision of a people called as a royal priesthood and sent as ambassadors of the King above all kings."[67]

Weaving is a fitting analogy as it involves the movement of integrated threads in and out of public life. Miroslav Volf explains how Christian identity involves many different postures with regard to culture: sometimes agreeing, other times dissenting, and usually involving a host of small alterations to the meanings of cultural givens."[68] Weaving helps explain some of what Volf is describing. You do not weave with just one thread or a single technique. It is a process of movement and dexterity. It requires an affirmation of publics as part of God's creation along with a critique of the ways they become idols in themselves separate from God.

Witness External to the Congregation

Local congregations do not just witness to publics as they gather, but more importantly, they do so through their scattering. We cannot allow our worship of Jesus as Lord to be separated from the proclamation of that kingdom within every aspect of life. The church is a public in the world in

sanctification to speak of public witness; see *God and Globalization*, ed. Max L. Stackhouse, vol. 4, *Globalization and Grace*, by Max L. Stackhouse (New York: Continuum, 2007), 226–29.

67. James K. A. Smith, *Awaiting the King: Reforming Public Theology* (Grand Rapids: Baker Academic, 2017), 53; he is summarizing his argument from a previous book, *Desiring the Kingdom: Worship, Worldview, and Cultural Formation* (Grand Rapids: Baker Academic, 2009).

68. Volf, *Public Faith*, 93.

its gathering, while the church is no less a public in the world by its collective scattering.

As parishioners are sent out into the public realm, they witness as an alternative public inserted into the world. They announce the in-breaking of Christ's kingship over every aspect of life and thus call the publics back to their origins as part of God's creation, positioned for the flourishing of the cosmos. They bless the rest of creation.

Congregations are "sent ones." They are apostolic communities that exist within and for their surrounding publics. "The church exists as community, servant, and messenger of the reign of God in the midst of other kingdoms, communities, and powers that attempt to shape our understanding of reality."[69] Our gathering is always for scattering. The local congregation is thus an eschatological community that shows the entire world that there is another way of being human. It does so while participating in the publics of this world, while parishioners are collectively straining their necks in anticipation of the coming kingdom of God (to bring heaven on earth).

As I explained in the introduction to the book, parishioners function as evangelists in and for their publics. For example, when we share the gospel with another person, we do so via the resources of our own humanity. This is what makes personal testimonies so effective, because we are explaining how the gospel relates to human existence. The more "parts of me" I can include in the personal testimony, and the more these are integrated into the lordship of Jesus Christ, the more effective I can be at demonstrating how the gospel reorients the fullness of human life.

If this is true for persons, it is no less true for congregations. As congregations are sent into the publics of their neighborhoods and cities, they witness through their collective imaging. They draw on the resources of work and family, while speaking into larger publics of sports and play. They are also positioned to address thicker narratives of ethnicity, freedom, and nationalism. The more a local congregation immerses itself in the inner life of the Trinity, and the more it inhabits the fullness of Christ's life through the Holy Spirit, the better equipped it will be to witness through its collective humanity. If the Holy Spirit within one person can produce great change, what about the Spirit within an entire community?

We need to send congregations to their surrounding publics. This is hard work since the public realm is inhabited by many rival gods. It is certainly not safe. And we cannot do this as individuals. If all we do in worship is make parishioners feel good about themselves (falling victim to "moralistic

69. Darrell L. Guder, ed., *Missional Church: A Vision for the Sending of the Church in North America* (Grand Rapids: Eerdmans, 1998), 110.

therapeutic deism"[70]), or treat our congregations as separate from the public realm (reverting back to the old Enlightenment dichotomies), we will never witness to the public realm—and we very well may open ourselves to being co-opted by the ideologies within the public realm.

We need to name the "powers" of the contemporary world and mobilize our collective humanity to witness to those powers. Public witness involves re-orienting our affections. While this undoubtedly takes place within the context of worship (as Smith's writings make clear),[71] the reordering of our affections can also occur in the public realm itself. We wrestle with poverty, struggle in the face of pernicious ideologies of race, and contend with a world that reduces everything to thin forms of materialism. "The souls of Christians may be shaped by their public engagement in ways that train their longings here, while also offering a foretaste of their participation in the eschatological kingdom to come."[72] The church is shaped not only in the gathered community but also through its scattered participation in the public realm. It needs to be sent as a blessing to its surroundings through the resources of God in its midst.

Public Witness

Let me conclude this chapter with a couple examples to show what this might look like in an actual congregation.

A young man wakes up Sunday morning and spends an hour perusing the internet to get caught up on the current political situation, while streaming the music of a local band. In the background of his mind, he is thinking about an important meeting he has at work on Monday, which involves a prospective business merger with a company in Seattle. This young man gets dressed in clothes he purchased yesterday at the mall. On the way to church, his mother calls to let him know that his father, with whom he has not spoken for several months, was taken to the emergency room in the middle of the night. He walks into the congregation carrying these things with him. He does not carry each of them individually, like assorted items in a grocery bag, but he carries them collectively. The pieces merge to form a general spirit of angst.

Once inside the church, the young man enters into an alternative story. He is drawn into it slowly, beginning with a few conversations with friends before the service, and then

---

70. This term was first used by Christian Smith and Melina Lundquist Denton in *Soul Searching: The Religious and Spiritual Lives of American Teenagers* (New York: Oxford University Press, 2005).

71. See his argument in *Desiring the Kingdom.*

72. Charles Mathewes, *A Theology of Public Life* (Cambridge: Cambridge University Press, 2007), 27.

more rapidly as the worship begins. Singing welcomes parishioners into the generosity of God's grace. The parts of the service weave together subthemes of love, generosity, and service, told through the story of Christ's encounter with the Samaritan woman, then punctuated by the cross. Our young man thinks of something brash he posted on Facebook, where he was reacting against the political leanings of an overzealous "friend." Collective anxieties build in his body. Songs and liturgy cause him to respond to those feelings of angst. He recites words that speak of the reception of grace and then sings songs that laud Christ's love. The pastor delivers an impassioned message about the kingdom of God inaugurated in human life (as part of a series on the supremacy of Christ). She speaks of the need to surrender everything to the lordship of Jesus, and specifically mentions work and family. The service concludes with a song reminding people that the Holy Spirit is the same power that raised Jesus Christ from the dead. At the end of the service, parishioners participate in the Eucharist. This young man recites the words "Pour out your Spirit on us gathered here, and on these gifts of bread and wine. Make them be for us the body and blood of Christ, that we may be for the world the body of Christ, redeemed by his blood."

Coming out of the service, he decides to visit his dad. He is not alone in his shifted thoughts and feelings. Other congregants have been forced to deal with their own anxieties by the cross, which releases them to be new people through the resurrection. A young mother examines her parenting. A medical doctor, her treatment of patients. An older man, his care for his physical body. Inside a congregation, publics get converted to the gospel of Jesus Christ. The congregants are then sent out as collective witnesses to the in-breaking of the kingdom of God in and through their own lives, which means confronting anxieties about families, jobs, and health. They show the world there is a different way of being human.

This story occurs in congregations all around the world. I purposely made the illustration ambiguous to show that even when a church is not intentional about speaking about specific public domains, they still get integrated into the story of the liturgy. What if churches were more forthright? What if liturgy asked people to reflect on their family relations in light the kingdom of God? Or if the pastor asked people to consider their workplace through Jesus's resurrection? Or if congregants' money got included within the open weave of doxology? Or if the Holy Spirit stood between us and our political ideologies? The more explicit we are in naming the publics, the greater the likelihood that these publics will be exposed to the worship of the congregation and thus released back into the world as agents of God's mission.

The above story focuses on one individual. However, it is possible to discern collective themes of the church sent. Let's consider what this might look like in three congregations.

A church is located in a low-income part of the city. While most parishioners commute from more affluent neighborhoods, the church has developed strong relationships with the local school district. Parishioners who teach and administrate in the district slowly develop a converted understanding of education—informed by the doctrines of creation, blessings, and the incarnation—while having their understanding of power reconfigured through the persons of the Trinity. As a result, several families decide to move into the neighborhood. Others forgo higher salaries to serve the people in that school district. One teacher regularly calls the parents of her middle school class and has developed good relationships with several single mothers. A couple of youth host mentoring sessions for struggling elementary school children after school. One school administrator advocates for increased funding to the public schools with the city council. Parishioners who are schoolteachers do not talk explicitly about their faith, and indeed cannot by school policy, but they teach "with difference." As a result, the habitus of the congregation leans toward education. Inside the church they accentuate spiritual formation and discipleship. Church leadership decides to open their Sunday school wing for after-school tutoring, along with providing free lunches during the summers. Several college students volunteer to serve as basketball coaches. Over time, the habitus of the congregation slowly influences the school district, reconfiguring the domain of education (along with how education relates to economics and politics) according to the kingdom of God.

Another congregation is surrounded by medical services. Parishioners work as nurses, doctors, and office administrators in neighboring health-care companies. Over time, the theme of healing becomes prominent within this congregation. The theme enters into the church from the parishioners' professions, where it thereafter becomes converted through contact with Christ's salvation. As people leave the congregation, they carry with them a broader view of health as a result of what they experience in the worship and sacraments. The nurses and doctors treat patients holistically. A few even probe spiritual health. One health-care company decides to offer free clinics to people living in lower-income areas. The church sends medical short-term missions teams to other countries, partnering with local health-care specialists in those areas. Church leadership decides they want to partner with an African American church across the street, broadening "health" to include reconciliation across racial divides. A few congregants work in agricultural arenas and connect food security with holistic needs. Through a process of years, salvation (as health) becomes the habitus of the congregation, woven into the surrounding publics, influencing social relations, economics, and even agriculture.

A third congregation abuts public land in a heavily populated part of the city. Local developers have been trying to purchase the land for commercial use, but the city council has been resistant because of the lack of green space in the borough. The congregation has parishioners who are businesspersons, civil engineers, and retired landscape architects, and one is a botanist. They all carry a shared concern for the environment into the congregation, which slowly becomes converted (and even sanctified) by the liturgy, songs, sermons, and sacraments. As a result, the leadership of the church decides to approach the city council with a proposal to turn the public land into a park. To their surprise, the proposal is accepted. The congregation donates its expertise, time, energy, and physical labor to work alongside the city council to create a nature reserve, walkways, an area where kids can play and learn about indigenous flora, and a "third space" for people to relax in the midst of a bustling, heavily industrialized city. Through the process, the congregation broadens its theological understanding of salvation to include people *and* creation, while the city receives new input into the underlying meaning of land and leisure.

These three examples illustrate a range of ways that congregations witness to publics through their collective humanity. The examples pertain to education, health, and the environment, but in reality all of these domains intermingle. In each of these examples, the local congregation "goes public" in life-giving ways. Their habitus develops certain characteristics *from* the public realm, and they use that habitus to witness *to* the publics surrounding the congregation.

Conclusion

I began this chapter asking us to hold two things together. First, the church is a different kind of public in the world. Second, as a public, the church exists in and for all of the surrounding publics, to witness to them from within.

We are constantly tempted in two directions. Either we retreat into heavily privatized ghettos we call the church, where the public realm is intentionally kept on the outside (while in reality it is only those publics we deem toxic to our own brand of faith that are kept out, and others are baptized with religious warrant), or we go public in the most radical ways but neglect the habitus of the worshiping, liturgizing, and sacramentalizing community formed around the persons of the Trinity. We need to hold these together through back-and-forth movement, which thickens the identity of the local congregation as it relates to the public realm. Local congregations are, in Newbigin's words quoted in this book's introduction, the "hermeneutic of the gospel" and thus the "basic unit of [a] new society."

Congregations possess the one thing all publics desire, an eternal center. This is not to say that publics are centerless, only that their center lacks solidity and immortality. Like the scarecrow from *The Wizard of Oz* who is on a never-ending search for a heart, the publics of this world attach themselves to anything giving the slightest appearance of an eternal center. A public's center might be fed by many elements, including ideologies. The goal of change, according to James Davison Hunter, "is to infiltrate the center, and, in time, redefine the leading ideas and practices of the center."[73]

Congregations witness to publics through a realignment of centers. Christ is the center of the church as well as the center of the world. But to make this point, we must unpack what we mean by a center. Christ's center is not an empirical center, which we can point to, touch, or tie a rope around to demarcate its exact geographical location. Christ's center is of a different kind, described best by the power-laden language of kingdom, reign, or rule. For such reasons, Christ's center poses a far greater threat to all the rival centers found in the world. If it were merely a geographic center, it would be far easier to deal with. One could ignore it, revile it, or seek to overthrow it by force. But Christ's center is not like that. Christ works in the world through local congregations, sowing seeds of kingdom slowly, quietly, and yet with world-defining power "to bring unity to all things in heaven and earth under Christ" (Eph. 1:10).

---

73. James Davison Hunter, *To Change the World: The Irony, Tragedy, and Possibility of Christianity in the Late Modern World* (New York: Oxford University Press, 2010), 43. William Lindsey intimates something similar in terms of the role of prophets in today's world: "Prophets are less preposterous lunatics crying the absurd from the fringes of society than [they are] people who have managed to invade the center successfully enough to mimic the speech of the center while absolutely refusing the logic that dominates that speech." "Telling It Slant: American Catholic Public Theology and Prophetic Discourse," *Horizons* 22, no. 1 (1995): 89–103, here 101, quoted in Hunsberger, *Story That Chooses Us*, 146.

Part 2

Congregations and Public Witness

6

How to Study Congregations

Even a plain church on a pale day catches one in a deep current of narrative interpretation and representation by which people give sense and order to their lives.

—James Hopewell, *Congregations*[1]

We now recognize that the church is both a theological and a sociological entity, an inseparable union of the divine and the dusty.

—David Bosch, *Transforming Mission*[2]

Local congregations function as agents of public witness. That has been the controlling argument behind this book. They witness out of different movements taking place in and around the church, and these movements produce a thickness that is woven into their surroundings. In the first half of this book, I dealt with theoretical matters, unpacking a public missiology of the local congregation. In the second half, I want us to walk into churches to see what it looks like in living color.

To make this shift, I first need to stimulate interest in studying congregations. Most people pass by the church without giving it a second glance. I

1. James Hopewell, *Congregations: Stories and Structures* (London: SCM, 1987), 11.
2. David Bosch, *Transforming Mission: Paradigm Shifts in Theology of Mission* (Maryknoll, NY: Orbis, 1991), 389.

know this was the case for me. It is exciting to study things *in* the public realm, such as political elections, festivals, global conferences, and media events. We assume this is where the real action lies. The world, we believe, is changed in and through the public realm. Meanwhile, we pass by churches without even considering them. We think of them as simple, private entities where people undertake "spiritual" aspects of life. To the extent that life revolves around the public realm, people escape life by attending church.

Nothing could be further from the truth. As I have argued throughout this book, the lines separating the local congregation from its surrounding publics are less like tall fences with heavily guarded gates and more like multilane highways with traffic moving back and forth in both directions. To study a local congregation is to examine how it relates to its surroundings. Meanwhile, by researching the public realm, we investigate what role churches have had in its formation.

Of course, what I just described occurs unevenly in most congregations. We know too well that some churches baptize select publics with religious meaning, making it more difficult for them to critique the public realm. Others work hard to restrict *any* publics from entering into the congregation (while in fact only keeping out those publics they deem hostile to the gospel, such as select political ideologies). Still others spiritualize everything and leave it up to the parishioner to make any connections between liturgy, sacrament, and preaching and everyday life. When this happens, publics sneak into the church unaware, hiding under the surface. Congregations do an assortment of all these. By describing the boundaries around a church as traffic moving back and forth in both directions, I am merely observing an empirical reality that needs to be studied. I am not saying every congregation accomplishes it well—and certainly not thickly.

Congregations come in millions of shapes and sizes. They "take on varied colorings in different times or cultures, but in every case they serve to perpetuate embodiment, which is essential for the whole church."[3] Rather than assume the worst about them, we need to study local congregations, asking specifically how they exist in relation to the public realm.

Why Study Congregations?

I came to the study of congregations reluctantly. I was a first-year PhD student trying to figure out how to approach my dissertation research. My interests

---

3. Martin E. Marty, *The Public Church: Mainline, Evangelical, Catholic* (1981; repr., Eugene, OR: Wipf & Stock, 2012), 45.

related to theological understandings of power within the context of African Christianity. I had immersed myself in the literature and was preparing to craft my methodology when my doctoral mentor suggested I undertake ethnographic research within three specific denominations in Kenya. My family was moving from England back to Kenya at the time, so his request was reasonable. But I was hesitant. I knew ethnography would be hard work. It is far easier to engage literature than to enter churches. One can also study written documents anywhere, but the study of congregations requires being immersed in a certain context over an extended period. Nevertheless, I finally agreed to his suggestion.

It's one thing to conjecture about the nature of African Christianity, or engage what scholars have written on the subject of power, but quite another thing to enter the churches and observe what is happening on the ground. John Mbiti offers a similar insight. He asks, "Will theological education in the West ever get out into the streets without an umbrella, get wet and hear the birds singing? . . . Much theological activity is taking place on the ground and in the streets, in the fields where people are, where the church is."[4] And surely Mbiti is right. We have been trained to study theology in libraries inside theological institutions. We associate it with brilliant tomes written in the serenity of a professor's study. Undoubtedly, there is a great deal we can learn from works written by scholars. However, the task of unfolding the many rich nuances of Christian witness requires tools with greater animation than words printed on a page. It requires something more active, like three-dimensional video. Or more sensory, like "scratch and sniff" prose. The study of churches must be experienced through all parts of our person, while being immersed in a specific community.

I have never looked back. After finishing my PhD, I applied for a research grant to enlist students at my institution in Africa in a broader study of various congregations throughout Kenya. Since returning to the States, I have required all of my students at Asbury Theological Seminary to study a local congregation for an introductory course on missiology. Not only have I benefited personally from the study of local congregations all around the world, but the process has also opened the eyes of my students to the beautiful complexity found in and around churches.

Let me suggest why we should study congregations. In many ways, the reasons relate to the problems I introduced in the first chapter. In the face

4. John Mbiti, "When the Bull Is in a Strange Land, It Does Not Bellow," in *God and Globalization*, ed. Max L. Stackhouse, vol. 3, *Christ and the Dominions of Civilization*, ed. Max L. Stackhouse and Diane B. Obenchain (Harrisburg, PA: Trinity Press International, 2002), 145–70, here 170.

of the separation of theology from public life and the tendency to look for simple, individualistic answers to complex social problems, the study of congregations offers us some of the greatest hope.

Making Sense of Complexity

We live in a complex world. That fact is unavoidable. However, we love to paint with broad strokes when dealing with highly complex entities. We are reductionists by nature. Whether referring to "cultures" in terms of bounded wholes or employing the language of "people groups" to lump diverse communities into categories of shared traits, we constantly want to reduce complexity to a form we can easily understand (and control?). We are ill-equipped to face the messiness of everyday life, and these efforts make the world appear less complex.[5]

By studying local congregations, we are in fact studying a group of people living in the midst of complexity. Yet even here we project our desire to tame complex realities onto the subject of the church. We refer to congregations in terms of sweeping generalizations in an attempt to wrap our hands around them like a hot cup of coffee on a wintry morning. We say, "That's the Baptist church on the other side of Main Street," or ask, "Are you talking about the Hispanic congregation meeting in St. James Anglican Cathedral?" However, neither of these simple descriptors accurately captures the inner essence of the local congregation. Life is always messier than such generalizations let on. It's not just a Baptist church; the origins of the congregation go back to Wesleyan revivals that swept through the region in the late nineteenth century. The church still retains some of these traits but has recently embraced aspects of neo-Calvinism within the Southern Baptist Convention while simultaneously being influenced by charismatic elements people carry with them from other churches. Meanwhile, the Hispanic congregation meeting in St. James Anglican is actually the amalgamation of three churches, with congregants from Cuba, Mexico, Honduras, and Panama. The pastor (and many of the parishioners) came out of the Roman Catholic Church but recently embraced Pentecostal, evangelical characteristics. Most of the congregants retain strong ties with their home countries, unsettling any attempts to refer to this congregation by means of "people group" language.

5. Clifford Geertz remarks, "They are not, these separated 'cultures,' or 'peoples,' or 'ethnic groups,' so many lumps of sameness marked out by the limits of consensus: they are various modes of involvement in a collective life that takes place on a dozen different levels, on a dozen different scales, and in a dozen different realms at once." *Available Light: Anthropological Reflections on Philosophical Topics* (Princeton: Princeton University Press, 2000), 254.

I hope you see my point. It is not wrong to study "cultures" or "people groups," but it is always preferable to research specific communities living in particular locations. The study of local congregations enables us to do exactly that. It also helps us analyze how theology relates to sociological realities, and how sociological facets arise from theological characteristics. As David Bosch says, "The church is both a theological and a sociological entity, an inseparable union of the divine and the dusty."[6]

The study of local congregations can best be described through different images of movement. In the last chapter, I described some of these in terms of ecology, narrative, and weaving. Clifford Geertz says something similar in regard to understanding the complexity of contemporary culture. To delve into the intricacies of global society, Geertz explains, one needs to discover "the overlappings of different threads, intersecting, entwined, one taking up where another breaks off, all of them posed in effective tensions with one another to form a composite body, a body locally disparate, globally intertwined." Hence, the goal of studying a local congregation, if I might continue borrowing from Geertz, is that of "teasing out those threads, locating those intersections, entwinements, connectings, and tensions, probing the very compositeness of the composite body, its deep diversity."[7] All congregations weave, or dance, or relate within their environment like an organism in an integrated ecology. The challenge is for us to understand *how* local congregations do so, in order to strengthen (or thicken) their witness in and for their surrounding publics.

Implicit Theology and Movements

One way of studying how a congregation relates to its surrounding environment is to examine its implicit theology. When we hear the word *theology*, we immediately think of historical creeds, doctrinal statements, or impressive theological treatises written by scholars. Our minds drift toward large (often obscure) words that only make sense to professionally trained scholars. However, most of the theology occurring in and around the church is of a different kind.

In a local congregation, we find both explicit and implicit theology. Churches use explicit theology to communicate what is important to them. Explicit theology tends to rest on carefully worded statements—often heavily vetted by church leadership. The explicit tells us what a church believes, or what it wants others to know it believes. We discover it on websites or in official documents. It lies before us in plain sight.

6. David Bosch, *Transforming Mission: Paradigm Shifts in Theology of Mission* (Maryknoll, NY: Orbis, 1991), 389.
7. Geertz, *Available Light*, 227.

Meanwhile, implicit theology broadens the scope of what a congregation believes. If explicit theology is largely based on material written by specific persons (i.e., professionally trained clergy), implicit theology includes all the people in the congregation (including parishioners). If explicit theology favors cognition (what people think about God), implicit theology broadens the resources for doing theology, including the social imaginary (who the community envisions themselves to be in relation to God and others) and embodiment (how a congregation worships or lives out its faith).[8] If explicit theology focuses on coloring within the lines of an established theological tradition, implicit theology paints across lines to make vital connections with the local congregation's surrounding culture. If explicit theology wants to be seen, implicit theology loves hiding behind the scenes in symbols, art, gestures, and other subtle means.[9]

Both are important. In many ways, implicit theology helps us test the veracity of explicit statements of belief. For example, let's imagine a local congregation says they are "missions-minded" but then defines what they mean by that in terms of overseas missions work, highlighted during certain times of the calendar and accomplished only by particular people, but without it ever influencing the nature of the congregation as a whole. In such a case, the explicit functions more as a projection of self-identity than of reality. Another congregation talks explicitly about the priority of preaching God's Word, but congregants in the church regularly minister to people in the community and welcome refugees and immigrants into the body. They pray in every service for the marginalized and weave matters of social justice within their liturgy. In this instance, implicit theological practices broaden our understanding of what the church actually believes. When we study a local congregation, we need to lay explicit beliefs alongside implicit theological practices and see how they align (or how they don't align).

When it comes to research, it's relatively easy to study a church's explicit beliefs. All you have to do is visit a website, request official documents from the church, or visit the archives of the denomination. It is much more difficult

---

8. Agbonkhianmeghe Orobator refers to theology as "faith seeking understanding, love, hope, prayer, praise and worship" to show how it is something we do in church. See *Theology Brewed in an African Pot* (Maryknoll, NY: Orbis, 2008), 21.

9. Robert Schreiter defines implicit theology as "theologies or fragments of theologies that inform the congregation's life but are not necessarily acknowledged or overtly expressed. They may be only half-formed and only present in certain sectors of a congregation. They may be present in a variety of places and activities in the congregation: in the stories a congregation tells about itself, in styles of leadership, and in the many ways it chooses to arrange its life." "Theology in the Congregation: Discovering and Doing," in *Studying Congregations: A New Handbook*, ed. Nancy T. Ammerman et al. (Nashville: Abingdon, 1998), 23–39, here 31.

to study implicit theology. Martyn Percy defines the word *implicit* from its Latin origins in the word *plicare*, which refers to weaving or folding, "in the sense of mixing and combining, rather as one might expect to 'fold' an ingredient into a recipe."[10] This colorful word picture underscores what I have been saying throughout this book. All congregations weave or fold elements together within highly complex movements.

Explicit theology tends to be relatively static (i.e., doctrinal statements don't normally change much). Implicit theology attends to connections. "Folding" is a slow, subtle process that happens beneath the surface. Percy explains that all congregations fold, or knit, and by this he means they use material at hand to influence their surroundings. For example, local congregations will employ insider language drawn from the surrounding culture. Worship is filled with rich, textured weaving, drawing together disparate threads into a colorful tapestry of doxology. The threads might be fragments of doctrine, combined with flecks of color drawn from cultural norms, while performed through the resources of the body. Rather than these things making worship unintelligible, congregants not only interpret what is happening but derive great theological meaning from the flow. Despite the Enlightenment heritage of mapping out the world according to strict binaries, implicit theology reveals that congregations weave together sacred and secular or private and public with far greater fluidity.[11]

Theology within Community

Studying congregations helps us see how theology is performed by an entire community. Whereas explicit theology is usually done by a single author (or a group of individuals), implicit theology is dramatized by all the persons in the congregation.[12] They perform theology, drawing on an array of threads

10. Martyn Percy, *Shaping the Church: The Promise of Implicit Theology* (Surrey, UK: Ashgate, 2010), 1–2.

11. Percy explains more what he means by implicit theology: "That is to say, it is entangled, entwined and involved in the life of local congregations; that it is engaged in areas of overlap and hinterlands between the life of the church and the world. Implicit theology, as the term suggests, understands that most of what is expressed theologically is implied rather than plainly expressed." *Shaping the Church*, 161.

12. Kwame Bediako makes this argument: "Because of the strong element of 'the experience of community' in the theologies of the South, these theologies have a distinct inclination to be 'ecclesial' theologies, which is not to say that they are confessional or denominational. Rather, this simply expresses the way in which the theologies of the South are rooted in the churches, and are produced from within the churches, to the extent that they proceed on the basis of seeking to understand and articulate the longings and aspirations of the communities they present." *Christianity in Africa: The Renewal of a Non-Western Religion* (Maryknoll, NY: Orbis, 1996), 162.

from Scripture, tradition, and the surrounding culture.[13] And they do this together while located within a specific context.

By studying local congregations, we observe new vistas for theological exploration. For example, if we think of theology only according to Western systematic theology categories, then our primary themes of analysis will be limited to doctrines of creation, sin, election, redemption, and eschatology. If we include theological categories emanating from local congregations, the variety of themes might increase to include hospitality, belonging, healing, forgiveness, and freedom. If we extend our analysis to local congregations around the world, our list expands exponentially. We will be forced to consider land, place, and reconciliation (all themes I will highlight in the following chapters), along with many, many other themes, such as power, blessings, and cosmology. None of these need to take us away from Scripture, but they help us ponder how Scripture relates to the matters of importance to the local congregation.

Furthermore, by studying local congregations we do not just consider these categories theoretically but consider how they are sung, danced, and dramatized through the resources of our collective humanity. It expands the scope of our analysis. Congregational study should lie at the very heart of how we study all the incredible resources found within world Christianity. It's one thing to study a book written by a global scholar. But that scholar is speaking to a specific audience, and that audience is more likely than not to have an eye directed toward Western readers and to be composed of fellow scholarly elites.[14] While this is helpful for translating African or Asian or Latin American theology for a Western audience, it is limited in scope. By way of contrast, the theology emanating from a local congregation is always directed *within* and *for* a specific community. We discern new ways of thinking about God, expressed through doxological rhythms and cadences, and woven together with public elements surrounding the church. Parishioners do not just think about God with their minds but dramatize their faith through their bodies. They are

---

13. Kevin Vanhoozer says, "Indeed, if the church is a community of interpreters—of Scripture and of culture—it is for the sake of becoming an effective community of cultural agents." "What Is Everyday Theology?," in *Everyday Theology: How to Read Cultural Texts and Interpret Trends*, ed. Kevin J. Vanhoozer, Charles A. Anderson, and Michael J. Sleasman (Grand Rapids: Baker Academic, 2007), 55.

14. Kwame Anthony Appiah makes a similar argument about postcolonialism. He says, "Postcoloniality is the condition of what we might ungenerously call a comprador intelligentsia: of a relatively small, Western-style, Western-trained group of writers and thinkers, who mediate the trade in cultural commodities of world capitalism at the periphery." See "Is the Post- in Postmodernism the Post- in Postcolonialism?" In *Contemporary Postcolonial Theory: A Reader*, ed. Padmini Mongia (London: Arnold, 1996), 62–63.

singing, dancing, preaching, and relating with others within a location. Or as Percy explains, "The belief that God is Father, Son and Holy Spirit is not an arid set of directives, but rather a faith that is embedded in a community of praxis that makes beliefs work, and gives shape and meaning to the lives that believe."[15] By studying the theology emanating from local congregations, we gain new insights into world Christianity.[16]

Finally, the theology found in local congregations is already contextualized within particular situations. By saying it is already contextualized, I do not mean to suggest it is always faithful to Scripture, or reflective of historical traditions or orthodoxy. I merely want to highlight that it involves weaving explicit theological material with implicit cultural sources, while interlacing these with the surrounding publics. Congregational theology is what Robert Schreiter calls "local theologies."[17]

Theology in Relation to Surrounding Publics

Congregational theology relates intimately to its surrounding publics. Clergy may "police" the church's borders, or a congregation may interpret itself as "set apart" from its surrounding culture; however, all churches possess an open weave.[18] We need to investigate *how* a particular congregation weaves into its surroundings rather than assuming it is inward.

PUBLICS WITHIN THE CONGREGATION

By studying congregations we gain insights into *how* publics surrounding the church enter into the liturgy, preaching, organization, dress, songs, and other aspects of the congregation. Parishioners bring their publics with them. They do not check them at the door of the sanctuary or keep them locked in the safety of their homes. Publics travel with people in the form of narratives, myths, or ideologies. They are not garments people put on and take off at will. When we belong to a public, it becomes part of our human identity. Studying congregations helps us see our surrounding contexts in new ways, like standing in front of a mirror for the very first time.

15. Percy, *Shaping the Church*, 4.

16. Princeton Seminary recently hosted a conference on world Christianity and ethnography. I suspect that this approach will generate incredible new insights into the diversity, complexity, and beauty of World Christianity in the years to come.

17. Robert Schreiter, *Constructing Local Theologies* (Maryknoll, NY: Orbis, 1985).

18. Percy says, "Places and churches exist on many levels, and their boundaries, though real, even perhaps geographical and firmly fixed in culture, are nevertheless subjective and porous." *Shaping the Church*, 165.

We often interpret this negatively. Scholars will bemoan the church's domestication by Western culture or Christianity's complicity with political ideologies. We can rightfully challenge congregations for their "vendor-shaped ecclesiology"[19] or their infatuation with Christendom models.[20] We know too well the extent to which some churches reinforce (rather than challenge) existing stereotypes and in some cases perpetuate societal injustices. The publics *around* the church can easily co-opt the gospel of Jesus Christ.

However, as we saw in the last chapter, a congregation's proximity to its surroundings can also be one of its greatest strengths. Publics are more than just the negative ascriptions of everything we deem wrong about culture. They are an important part of our humanity. Publics relate to how humans configure power, think of freedom, and give meanings to things like money, status, or technology. Kevin Vanhoozer explains, "[Publics] give us new capacities for knowing ourselves, new possibilities of being human." He continues, "In a real sense, in choosing how to respond to the texts of popular culture—to their propositions and to their projection of a proposed world—I also choose myself."[21] This is an important lesson that lies at the heart of this book. By witnessing to publics we are witnessing to our humanity, along with God's intentions for the flourishing of life. When we neglect publics and focus only on individuals, we not only truncate the gospel to fit one aspect of humanity (i.e., souls) but leave publics to roam unfettered, constantly looking for anything big and strong enough to give them meaning and cohesion with the rest of life.

The more we attempt to keep publics out of local congregations, the greater the likelihood we will be enticed by a vision of "pure" theology, which, as history shows, leads to increased violence against others.[22]

We actually want publics to enter into the liturgy, sacraments, worship, and preaching of the local congregation. Once inside, publics are exposed to the movements of the persons of the Trinity and come into contact with the totality of Jesus Christ's life. We introduce them to the only thing big and strong enough to give them meaning and cohesion with the rest of life: "bring[ing] unity to all things in heaven and on earth under Christ" (Eph. 1:10).

19. E.g., George Hunsberger, "Sizing Up the Shape of the Church," *Reformed Review* 47, no. 2 (Winter 1994): 133–44.

20. Stuart Murray, *Post-Christendom: Church and Mission in a Strange New World* (Eugene, OR: Cascade, 2018).

21. Vanhoozer, "What Is Everyday Theology?," 53.

22. Percy says, "Religion, in other words, when un-earthed and de-coupled from social and cultural contexts, has a greater potential to become toxic and self-absorbed." *Shaping the Church*, 163.

Public Witness around the Congregation

Not only do we study publics within the congregation, but we study how the church goes public. This might happen through outreach events. Or it can occur implicitly, and even symbolically. "By the very presence of their buildings, their steeples and stained glass, they call people beyond themselves."[23] This does not mean congregations always influence a community positively. We know too well the sordid history of Christianity (or any religion) as it relates to the public realm. However, acknowledging the potential harm a religion brings to the public sphere is not the same as calling for the "bracketing out" of religion from public life. Even if we were to successfully keep religion out of the public sphere, many other pseudo-religious entities would fill that vacated space, and the end result could be worse than the original state.[24] The question is not *whether* religion goes public but *how*.

Congregations are, as I have been saying throughout this book, the hermeneutic of the gospel, and the basic unit of a new society. They facilitate public witness first by helping us think about religion differently—not as a cluster of beliefs but as "lived religion" or "embodied theology." For example, doctrines do not just hang in the air like Gnostic ghouls but function as "dramatic scripts which Christians perform and by which they are performed."[25] Parishioners do not philosophically muse about doctrines such as creation, sin, and redemption, or about the persons of the Trinity. They dramatize doctrines through liturgy and song.[26] David Ford describes lived theology as "the adoption of habits of thought, imagination, feeling and activity, which are assimilated through participation in a community's life."[27]

This leads to the subject of a habitus. As you will recall, I suggested in the last chapter that the early church witnessed to its surrounding publics by means of its habitus. I explained how a habitus arose in the early church from small, seemingly insignificant actions local communities performed over time, such as catechesis, worship, and the eating of meals together. It trained them in certain ways. Drawing on Pierre Bourdieu's work, Christian Scharen refers

23. Ammerman et al., *Studying Congregations*, 8.

24. Miroslav Volf explains, "When religion leaves the public sphere—or is driven from it—the public square doesn't remain empty. Instead, it becomes filled with a diffuse phenomenon called secularism." *A Public Faith: How Followers of Christ Should Serve the Common Good* (Grand Rapids: Brazos, 2011), 124.

25. Percy, *Shaping the Church*, 11.

26. Kevin J. Vanhoozer, *The Drama of Doctrine: A Canonical-Linguistic Approach to Christian Doctrine* (Louisville: Westminster John Knox, 2005).

27. David Ford, "Theology," in *The Routledge Companion to the Study of Religion*, ed. John R. Hinnells (New York: Routledge, 2010), 61–79, here 62.

to a habitus as "a particular but constant way of entering into relationship with the world the body inhabits," or as a "mode of being in the world, by which we practically navigate day-to-day life."[28] James K. A. Smith refers to it as "a complex of inclinations and dispositions that make us lean into the world with a habituated momentum in certain directions."[29] In other words, we do not have to choose between worshiping God and living in the world. Whatever parishioners do inside a congregation inevitably goes public. We carry a habitus with us wherever we go.

By studying a congregation's habitus, we discern rhythms, patterns, and meanings nurtured within the faith community. We also explore how the congregation relates to its surrounding communities through the scattering of parishioners into neighborhoods, places of work, and "third places." This might involve how the habitus of a congregation diffuses into a local community with "patient ferment" (to use Kreider's phrase again) to influence the ways a neighborhood thinks about itself. Sociologists refer to this as "social capital." We can also investigate how the congregants are sent out as evangelists in and through their publics, to witness to the in-breaking of the kingdom of God within the context of public realities.

By studying a congregation, not only do we understand publics better (especially as they enter the church with all their complexity), but we discern how the congregation relates to its surrounding publics in its scattering. We discern connections and movements between the two. It helps us weave.

The Study of Congregations

Before I get to the practical how-tos of studying a local congregation, let me begin with some theoretical considerations. I begin theoretically because of historical ways we have been trained to do theology. Theology in the West has focused on one primary disciplinary dialogue partner, and that is philosophy. Philosophy helps us think of theology as related to what is good and true, but struggles, in the words of Mbiti from above, to "get out into the streets without an umbrella, get wet and hear the birds singing."[30]

This does not mean we jettison philosophy. We just need new dialogue partners. Kevin Vanhoozer bemoans Western theology's preoccupation with

---

28. Christian Scharen, *Fieldwork in Theology: Exploring the Social Context of God's Work in the World* (Grand Rapids: Baker Academic, 2015), 15.

29. James K. A. Smith, *Imagining the Kingdom: How Worship Works* (Grand Rapids: Baker Academic, 2013), 79.

30. Some scholars have recently sought to make stronger connections between theology and wisdom, which might help theology "get out into the streets" more than it currently does.

philosophy.[31] He asks the probing question of "whether, and why, Christian theologians from other parts of the world must play by Western Christianity's rules in order to do theology."[32] Vanhoozer suggests that global Christianity ushers in an era of "after method,"[33] where no particular methodology rules the roost. He asks why scholars in other parts of the world cannot develop their own unique methodologies. "The key methodological issue [for them]," he proposes, "is no longer that of right procedure (how?) but location (where?) and position (who?)."[34] He is not suggesting we abandon existing methods or move away from the text of Scripture. Vanhoozer is rather highlighting the need for us to develop methodologies that probe the valuable contributions of *location* and *position* in theological research. And for that we need the social sciences.[35]

Let me say up front that any dialogue with the social sciences comes with its own risks. By beginning with culture, it is easy to allow context to become determinative or accept secularistic assumptions found within the social sciences. Interaction with any discipline does not mean wholesale embrace of everything found in that discipline.[36] I am rather suggesting that to discern the theology found within congregations, we need other tools. We cannot just read about salvation, for example, but need to study it *in* local communities.[37] The same is true for a habitus. If a habitus is our "mode of being in the world, by which we practically navigate day-to-day life,"[38] or "a complex of inclinations and dispositions that make us lean into the world with a habituated momentum in certain directions,"[39] then we cannot study a habitus in a textbook. We need to enter the churches.

31. Some of the material in this section first appeared in my book *Re-imaging Modernity: A Contextualized Theological Study of Power and Humanity within Akamba Christianity in Kenya* (Eugene, OR: Pickwick, 2012), 31–32.

32. Kevin Vanhoozer, "One Rule to Rule Them All: Theological Method in an Era of World Christianity," in *Globalizing Theology: Belief and Practice in an Era of World Christianity*, ed. Craig Ott and Harold A. Netland (Grand Rapids: Baker Academic, 2006), 85–126, here 88.

33. Vanhoozer, "One Rule," 91.

34. Vanhoozer, "One Rule," 95.

35. Christian Scharen says something similar: "Whereas theology had for many centuries turned to philosophy as its main conversation partner, theology since the 1960s has experienced what Kathryn Turner has termed a 'turn to culture.'" *Fieldwork in Theology*, xvi.

36. A colleague of mine, Steve Ybarrola, notes this is as true of philosophy as it is of the social sciences. All disciplines come with their own presuppositions and "plausibility structures."

37. Timothy Tennent explains, "Indeed, there are aspects of salvation that can be experienced and known only within the church as the redeemed community and cannot be realized in isolation from that community." *Invitation to World Missions: A Trinitarian Missiology for the Twenty-First Century* (Grand Rapids: Kregel, 2010), 62.

38. Scharen, *Fieldwork in Theology*, 15.

39. Smith, *Imagining the Kingdom*, 79.

Theology and the Social Sciences

Andrew Walls makes the point that "when theological studies cut themselves off from other branches of learning, they lose opportunities to renew their own streams with fresh, clear water."[40] Innocuous as this statement appears, there are certain predispositions within Christianity in which any suggestion that theology might need help from other disciplines is met with varying levels of resistance.[41]

Evangelicals, in particular, have been tentative, and sometimes hostile, toward any suggestion of theology needing renewal from the outside. Some theologians might fear that this would be tantamount to saying that "God is not sufficient" for the needs of humans, or others might question whether mixing theology with another discipline will inevitably compromise God's character, leading to "secularism" or "syncretism," or deemphasize the centrality of the Scriptures. Each of these concerns arises from the history of evangelicalism's uneasy relationship with modernity, and especially liberal Christianity's accommodating posture toward culture from the late nineteenth century.

As I probe the relationship between theology and the social sciences, I should make clear I am not doing so as a social scientist. I am a missiologist who has enjoyed having my own streams renewed with fresh, clean water in dialogue with the social sciences. Let me briefly summarize some of the scholarship that integrates theology with the social sciences, and then use that as a springboard to examine the study of local congregations.

Sociology and Theology

Sociology and theology interrelate in a number of ways. Robin Gill provides a typology for examining the possibilities. He adds his voice to those of David Martin and Peter Berger, who have likewise contributed to the growing body of knowledge in this area. Gill presents three possibilities for how sociology contributes to theological research (ultimately suggesting all three are inseparable, leading to what he calls "an interactionist approach").[42] The first is to examine the social determinants of theological positions and explore ways that theologians are influenced by their society. When I talk about publics

---

40. Andrew Walls, "Globalization and the Study of Christian History," in Ott and Netland, *Globalizing Theology*, 70–82, here 78.
41. Some of the material in the section "Theology and the Social Sciences" first appeared in my book *Re-imaging Modernity*, 25–30.
42. Robin Gill, "Three Sociological Approaches to Theology," in *The Social Context of Theology*, ed. Robin Gill (London: Mowbrays, 1975), 3–14.

entering into congregations, this is what I am describing. We never theologize in a vacuum. By studying the theology of a local congregation, we are trying to pay attention to how theology is shaped by its local context, which means its surrounding publics.

A second possibility, Gill suggests, involves the social significance of theological positions, which looks at the other side of the relationship: how theology goes public. This is roughly similar to what Max Weber postulated when he argued that Calvinistic theology was, in part, responsible for the inception and growth of capitalism in Western societies. This perspective promotes the frequently overlooked possibility that theology functions as an independent variable, and it underlies the main contention of this book: congregations always go public.

The third possibility proposed by Gill employs sociological methods in the service of understanding the social context of theology. In this case, sociology offers its tools and resources for explicating the social context around the local congregation. In this chapter, I am essentially laying out a very rudimentary pathway for what this looks like.

Anthropology and Theology

If sociology relates to theology in different ways, the same can be said for theology and anthropology. We see this especially in the emerging field of the anthropology of Christianity. This new discipline examines Christian faith communities around the world.

In the book *On Knowing Humanity: Insights from Theology for Anthropology*, a collection of theologians and anthropologists dialogue for mutual benefit. They begin by examining some of the basic assumptions behind the social sciences, arguing that if anthropology is going to take Christianity seriously (and not just treat it as a social phenomenon to be studied), it must make room for religious belief. With its origins in the Enlightenment, anthropology has historically divided up the world into two separate realms: natural and supernatural. As the authors explain, "[Anthropology] has used this division as an operating assumption, relegating all observable phenomena of human life to the former as the object of study, and declaring agnosticism with regard to the latter."[43] However, the authors want to show that religious belief is not at odds with science (as Michael Polanyi's work reveals), nor is it possible to occupy a position of pure objectivity (as Western modernity

---

43. Eloise Meneses et al., "Engaging the Religiously Committed Other: Anthropologists and Theologians in Dialogue," in *On Knowing Humanity: Insights from Theology for Anthropology*, ed. Eloise Meneses and David Bronkema (New York: Routledge, 2017), 10–30, here 11–12.

has assumed). Anthropologists can actually use their belief systems to their advantage, and theologians can use the tools of anthropology to exegete cultural contexts.

I am also encouraged to see anthropologists and theologians dialoguing around the field of ethnography. In the past, we have tended to see ethnography solely as a social science tool. Theologians have been hesitant to use any methodology developed by the "secular" social sciences. However, as James K. A. Smith explains, "Any theology that refuses Gnosticism needs to be somehow accountable to empirical realities."[44] If Christianity represents an embodied belief system, and theology is the study of God in actual situations, then we must develop tools for the sake of studying theology in human contexts.[45]

My approach roughly parallels the work of Agbonkhianmeghe E. Orobator, a Jesuit priest who studies the church in Africa as it pertains to HIV/AIDs, refugees, and poverty.[46] Orobator begins with the assertion that the complexity of the church demands a multidisciplinary methodology. One of the reasons theology proves insufficient to these ends is that "church" represents an entity with "two sides: one theological, the other social."[47] Theology employs its methodology for the spiritual dimensions but misses the social, public aspects of faith. Orobator contends the church must be seen as "an open human community of faith, that is, open to society, to its social environment."[48] An integrative ethnographic/theological method helps us understand how a local congregation relates to its surrounding publics.

By nurturing relationships with the social sciences, theology is able to gain critical insights from different contexts. For example, if Africans were to construct their own systematic theology, drawn from their own cultural values (as we in the West have done), they might begin with power and blessings. Both of these themes arise from the *missio Dei*. However, we rarely talk about power or blessings in Western contexts, except perhaps in Pentecostal or black congregations. Our systematic theologies are constructed through our own cultural lenses. This does not mean they are wrong. Our theological lenses are merely limited by the categories our culture offers us to interpret

44. James K. A. Smith, foreword to Scharen, *Fieldwork in Theology*, xii.

45. Smith explains further: "Theology as ethnography complicates any easy bifurcation between church and world without simply eliding the two. This is honest theology that can still be a gift to the church—or more specifically, to real, tangible, messy congregations you find down the street." Foreword, xii.

46. Agbonkhianmeghe E. Orobator, "Ecclesiology in Crisis: A Contextualised Theological Study of the Church of Africa in the Situation of HIV/AIDS, Refugees and Poverty" (PhD diss., University of Leeds, 2004).

47. Orobator, "Ecclesiology in Crisis," 14.

48. Orobator, "Ecclesiology in Crisis," 15.

the world. By studying congregations, we gain insights into the theology that matters to people on the ground and broaden our theological framework as we listen to communities around the world.

How to Study a Congregation

Let me devote the rest of this chapter to describing *how* to study local congregations. This is a topic of increasing scholarly interest. We can find many good books that nurture a dynamic relationship between theology and ethnography. The most accessible and readable among these is the edited volume *Studying Congregations*.[49] Other possibilities include Mary Clark Moschella's *Ethnography as a Pastoral Practice*,[50] which is a good supplemental text. For students interested in exploring more deeply the various intersections between theology and ethnography, I would recommend Christian Scharen's *Fieldwork in Theology*;[51] in the series Studies in Ecclesiology and Ethnography, which includes the volumes *Perspectives on Ecclesiology and Ethnography* (edited by Pete Ward)[52] and *Explorations in Ecclesiology and Ethnography* (edited by Christian Scharen);[53] and Martyn Percy's *Shaping the Church*.[54] We have also seen the inception of the journal called *Ecclesial Practices*,[55] which allows for increased opportunities to examine the subject. Finally, if you are looking for a good example of what theology and sociology can produce, I would recommend Christopher James's fine book *Church Planting in Post-Christian Soil*.[56]

How then do we study local congregations? I will keep this section fairly basic. I have taken courses in social science methods at three institutions and am now a professor at a fourth. Each of these institutions teaches ethnographic research in slightly different ways. The fundamental goal of ethnography is to understand a context from within sustained, immersed observation,

49. Ammerman et al., *Studying Congregations*.

50. Mary Clark Moschella, *Ethnography as a Pastoral Practice: An Introduction* (Cleveland: Pilgrim, 2008).

51. Scharen, *Fieldwork in Theology*.

52. Pete Ward, ed., *Perspectives on Ecclesiology and Ethnography* (Grand Rapids: Eerdmans, 2012).

53. Christian B. Scharen, ed., *Explorations in Ecclesiology and Ethnography* (Grand Rapids: Eerdmans, 2012).

54. Percy, *Shaping the Church*.

55. *Ecclesial Practices: Journal of Ecclesiology and Ethnography*, http://booksandjournals. brillonline.com/content/journals/22144471.

56. Christopher B. James, *Church Planting in Post-Christian Soil: Theology and Practice* (New York: Oxford University Press, 2018). James refers to his work as "practical ecclesiology," which relates to "an ecclesiological method that utilizes study of concrete churches and to the written products of such work" (6).

while allowing people on the ground to provide meanings to any of the data that emerges.

When I teach on this topic, I usually begin by asking my students the following questions: If you were posted as a pastor to a new congregation, what would you want to know about the church? Where would you look for information? Who would you talk to and why? And what questions would you ask them? My students initially gravitate toward the explicit. They want to look at the church's mission and doctrinal statements. They express interest in reading any historical documents that exist. Others talk about interviewing church leadership, including former pastors. One says he wants demographic information of the church and of the surrounding city. These are good answers. After a few moments, a few intrepid students shift toward implicit matters. One says she would participate in a worship service to see how the congregation prays, sings, and preaches. Another would study a local newspaper. Others talk about their desire to interview parishioners in the church. When I ask them who they would interview, some say those who have attended the church longest, while others say they would want to talk with those who attend infrequently. One explains he would want to interview those who have left the church. All of these answers show that the greater the diversity of those interviewed (whom social scientists call "respondents"), the stronger the overall research.

It's a profitable exercise. It helps us begin thinking about the formal study of a local congregation. Let me offer a series of steps for studying a local congregation. I am intentionally keeping this simple, desirous to make such an exercise accessible to anybody within the church: lay leaders as well as clergy. If you want to go deeper, I would strongly recommend you pick up a copy of *Studying Congregations* edited by Nancy Ammerman, Jackson Carroll, Carl Dudley, and William McKinney and follow the steps they provide.

Study Material about the Local Congregation

The first step is to get your hands on anything written about the local congregation. This might entail visiting the church's website (if they have one) or reading historical accounts, the Facebook page, or anything about the church appearing in the local newspaper. As you peruse these sources, ask yourself the questions, Who do they say they are? What are their explicit beliefs? Who are the official leaders? And what ministries are highlighted (meaning ones they want you to know about)? A person can learn a lot about a church from this simple exercise. Does the congregation have a doctrinal statement? What elements do they include in their statement? And what elements do they omit? From there we can probe other questions. Are all official leaders male? Where did the pastor (or pastors) study? Do the leaders introduce themselves on the website? How do they self-identify? And how did the church begin, and by what families?[57]

By exploring these questions, we gain valuable insights into what the congregation wants people to know about them. Material on a website is not just for transmitting information; every church uses its website to project a public image as well. What image are they projecting? And to what public(s)? People outside the church? Those disillusioned by other churches? The parishioners themselves? Or a particular segment of society? A church's audience provides valuable information into what is important to them. For example, when a congregation says, "We're a friendly church," they might be catering to those new to the city, or such a statement might address a felt need within the culture. Throughout the process of our research, the goal is to understand what the church means by "friendly," why that is important to them and whether such a statement aligns with their belief in God, how the congregation worships, and how the church relates to the broader community.

Study Material about the Church's Social Location

After studying any written material, we should investigate the immediate context around the church. Social location is critical for understanding a congregation. By studying the context surrounding a local congregation, we are learning about the church itself. If it's a commuter church, this entails learning about the entire city; or if it's a parish congregation, we can focus on the neighborhoods, places of work, and "third places" around where the congregants meet for worship. One of the best things to do is to walk around the community and study the publics surrounding the church.

There is no end to what we can study about the social location around a congregation. Nancy Eiesland and Stephen Warner use the term *ecological frame* "to speak of the social fabric of any community as a complex web of people, meanings and relationships, alterations in any one of which can result in social ramifications elsewhere."[58] The first layer is demographic, the second is cultural, and the third they describe as organizational. Every

---

57. At least in many parts of Africa, the family that gives the property for the church always has more power in the congregation. This may have something to do with the importance of land, along with the cultural value given to the past and origins.

58. Nancy L. Eiesland and R. Stephen Warner, "Ecology: Seeing the Congregation in Context," in Ammerman et al., *Studying Congregations*, 40–75, here 42–43.

congregation exists within a delicate ecology made up of social, ethnic, and institutional networks. Our goal is to understand these layers, and especially how they interrelate.

READ A LOCAL NEWSPAPER

To study the ecological frame, the first thing we can do is read a local newspaper. Media focuses on topics important to people in any given location. By scanning the headlines, we are given critical insights about what people value, along with what issues provide meaning to people living in a particular place. For example, if the newspaper talks about a local sports team or a public debate, such as the opioid crisis occurring in the United States, then it is likely that the team or debate carries important cultural information. For example, I currently live outside Lexington, Kentucky, and the University of Kentucky basketball team is more than a topic of local entertainment but a cultural theme that carries valuable social identity for people living in this region. It is also helpful to read letters to the editor. What are people upset about? What topics do they care about? It is probable that whatever is showing up in the newspaper will eventually make its way into the local congregation. People carry their publics wherever they go.

INVESTIGATE DEMOGRAPHICS OF YOUR LOCATION

Next, get demographic information about your community. Many times this can be found through a simple internet search; if it cannot be, go to the local library or government offices. You will want to obtain demographics about per capita income, population, median age, poverty rate, race and ethnicity, employment by occupation, and other helpful information. I would especially recommend studying demographics for specific districts in your city. Where is growth occurring, and what kind of growth is happening in those locations—population, job creation, new business, or ethnic migration? Where is decline occurring? And what kind of decline—population, employment, graduation rates, or housing markets?

By studying demographics, we are taking note of shifts (or, in the language of this book, movements or weave). Are neighborhoods gentrifying? If so, who is moving into those communities, and where are the original residents going? If international migrants are moving into your city, where are they coming from, and why? And what kinds of relationships do they retain with their countries of origin? The answers to these provide us with critical information. Demographic shifts help us understand not only the current state of the region but also future trends we should be aware of.

STUDY OTHER CHURCHES IN YOUR REGION

Not only can we study demographics, but we can do an analysis into the different types of churches (or other religions) in our city. The presence of other faith communities provides us with critical information about the religious frame. They point to historical layers of religious tradition. For example, can you narrate the religious history of your city? Indigenous beliefs? Colonial heritage? Missionary presence? Denominationalism? Secularization? Changes brought about by migration? New religions? As you outline this history, think of it according to layers, with each layer informing the others. By studying the religious-ecological frame, we gain insights into the intersecting layers of belief within a certain location.

Every congregation exists within a delicate ecosystem. As Nancy Eiesland and Stephen Warner explain, "A congregation is linked to networks and events across geographic and temporal space. Communities are not only discrete localities with stable boundaries and fixed constituencies, they are also characterized by shared conversations, common practices, and structures that promote cooperation and exchange."[59] Think of a giant spider's web or an elaborate ecosystem. We sometimes think of congregations as "private" entities, "set apart" from larger public domains; however, every church exists in intimate relationship with its surroundings, like one strand within a complex web. Change occurring in one place will trigger change across the whole.

Do a Mapping Exercise

The next step is to map your location. Even the most insular congregation exists within a vibrant social ecology. A church might self-define in contradistinction to its surrounding "culture." They might sing, pray, and preach in ways that imply discontinuity from the world (e.g., "I'll fly away, oh glory"); however, the parishioners are still farmers, shop owners, factory workers, schoolteachers, students, lawyers, stay-at-home moms and dads, and medical professionals. Because of this, the congregation is linked with land, economies, educational institutions, legal systems, houses, playgrounds, and hospitals. Furthermore, even when parishioners are not members of a given social organization (such as the city council), the church's proximity to that institution is still an important piece to analyze. The threads connecting a church with its social ecology are not just empirical but are also invisible. A church's vicinity to the city council, for example, might make

---

59. Eiesland and Warner, "Ecology," 41.

the community more conscious of its political identity. Influence between a church and its surrounding publics can still occur even when there is not direct contact.[60]

It is important to visualize what this looks like. One easy way of doing this is to take a map of your area, circle your church location, and then mark various things on the map. Use different colors to help differentiate between the categories. For example, begin with the following:

- For every member of your congregation, place a black dot next to where they live.
- Do the same for where they work, but this time drawing a black circle around the location. (If interested, you could draw black lines between where the members live and work to show their fields of influence between home and employment.)

Even doing this simple mapping exercise will help you visualize your congregation's potential web of influence. Are members clustered around one area? Do the lines thicken around the local congregation, or do they stretch far and wide across an entire city? By drawing this on a map, it helps us see the connections (movements) the church possesses.

Next, add public institutions. Mark colors for the following public domains on the map:

- Place a red mark for medical fields.
- Place a blue mark for businesses.
- Place a yellow mark for legal entities.
- Place a green mark for agricultural entities.
- Place a purple mark for political entities.
- Add any other public domains, depending on your specific context.

Note: referring to these as specific domains (with unique colors) does not mean they are discrete from other publics. Medical fields are heavily influenced by economics. Agriculture and politics relate to each other dynamically. Paying attention to specific domains just helps us see different thematic elements that we perhaps have never noticed before. Do congregants work in specific domains, such as medical or agricultural? What public institutions surround the local congregation? And to what extent do these public

---

60. Eiesland and Warner further explain, "Both religious influence and social causation are sometimes open and visible, other times more hidden and subterranean." "Ecology," 42.

domains overlap each other? For example, are there businesses in proximity to the town or city council? Or do educational institutions exist close to medical facilities?

It is also important to map "third places" in the city, identified as locations where people spend time outside of work and home. Third places might include parks, pubs, coffee shops, public libraries, or other locations where people congregate. If you wanted, you could draw square boxes around third places. Marking these locations helps us see where people spend their leisure time.[61]

You can expand the map to include demographics, helping you notice the populations of different communities in various parts of the city and think about how that relates to where your congregants live, work, and play. Write such details into neighborhoods or sections of the city. Another significant measurement tool is to obtain economic data and provide that as a different layer on your map. Which businesses are growing, and which are declining? Which neighborhood incomes are changing, and how?

If you wanted, you could include on the map "transnational circuits of relationship."[62] Every congregation exists in one particular location but possesses webs of influence across the globe. You can draw lines from your congregation to international cities where you have vibrant relationships. Lines are not one-directional, so it might be helpful to place arrows on both ends. For example, you might support a missionary in Uruguay and assume the influence moves from your church to that country, but all relationships, if they are healthy, travel back and forth. People in that church pray for you. They might even come to speak in your congregation. Alternatively, you probably have members of your church who work for transnational corporations such as BMW and regularly travel to Germany, the United Arab Emirates, or South Africa. The same is true for short-term mission trips. These partnerships strengthen "transnational circuits of relationship" between your church and international congregations. The best example of such global flows would be if you are blessed with immigrants who have immigrated to your city and attend your church. Transnationalism connects your congregation with people all around the world.

The longer you think about it and work on your map, the more lines stretch out across your city and around the world. Colors bleed into each other across the map. Demographics highlight critical shifts occurring. A simple

---

61. There might be repetition between some third places and businesses, especially if people congregate in pubs or coffee shops.

62. Eiesland and Warner, "Ecology," 41.

mapping exercise helps us visualize a local congregation's complexity. This is true for all churches, not just those residing in urban "gateway" cities. A congregation's complexity is a gift to its surrounding publics. The thicker the lines existing in and around any location, the greater the likelihood for public witness.

Know Yourself

Before actually entering the church, it is critical to know yourself. The better you know yourself, the better you will be able to observe the church without projecting your biases onto them. Everyone views reality through his or her interpretive frame. This is a "natural" part of being human. However, our lenses not only help us see but also can restrict our sight. Cultures function as blinders as well as flashlights. You may have a visceral reaction to what you experience in a church, whether overly positive or quite negative. In both cases, it is important to suspend interpretive judgments in order to observe as much as possible. Of course, no one can obtain pure objectivity. That's a myth straight out of modernity. But by knowing ourselves, we can alleviate biases we bring into the process of research. Social scientists call this "reflexivity."

For example, I am a tall white man with titles and degrees. When I undertook research in Africa, my height, skin color, and academic credentials influenced how others perceived me. Sometimes respondents gave me answers they thought I wanted, and in other instances they were guarded in speaking with me. In knowing ourselves, we can take steps as researchers to mitigate these influences. For example, when I attended a new church (to me), I would go with a member of that church and ask them to introduce me to the church leadership. I conducted interviews in focus groups to lessen any discomfort people might have, while trying to be sensitive to power differentials. In some cases, we can hire research assistants. We cannot stop being ourselves, nor can we acquire complete objectivity. In knowing ourselves (and how others perceive us), we can make adjustments to our research methodology in order to get more accurate data.

Attend the Church and Observe (and Write Down) Everything

The next step is to actually enter the church. We don't study from afar, like astronomers examining distant galaxies through the means of high-powered telescopes. We observe by participating in the life of the congregation, which social scientists call "participatory observation."

Moschella describes participatory observation as a "pastoral practice [that] involves opening your eyes and ears to understand the ways in which people practice their faith."[63] Since faith is always an embodied practice, it is necessary to adopt tools of analysis that take seriously how faith is sung, preached, prayed, liturgized, and performed by the entire community. Participatory observation is "intentional and systematic investigation and description of what takes place in a social setting."[64] Understanding a church involves affections, bodies, and social relationships within the context of a communal setting. By participating in the community, we broaden the scope of our knowing; or, we could say, by doing ethnographic observation, we know through greater parts of our personhood.

For some congregations, it might be helpful to introduce yourself and ask permission to study the church. This is especially the case when the congregation does not regularly host visitors, or if there is a strong "gatekeeper" presence in charge of the church (such as a clergy member or ranking elder). Other congregations actively court visitors and thus are more amenable to someone coming and doing participatory observation.[65]

Purchase a small notebook for your observations. The goal of ethnographic observation is to observe as much as possible and write it down. Of course, you will not be able to record everything. Some people choose to use an audio recorder (with permission). This helps them hear everything, but it does not help with visual dimensions of the congregation. I prefer a small notebook, which I sometimes supplement with an audio recorder. Attempt to see the congregation as an outsider, even if it's your home church.[66] You will want to attend the service numerous times and sit in different locations. The goal of observation is to see patterns, and it is hard to see patterns when you only attend once or observe the service from a single vantage point. Patterns arise from repetition. If you attend the church only on Easter Sunday, you might think the congregation always focuses on the resurrection. The more times you visit, the more likely it is that you will see patterns that give insight into the real identity of the church.

63. Moschella, *Ethnography as a Pastoral Practice*, 4.

64. Scott L. Thumma, "Methods for Congregational Study," in Ammerman et al., *Studying Congregations*, 196–239, here 199.

65. If you are uncertain, it is always best to ask for permission. In asking, you will be perceived in different ways than if you were just a visitor. But you want to make sure you do not violate any ethical standards of research protocol by researching a church against the wishes of the clergy or persons in charge.

66. It is often easier to "see" and "hear" things when the church is completely different from what you are accustomed to. If you attempt this with your own local congregation, your own lenses can impede your ability to observe. Your interpretive mechanisms will get in the way. It is still possible, but you will need to be much more intentional about "seeing the familiar as strange."

What can you observe? Begin by looking at the physical location of the congregation. Sketch how the church relates to its surrounding community. If it is a parish church, sidewalks will connect pedestrian traffic with shops, parks, and city transport (such as we will see in chap. 8). If it is a commuter congregation, the first thing one may notice is a large parking lot, with buildings set back from the road (as in chap. 9). Is the church connected to its social ecology by roads, highways, and sidewalks, or by lush gardens (as in chap. 7)? When you first arrive at the location, what signage appears? Who is there to greet you? What do people say when they greet you? As a visitor, do they give you any written material or introduce you to anybody in particular? What about the architecture of the building? How or what does it communicate?

Once inside the church, sketch the use of space. I like to draw a picture of the inside of the building. Where do people congregate before and after the service? What is the physical arrangement of the sanctuary? All of this is important even if the church meets in a theater or a storefront. Sketching a visual diagram of the meeting space helps you see how everything is organized. It also communicates power dynamics (such as if the priest sits separately from the people, or if the pulpit is raised above the congregation). Observe how the church organizes space and what people do with that space. Also note social patterns of behavior. What do people do as they wait for the service to begin? Where do they sit? Who talks to whom? Are there any special pews? Does everyone want to greet a particular person? Are there children in the service? What about youth? Do people sit by families, by gender, or by ethnic similarity? What about their interactions with clergy? Do pastors greet people with familiarity, or is there a distance between clergy and parishioners?

Once the service begins, you will want to write down everything that happens: prayers, songs, liturgy, dance, and sermon. Unless you use an audio recorder, it is impossible to capture everything. Yet it is critical to get as much empirical data as possible. The first couple of times you attend the church, you will want to write down as much as you can. Do not interpret. Record word for word. If they pray, write down as much of the prayer as possible. If there is an official liturgy, see if you can get a copy of it. If they sing popular choruses, a simple internet search will procure the words of the songs. If the pastor preaches, write down as much as you can (and see if you can get a transcript of the sermon). Then pay attention to the specific elements of the service. How do they refer to God? What is the nature of their supplication: praise, petition, and for what needs? What announcements do they share? How does the pastor preach? We learn a lot from the images, language, and stories that someone uses to communicate God's Word. Do they draw on expository preaching or combine different texts into a whole? What sacraments are included? How do they refer to the sacraments? Then there is implicit material. Pay attention to nonverbal communication, including the use of symbols, art, and gestures (including how a pastor preaches). If you miss something, don't guess at what was said. Write down everything word for word. This becomes your data.

Look for Patterns

The goal of ethnographic research is to identify patterns. Patterns in congregational research are like foot traffic across a field. It is hard to see patterns after one or two people have walked through an area. But after an extended period, with literally hundreds of pedestrians traipsing across a barren field, one can physically observe the patterns of foot traffic. Patterns help us see where people have walked (and where they did not walk), along with which direction they were heading, and how their paths crossed with others. Congregations are integrated organisms. They are not a collection of random, independent agents but a community using theological and sociological resources to position themselves advantageously *with* God and others and *for* the world.

All churches possess patterns. The key is to understand what patterns exist and how the patterns highlight resources that facilitate public witness.

Discovering patterns means taking empirical notes and spending time analyzing the data (your notes). In social science research we call this "data analysis." We do not interpret *into* the data but allow the themes to emerge *from* the data. It is possible to find good computer software that will help with the analysis. But perhaps the easiest way is the tried-and-true method of using colored highlighters. We go back through all our notes and color a word (or phrase) with the same color. For example, if we consistently see a word or image that communicates "grace," we will mark that yellow. Or if we observe another word, phrase, or image signifying "healing," we will color every instance in blue. Patterns can be strengthened by architectural elements, such as some church buildings built in the shape of a cross. They can also be emphasized by colors, such as regal colors of purple reinforcing the theme of kingship.[67]

When a theme arises from multiple parts of a service, we say that it possesses *thickness*. In other words, a pastor might preach on the theme of grace, but if that theme arises in songs, in prayers by parishioners, on tapestry hung in the foyer, and in personal testimonies, we could say that the theme of grace

---

67. However, we will want to use interviews to see whether people interpret those colors in such a manner.

arises with thickness within the church. We want to identify thick themes. The thicker the theme, the more likely the congregation can use that theme to witness within and for its surrounding publics.

Interview People

Once you have identified themes that emerge from the data, you will want to discover the meanings of those themes. For example, if the kingship of God is a prominent theme in a congregation, we will want to make sure we are not projecting our own cultural understanding of kingship into that church. To get meanings, we need to conduct interviews. Our desire is for people themselves (and especially a diverse cross section of respondents) to give the meanings to a theme. When I did this in Africa, I noted a theme of power. I thought people would use that theme to speak of leadership. I was surprised when they began describing power in larger sociological terms, such as through development or education, or to express agency in the world. We need to allow people to explain themes for themselves and not assume we know what they mean.

To do so, you will want to interview a diverse array of people. It is always important to interview official leaders, such as the pastor or an influential elder. But you can get broader perspectives by interviewing lay leaders, long-time attendees of the church, and founding family members, along with people existing on the periphery, such as those who recently left the church. Interviewing a wide variety of respondents helps generate a thickness of meanings from diverse perspectives.

There are different kinds of interviews. The best is usually semi-structured and open-ended, where you go into the interview with prepared open-ended questions (not just yes-or-no questions) and allow the person to take the interview in whatever direction they find most helpful. As I explained in the introduction to this book, the best interview I ever did was with eight women attending a Pentecostal church in Kenya. I started with one question, and forty-five minutes later we ended the interview. I never spoke again during the entire time. The women gave their thoughts. Some disagreed with others. A few explained the reasons for their responses, speaking to each other more than to me. In the end, the women arrived at a position that allowed them to give "thick description" to the theme.

Provide Thick Description

After doing the research, analyzing the data to discern themes, and doing interviews based on the themes, you are now ready to write up the results. As stated in the introduction to this book, Clifford Geertz refers to this as "thick description," which means describing the congregation as holistically as possible to show the complexity of the church. Through thick description we want to show how a theme arises from many vantage points, along with the meanings given to that theme from a diverse array of people. Consider the theme of freedom in a North American congregation, or power in an African congregation. Both require thick description. You cannot explain either freedom in the United States or power in Africa thinly.

For example, congregants within a predominantly Anglo church in Lexington, Kentucky, sing about freedom as they rehearse God's saving work, and they pray for deliverance from their past mistakes. Songs are sung in the first-person singular to show that freedom is primarily interpreted by them individually: "set me free from the chains holding me," and "love came down and rescued me." They also practice personal choice in relation to church governance: voting for a new senior pastor. The goal of salvation, as explained by a recent sermon series, is "release" or "liberty" from our sins. "God wants you to be a new person," the pastor explains. "The world needs your freedom in Christ." As I talk with people after the service, they explain to me that many people come to the church with deep pains from their past. They need individual freedom from their guilt. Others talk about how Christ's freedom helps them become better mothers, friends, and business professionals in the "real world." They see themselves making an influence in the world through their individual lives. Freedom releases them "to be a new person" in the world.

Meanwhile, in a small congregation on the outskirts of Machakos, Kenya, parishioners sing about God's power—"the Lion of Judah has given us power; he has broken every chain," and "if Jesus says 'Yes,' nobody can say 'No'"—as they dance around the inside of the church. They shake their fists at Satan while imploring God to grant them power through the Holy Spirit. In prayers people cry out, "Mighty God," "Eternal King," "Mighty Everlasting Father," asking God for help, while doing so in "the Mighty Name of Jesus." The pastor delivers an impassioned sermon about deliverance from generational curses, and the need to receive the Holy Spirit. Regal colors fill the sanctuary. There is a tapestry hung on the wall with the words "Victory in the Spirit." A choir performs a song. Choreographed motions dramatize the choir bowing low before the throne of God. As the choir rises, they stand erect, looking up toward heaven with arms open wide. The pastor refers to the Bible as the "sword of the Spirit." After the service, the congregants explain that many people in the church feel defeated. They come to church to "tap the anointing" and experience power, which they carry to their homes, communities, and places of work. They depart the church filled with the Holy Spirit and confront spiritual forces in societal places through the kingship of God.

Both of these snapshots show a little of what thick description looks like. The next three chapters will go into greater detail. All congregations possess patterns, which need to be thickly described. I am interested in *how* congregations use their themes (or habitus) to position themselves as agents of public witness in and for the world.

Conclusion: Benefits of Studying Congregations

Inside congregations all kinds of exciting things take place. We may miss all of this good stuff if we think we know everything about a congregation because we have memorized the liturgy or attended the church since childhood. In fact, one could argue that someone deeply immersed in a given congregation may be less likely to see all the things taking place because of the ways their lenses have been shaped by that context. Hence, if you are studying your own church, the goal should be to make the familiar strange. You want to see it through new eyes. If you are studying a different congregation, it will be easier to see themes but will require help from others to interpret the meanings of the themes.

That is the point of this chapter. While it has become fashionable to say all kinds of despicable things about churches (many of them well deserved!), local congregations remain the bedrock of Christian faith around the world. We study them because of their theological significance; they are where doctrines become dramatized within embodied practice. We also analyze them for their thickness, to see how they make a difference in their publics. We can also study them out of intrigue. As the editors of *Studying Congregations* explain, "Any student who is curious about how ordinary people experience their religion would do well to begin his or her exploration in the gathered communities."[68]

Congregational research connects theory with practice, and theology with embodiment. Such a methodology takes the researcher by the hand and introduces her to the churches, where effusive worshipers sing and dance, pray with outstretched arms, and interpret Scripture through songs, prayers, and preaching. While the study of theology often revolves around scholars, the study of congregations focuses on parishioners, who draw on a rich array of language to reflect God's nature, often piecing together various attributes of God in a way that provides a thickness to their doxological flow. In this way, the study of congregations is more descriptive than prescriptive, more empirical than hypothetical, more critical than romantic, and specifically located in time and place.

68. Ammerman et al., *Studying Congregations*, 7.

The goal of a public missiology of the local congregation is to research how a congregation witnesses to its neighborhoods, city center, and third places. All congregations are, by nature, public. Let me now highlight the nature of that public witness through case studies involving three churches.

Note about how to interpret the next three chapters. The second part of this book aims to be more descriptive than prescriptive. In the first five chapters, I sought to make a case for a public missiology of the local congregation. Now I want to lead you on a tour of three specific churches.

Let me say up front that by foregrounding these congregations, I am not suggesting they are perfect or ideal varieties. That is a burden too great for any church to bear! I have purposely chosen examples drawn from three countries (Kenya, the United States, and Canada) on two continents (Africa and North America) to better illustrate the diversity in how the congregations witness into their surrounding publics. One is not better than the others. I merely want to identify different kinds of movements taking place in and around these churches. As you read, please interpret these chapters less as prescriptive examples for others to follow and more as thick, descriptive case studies of public witness.

I am focusing on the good found in these churches. In a different kind of study, I could offer a critical engagement of the faith communities. But that is not my intention here. I have visited each of these congregations on multiple occasions.[69] I have also drawn on research my students have done on these churches, giving them full acknowledgment in my citations where relevant. I am presenting these not as complete ethnographies but as case studies. They help connect the theory of a public missiology with congregational witness.

Let's now enter the churches.

---

69. For one of the congregations, some of my visits were done by watching the service on the church's website; however, I did physically observe two church services and used three ethnographic papers written by my doctor of ministry students.

7

Thick Doxology and Witness to Land—Africa Brotherhood Church, Machakos, Kenya

We want to go a step beyond the gospel and outreach the whole personality.

—Bishop Timothy Ndambuki

We're going to change this place religiously.

—Millicent Manesa

It's a Sunday morning in Machakos, Kenya. Machakos is a bustling city that lies seventy kilometers southeast of Nairobi. Normally, the city is teeming with pedestrian and vehicular traffic, but today the streets are empty. Shops are closed. The sun has yet to rise above the distant hills, but already there is song in the air. It's faint at first, but a slight breeze carries the first whispers of melody echoing across the Mua Hills. And with the song, the entire city comes to life, as if with the breaking of a trance.

It does not take long for people to begin streaming out of their homes, dressed in their finest garments. Women are adorned with brightly colored dresses, while men wear suits or African-style kitenge shirts. Young kids run around playing with each other. Everyone begins walking to church, and they are holding two books in their hands. One is a Bible, and the other is a hymnbook. Scripture and song flow organically into each other, forming the bedrock of African Christianity.

Music fills the air as with a gentle murmur. A Sunday morning in Machakos is like a majestic parade with people streaming in all directions.

My friends and I pass a host of churches. There is a Redeemed Gospel Church with spirited choruses reverberating out of its tin-walled structure. We stroll by an Anglican cathedral with regal hymns billowing from its lofty bell tower. Then we hear Kikamba (the language of the Kamba people living in the region) music arising from an old, seasoned Africa Inland Church. Congregations dot the landscape. They rise resplendent across inner-city skylines, meet in secondary schools across the country, and can be seen all across the distant terraced hillside. A Salvation Army band marches down the street, followed by throngs of parishioners dressed in their uniforms. We stop to watch the procession as it goes by.

Continuing down the street, we pass various shops and places of business. Their names suggest a long-standing Christian presence in the region—for example, Grace Butchery, Destiny Hair Salon, Canaan Shopping Center, and Mustard Seed Building. Vehicles carrying commuters stream past us with more powerful ascriptions, such as God's Power, Yesu ni Bwana (Jesus is Lord), El Shaddai, and Trumpet of Hope. If one did not know better, one would think that all the shops and vehicles have, like the people, put on their Sunday best. I purchase a newspaper from a street vendor and am struck by the first two headlines I read: "Raila quotes Bible to win over Anglicans" and "Women storm pub, convert husbands." Christian images spill over into public spaces like music flooding down the Mua Hills.

We arrive in Mumbuni, a small hamlet within Machakos city proper. Walking through the gate of the Africa Brotherhood Church, we find ourselves immersed in a lush garden, filled with sensory delights. Palm trees stretch to the heavens. Avocado, orange, mango, and papaya trees fill the courtyard. The walkways are meticulously lined with carefully pruned shrubs. Meanwhile, brightly colored flowers burst like synchronized explosions from bromeliad, hibiscus, plumeria, and bird of paradise plants, filling the garden with a profusion of sights and smells. Music streams out of the church building, beckoning everything to fruitfulness.

The contrast with the surrounding countryside is notable. Outside the gates of the church, the city labors under a prolonged drought. The short rains did not come, and the longer rains are past due. Ukambani (the place where the Kamba live) is considered an arid region in Kenya. The city of Machakos is little better. But walking into the courtyard of the church compound is like entering a hidden garden oasis. Plants fill the landscape with blooms as if emerging from the creational powers of song.

The Africa Brotherhood Church

The Africa Brotherhood Church (ABC) broke away from the Africa Inland Mission (AIM) in 1945.[1] At the time of its inception, Kenya was at the height

---

1. Some material in this chapter first appeared in my chapter "Africa Brotherhood Church: Self-Reliance and Development," in *Re-imaging Modernity: A Contextualized Theological*

of colonial activity. Western missionaries controlled many of the churches. People within Ukambani felt that mission-founded churches were not taking seriously the economic needs of the region. The ABC began with a vision for a church led by Africans and existing for Africans, bringing "brotherhood" and development to a part of the country beset with strife and poverty.

The early leaders of the ABC came out of evangelical churches, most notably the AIM (a faith-based mission) and the Salvation Army. As a result, the ABC combines spirited evangelical beliefs (which include a robust biblicism and priority given to accomplishing the Great Commission) with Akamba values of hard work, respect for authority, responsibility, and the importance of land. The ABC thus represents what scholars of African Christianity refer to as an older, Ethiopian-style African church that borrows and subsequently revises the heritage they received from the early missionaries.

Ostensibly, Kenya is a Christian nation. Eighty percent of citizens claim to be Christians. It is not unusual to hear the Bible quoted by political leaders. As Jon Lonsdale explains, "The Bible may not be taken by all Kenyans to be God's word, but its images are certainly at the center of their political culture—if in a rather ambiguous way."[2] We see this in newspaper headlines, along with ascriptions on shops and public service vehicles. Simplistic private-public, sacred-secular dichotomies are not sufficient to capture the complex cartography of African Christianity.[3] Birgit Meyer differentiates between *going public*, where Christianity makes a public appearance, and *making public*, where private, sacred realities are purposely oriented for the public sphere.[4] The former is an undeniable reality throughout sub-Saharan Africa; the latter is the subject of inquiry for this chapter. How do "private," "sacred" elements of worship "make public"? And in what kinds of ways?

Study of Power and Humanity within Akamba Christianity in Kenya (Eugene, OR: Pickwick, 2012), 115–44. For more on the Africa Brotherhood Church, see "African Brotherhood Church," *Ecumenical Review* 24, no. 2 (January 1972): 145–59.

2. Jon Lonsdale, "Compromised Critics: Religion in Kenya's Politics," in *Religion and Politics in Kenya: Essays in Honor of a Meddlesome Priest*, ed. Ben Knighton (New York: Palgrave Macmillan, 2009), 55–94, here 85. Earlier Lonsdale says, "Biblical texts and images give Kenyans a moral and political language that most of them share, so that no matter what their ethnicity, they can understand each other on matters of personal and public morality well enough to agree on what they disagree about" (80).

3. As Harri Englund explains, "Ideas expressed in, and actions taken within, apparently different domains and institutions feed into each other, and what belongs to the public sphere or the private sphere is to be investigated and not assumed." Harri Englund, ed., *Christianity and Public Culture in Africa* (Athens: Ohio University Press, 2011), 2.

4. Birgit Meyer, "Going and Making Public: Pentecostalism as Public Religion in Ghana," in Englund, *Christianity*, 152.

We enter the sanctuary. A large crucifix hangs in the front of the church. The podium and chairs are decorated with special white cloths with a banner that reads *Fanyeni hivi kwa kunikumbuka* (Do this in remembrance), reciting Jesus's words from 1 Corinthians 11:24. On each side of the verse is a dove that symbolizes the Holy Spirit. Streamers hang from the rafters of the sanctuary as lingering remnants from a wedding celebration the previous day. I am handed a bulletin with the logo of the denomination. There is a badge on it with a cross. Mark 16:15–16 is listed on the logo: "Jesus said, Go ye into all the world." A dove hovers above the badge, with the words "HOLY SPIRIT."

The congregation has been worshiping for some time. The pastor has yet to arrive, but music floods throughout the quiet hamlet of Mumbuni, calling the entire neighborhood to praise. As parishioners settle into their pews, they kneel down, say a brief prayer, and then take their seats, sitting mostly by family groups. Various groups come to the front of the sanctuary to perform a song. Like most churches throughout Kenya, the congregation has multiple choirs. The better ones compete with other church choirs across the country in a yearly competition. On this Sunday, a microphone is shared by different groups: older men, some youth, a women's fellowship, and even a couple nervous children come to the front to sing. Music is open to all, transcending age or socioeconomic status. It is the great equalizer. Between songs, lay leaders offer prayers. We pray the Lord's Prayer, followed by another song performed by the choir; and then Bible reading, and more singing. Scripture and song interrelate in an intimate dance.

In every service, the ABC sings a hymn the early founders composed. One of the stanzas says, "God the Father, Son, and Holy Spirit, let us see your power in this service." Directly afterward, a choir comes to the front and performs a chorus about Jesus's victory over Satan. The lyrics correspond to bodily actions, where word and dance choreograph a story signifying Jesus's victory through the cross. Choir members' fists are clenched. They interlock arms to signify their collective will against evil. At the name of the devil, the choir collectively stomps their feet to the ground. The congregation breaks into spontaneous applause.

We continue to sing choruses, such as "The Lion of Judah has given us power, has given us power, hallelujah, day by day." As we sing, the congregants parade around the sanctuary, giving each other high fives as if celebrating the efficacy of the words. Other choruses laud God's attributes, laying characteristics of the divine on top of others as if building a scaffolding of ascriptions to the sky. We praise God, singing of him as the "Alpha and Omega" whom we worship as the one "worthy of our praise." We follow this with singing, "How excellent is your name, O Lord" and *Anaweza, anaweza Bwana*" (You are able, you are able, Lord).

At some point in the singing, the pastor and lay leaders come into the sanctuary. They sit up front, but their presence does not impede the worship, except that if people are sitting, they stand to their feet. The bishop, Timothy Ndambuki, enters and sits in a special elevated chair in the front right corner.

The congregation continues to worship, singing songs that laud God's character. Attributes of the divine are applied to all facets of the world. We sing: "Up the mountains, down the valleys, on the land and in the sea, the Lord is my shepherd in the land of the living, the Lord is good forever more." And then: *Hakuna mungu kama wewe . . . nimetumbea kotekote, nimetafuta kotekote, numezunguka kotekote, hakyuna na hatakuwepo* (There is no God like you. I have walked or traveled in places searching and have gone around but have never seen one like you). Followed by: "What a mighty God we serve; angels bow before him [at this point in the song, the parishioners bow low to the ground]; heaven and earth adore him; what a mighty God we serve."

Publics inside Congregations

Through song, God's attributes get applied to all parts of the cosmos. Things outside the church are naturally brought inside. Through these songs, parishioners name such things as mountains, valleys, land, seas, heaven, earth, and other parts of the physical world. Physical aspects of the world are carried into the service and placed in direct contact with God's attributes. All the things people care about (for the ABC: drought, poverty, agriculture, and nation building) make their way into doxologies, and, through contact with God's ascriptions, they become transformed. This is true for many churches throughout the region. Public realities are regularly carried into congregations. People pray and sing about sickness, poverty, greed, wealth, and tribalism. Occasionally, songs will mention political strife, such as what happened during the 2008 postelection violence that hit Kenya. However, most congregations avoid such topics for fear of upsetting delicate patron-client relationships.[5] It is more common to hear songs and prayers address sickness, drought, poverty, drunkenness, and other social ills.

In order to address drought and poverty, the ABC constantly talks about land. The mere mention of mountains, valleys, land, and seas in the words of the songs might not initially appear significant. One could argue they are just borrowing the words of well-known songs. But the members of the ABC give these words different meanings. When they mention any aspect of the physical environment, they are doing so intentionally for the sake of allowing God's character to enliven it. Anything that enters the open weave of doxology becomes freed and is thereafter released as a blessing for the rest of the world. By including physical creation in their doxology, they become agents of witness to the physical world.

5. Paul Gifford asserts that patron-client relationships undergird much of Kenyan Christianity. See *Christianity, Politics and Public Life in Kenya* (London: Hurst, 2009).

A lay leader comes to the front to give announcements. He talks about a medical mission trip to Rwanda and an upcoming choir competition in Taveta. Speaking about the choir competition, he explains, "If no one becomes saved as a result of this trip, the entire competition will be a waste of time." He then requests prayer for students who are about to sit for their secondary school exams and mentions financial requests for the deaf school sponsored by the ABC. The lay leader then introduces Bishop Timothy Ndambuki, who approaches the pulpit and greets the congregation with an affable smile. He tells the church that "the ABC is about sending people into the communities."

The worship leader comes to the front and guides people in prayer. He prays, but all the congregants spontaneously verbalize their personal supplications from their own pews. I can't hear everything being prayed, but I sense urgency and emotion, where parishioners are pleading with God through a cacophony of voices: shouting words of desperation interlaced with statements that attest to God's character. I hear people crying out, "Thank you for the gift of life" and "Grant us your blessings," along with "Defeat the devil" and "Bind him." After approximately ten minutes, the leader continues praying. He says, "Our dear heavenly Father, King of kings, Lord of lords, Priest of priests, and God of gods, we come before you humbly this morning; we give thanks. Thank you so much for the gift of life, and thank you for the gift of salvation, and now we want to start our fellowship. Be with us; we need your Holy Spirit in this period; be with our speaker, song leader, and programmer. In Jesus's name we pray. Amen!"

We sing another song, *Sisi wanawako tumekusanyika angalia Bwana* (We are gathered here as your children, look at us, Lord), and then *Tembea tembea Yesu tembea tukuone* (Move, Jesus, so that we can see you).

We then recite the Apostles' Creed. At this point the pastor comes to the pulpit and thanks everyone for coming to church. He reminds us that this is a holy place and that the Holy Spirit dwells in our midst.

Doxology and Social Texts

The narrative above highlights the importance of song and prayer within the ABC. It is virtually impossible to say anything credible about African Christianity without mentioning the importance of doxology. As I shared in the previous chapter, all congregations fold, or mix, or weave, or dance different elements together through complex movements. African Christianity does so through doxology.

In the West we think of doxology as a "private," "spiritual" act that sits comfortably inside a congregation. In Africa, by way of contrast, doxology possesses a more "public" role. Praise and prayers are found everywhere throughout Kenya. We hear praise songs in grocery stores, blasted by high-powered speakers in city markets, and even sung by travelers during the night when traveling on cross-country buses. Prayers occur before the planting of crops and when government leaders gather together. This is similar to what Birgit Meyer refers to as *going public*. Doxology inevitably makes its way into public places. However, I am interested in a different kind of publicness, best described by Meyer's *making public*: "the public expression of matters that hitherto were not open and accessible."[6] Congregations such as the ABC welcome public elements, such as land, poverty, and sickness into their doxology. What happens inside the congregation shapes their public witness in profound ways. Let me explain what this looks like.

Different Kinds of Texts

Initially, we need to understand doxology as a kind of "text." Rather than interpreting "texts" as words written on a page, Karin Barber broadens the meaning of a text to "a tissue of words"—building on the etymological meaning of the Latin *texere*, which means "to weave" or "bring things together."[7] If a text is a tissue of words, then it is possible to envision many different kinds of texts within a church service: oral, written, and embodied. Inside congregations, people sing, speak, read, and dance. Churches such as the ABC worship with two books, the Bible and a hymnal, weaving together written texts with oral ones, while performing these texts through carefully choreographed, corporate dance.

Barber explains the long-standing African tradition of constructing "praise poetry," which she labels as "Africa's master genre." She describes it in terms of its "fluid, disjunctive form, its vocative second-person address and its simultaneous evocation of the past and present, bringing the powers and potentials of dead predecessors into the centre of the living community."[8] In days past, Africans composed praise poetry to ancestors, heroes, or even, such as with the Dinka of South Sudan, cattle. Today, African Christianity has given different meanings to praise poetry. Church communities piece together the different attributes of God into a singular, doxological flow, which they perform through the body. The more attributes, along with the greater movement between the parts, the thicker the doxology.

6. Meyer, "Going and Making Public," 152.
7. Karin Barber, *The Anthropology of Texts, Persons and Publics: Oral and Written Culture in Africa and Beyond* (New York: Cambridge University Press, 2007), 1.
8. Barber, *Anthropology*, 74.

THICKNESS OF DOXOLOGY

An example could be the first prayer above, in which the supplicant weaves together a variety of divine titles, such as "Our dear heavenly Father, King of kings, Lord of lords, Priest of priests, and God of gods." This is an example of what Barber calls "entextualization," where people borrow bits and fragments of texts drawn from other sources and weave them together into a new text.[9] In days past, people would do this using proverbs, epics, or other oral and written sources. Today entextualization occurs in the churches through doxology. To enter a church is to experience rich, textured ascription of God's character. Song, prayer, choir performances, and even preaching saturate the service with a deeply imaginative construal of the divine nature, with layer on layer until it would seem the building is going to burst.

To explain the significance of this, we need to first understand that names in Africa carry power. To state someone's name is to "tap into" that person's power.[10] Most of the favorite titles for God in the ABC relate to his power. People cry out "Yahweh," "mighty God," "Creator of heaven and earth," "King of glory," "Lord of hosts," "God of wonders," "everlasting God," and "Alpha and Omega." Meanwhile, parishioners laud God's supremacy (*hakuna mungu kama wewe*, there is no God like you), accentuate his power (mighty name of Jesus, mighty God, all-powerful), or set him in reference to patriarchs in the Bible (Father of Abraham, Isaac, and Jacob). Parishioners will also use Hebrew or Greek biblical names in order to appropriate "private" knowledge of God's nature, referring to him as "Jehovah God," "Jehovah Jireh," or "Abba Father." Repetition of one of God's names increases its potency, where people cry "God of gods," "Lord of lords," and "Master of masters."

However, not only are divine names powerful, but they have an open weave to them. We can inhabit another person's name. By chanting ascriptions of a "more powerful" figure, singers come into contact with the object of the praise. All of this is possible because names are more than words and carry deeper meanings. Barber explains, "Names are the heart of identity; but names

9. Barber explains entextualization as a process that involves lifting specific texts out of one context and combining them with others in a new context: "Entextualisation may involve detaching stretches of discourse in order to freeze them: but it often involves setting stretches of entextualised discourse in motion, actively redeploying and 'quoting' them in such a way as to highlight the fluidity of performance." *Anthropology*, 23.

10. In a similar way, Agbonkhianmeghe Orobator says, "In Africa a person's name is the carrier of hope for his or her future. . . . Names confer identity and personality on us and allow for the possibility of entering into a relationship with other people, other names." He continues, "If you are interested in knowing what Africans believe about God, we should look at three sources that are native to Africa: proverbs, songs, and names bearing 'God,' that is, theophoric names." *Theology Brewed in an African Pot* (Maryknoll, NY: Orbis, 2008), 28.

. . . are also separable from individual persons and can function as external, enduring 'slots' through which a person passes."[11] By uttering divine titles, and especially through constructing praise poetry, parishioners pass through the identity of the divine—and by passing through it, they benefit from contact with the one whom they praise. The more names of God involved in the praise poetry, the thicker the weave; the thicker the weave of the doxology, the more people grow from their contact with God's nature.

Movement across the Realms

Not only do parishioners weave together the names of the divine into a thick text, but they move back and forth between human and divine realms. Consider the following prayer, in which the supplicant combines human action with divine action:

Father, we exalt your name, a name above all other names. Redeemer, we lift you, we cleanse you, we come into your presence to offer ourselves as living sacrifices; see us through, really, God, in the name of Jesus we exalt you; cleanse our hands in the name of Jesus; we love you, we need you, my Father, my God, we uplift you high; thank you for coming in splendor; we glorify you, we honor you, glorify yourself, you never share your glory with anyone. Lift us to your glory, we appreciate you, no one is like you, you enabled us to see another day, meet our needs, you know them, you know us well, you know our thoughts, we worship you. We pray all this in Jesus's name. Amen.

In this prayer, the supplicant begins with human action: "we exalt your name," "we cleanse you," "we come into your presence," "we love you," "we need you," "we uplift you high," "we glorify you," and "we appreciate you." Lifting God higher makes him more accessible to human need. The supplicant then anticipates a divine response, where he asks God to "see us through, really, God, in the name of Jesus," "cleanse our hands," and "lift us to your glory," and concludes by saying, "You enabled us to see another day, meet our needs." Doxology moves back and forth between these elements. Parishioners come to God ("we come in your presence") *so that* God will carry them to his presence ("lift us to your glory"). By exalting God ("we glorify you, we honor you") or appealing to his sovereignty ("you never share your glory with anyone"), supplicants expect God to help them in the everydayness of life ("meet our needs, you know them, you know us well").

African Christianity moves back and forth across divine and human realms like heavy traffic on a busy thoroughfare. In the West, we navigate them

11. Barber, *Anthropology*, 112.

selectively. Not so in Africa. What happens in the divine is for making sense of the human. Doxology is for the purpose of reanimating life. "The frontier between the empirical world and the spiritual world was [and is] being crossed and re-crossed every day and in both directions."[12] We see this in the prayer above. The lay leader moves between the realms. He weaves the attributes of God with human needs, nurturing a highly dynamic relationship between the divine and public realities.

Making Public

Christianity goes public in different ways in Africa. One of these ways is overt, where Christian images naturally make their way into public life. I have already explained that Kenya has a long, ambiguous history in this regard. David Maxwell refers to Scripture as the "preeminent African text,"[13] while Jon Lonsdale describes the Bible as "the only universal literature Kenyans possess."[14] The publicness of Christianity is not a matter of debate. Bible and doxology naturally make their way into public life. However, these resources do not always go public in healthy ways. Political agents can use the Bible or doxology for their own purposes. For example, when Uhuru Kenyatta returned from a trip to the Hague, where he was brought up on charges of contributing to the 2008 postelection violence, he is quoted as saying, "We want to thank God for having seen us through this. . . . Many said that we shall go to the Hague and not come back. We have now proved them wrong. . . . The devil has been defeated."[15] As this statement suggests, political elites use Scripture to intimate they are on the side of God. When this happens, no one can accuse them of any wrongdoing.

In this chapter, I am interested in another kind of public engagement, which Meyer refers to as *making public*, where "private" things inside the congregation make their way out into public life to create a different kind of public. It is harder to see this take place, and yet it is there in abundance. From what I have shared above, churches such as the ABC *make public* through the thickness of their doxologies.

12. Andrew Walls, "Christian Scholarship in Africa in the Twenty-First Century," *Transformation* 19, no. 9 (October 2002): 217–28, here 224.

13. David Maxwell, "Introduction: Christianity and the African Imagination," in *Christianity and the African Imagination: Essays in Honour of Adrian Hastings*, ed. David Maxwell with Ingrid Lawrie (Leiden: Brill, 2002), 1–25, here 13.

14. Jon Lonsdale, "Kikuyu Christianities: A History of Intimate Diversity," in Maxwell with Lawrie, *Christianity and the African Imagination*, 186.

15. Peter Leftie, "Uhuru and Ruto Vow to Preach Peace," *Daily Nation* (Nairobi), April 11, 2011.

To understand what this looks like, we need to think of texts differently. They are not just what people read but how people perform agency in the world. Barber argues that people do things with texts to help them make sense of the world: "Texts are used to do things: they are forms of action."[16] While written texts inspire people to see the world differently (think of reading a compelling novel such as Charles Dickens's *David Copperfield*), oral texts engage people at a deeper level, since they require an entire community to generate, perform, maintain, and bequeath them to subsequent generations. Barber says that "oral texts are the outcome of a concerted effort to fix words and make them outlast the here-and-now."[17] African Christianity has long used praise poetry to provide agency in the world. Singing and praying ascriptions of the divine represents a form of collective action.[18] In days past, oral texts might have included myths, riddles, and songs boasting of the prowess of heroes, while in more recent days African Christianity uses prayers, choruses, and choirs as a form of collective agency.

As I explained above, the ABC does this by bringing public realities into the open weave of the doxological flow. They incorporate land, mountains, valleys, and other facets of the material world into their songs. Thus "natural" things are brought into contact with the "supernatural." Earthly affairs are transformed as they enter into the open weave of praise poetry. By entering into praise poetry, the ABC thinks about and engages the natural world differently.

Whenever people sing, they also dance. Word and embodiment flow together into a symphony of orchestrated movement. Choirs perform songs through collective action, reinforcing the words of the song "from kinetic, visual and physical senses."[19] Dance takes seriously the beating of the drum, the cadence of the music, inflections of speech, and embodiment of a narrative. Michael Jackson and Ivan Karp thus describe dance as "metaphorical in character, creating links between the vital energy of the individual body, the social body, and the cosmos."[20] Through dance, parishioners act out cosmological warfare. They "step" on Satan (as the previous narrative shows). They

16. Barber, *Anthropology*, 3.

17. Barber, *Anthropology*, 67.

18. See Gregory Barz, *Performing Religion: Negotiating Past and Present in Kwaya Music of Tanzania* (Amsterdam: Rodopoi, 2003). He explains choirs in Tanzania as undertaking "a process of community formation, the process of communities performing themselves into being on a regular basis" (86).

19. Jean Ngoya Kidula, "Music Culture," in *Music in the Life of the African Church*, ed. Roberta King (Waco: Baylor University Press, 2008), 37–56, here 45.

20. Michael Jackson and Ivan Karp, eds., *Personhood and Agency: The Experience of Self and Other in African Cultures* (Stockholm: Almqvist & Wiksell, 1990), 22.

bow low before God and join hands in corporate praise. And when they leave the worship service, they function differently in the world.

For example, a choir performed a Swahili song that says, "*Namwabadu Mungu mwenye nguvu, ataukiwa mgonjwa, kakosa kazi, Mwanangu ambia Mungu ananweza, hakuna jambo lolote la kumshinda mwenyezi Mungu*" (I worship a powerful God; even if you are sick, or unemployed, my child, tell God; he is able, there is nothing that God cannot do). The song begins with God's attributes ("I worship a powerful God") and then moves to sickness and the need for a job, and then back to God's power ("he is able, there is nothing that God cannot do"). The choir dramatizes the words of the song through corporate, embodied actions. They bow low before God's power. They plead with God with outstretched arms for the sick and unemployed. The choir praises God at the end, proclaiming him victorious. The more attributes of God included in the song, the thicker the weave; the thicker the weave, the more parishioners are trained for corporate agency back in the world.

In such ways, doxology enables humans to be social actors. When they leave the church, they do so *through their doxology*. Private things do not stay private but *make public*.[21] (This is similar to what I said in the previous chapters about a habitus.)

I should mention that this kind of doxological weaving does not always address the most critical issues experienced in the public realm. As I explained earlier, the ABC purposely avoids any direct confrontation with political authorities. They may talk about politics or pray for political leaders, but they hesitate mentioning overt political themes in their doxology (unlike what they do with agriculture, poverty, or healing). The ABC actually mentions politics more than what I have observed among mission-founded churches, but, similar to the others, the ABC resists any overt mention of political agents. Until this happens, the ABC (and other congregations) will continue to be co-opted by the political machinations of the current political system. Politics needs to enter into the open weave of doxology, to be converted from within.

The preacher for today is a sister.[22] Her sermon is from Genesis 12. She recounts God's blessings to Abraham, explaining that God's original intention for creation was to bless

---

21. Birgit Meyer says something similar about Pentecostalism in Ghana: "One intriguing aspect of current Pentecostal modes of public appearance is that personal, intimate, or secret matters move center stage, becoming prime matters to be made public. Far from being a merely personal affair, conversion implies that people are on the move and articulate their new identity to the outside world." "Going and Making Public," 158.

22. This is similar to the Roman Catholic title, showing how the ABC borrows widely from different ecclesial traditions.

humans and provide everything they need for goodness and growth. She then explains, "When someone says to you, 'Be blessed,' they are asking God to give you all that is good: food, wealth, happy life, even eternal life." She goes on to explain to the parishioners that Christians, because of the salvation we have received from Jesus Christ, should be the main instruments of blessing to all people, even to the extent that they "should be the first people to contribute to nation building."

The sermon ends with three questions, which are asked at the completion of every service: (1) "Do you want to receive Christ as your Lord and Savior?" (2) "Do you want to repent of your sins?" and (3) "Do you want to formally join the Africa Brotherhood Church?" Those who raise their hands to any of the questions get prayed over by the leaders. The pastor prepares for the Lord's Supper. After the two officiates partake of the bread and the wine (juice), the parishioners come forward to the front of the church, where they kneel and are served the elements. The offering is taken after the sermon, where people once again come to the front of the church and place their tithes and offerings into baskets. At the end of the service, we sing the final traditional hymn, "Lord, dismiss us with thy blessings."

After the closing song, parishioners stream out of the back doors and into the garden-like atmosphere of the compound. I stand around talking to various leaders, surrounded by the dense foliage. Bishop Ndambuki joins me. He explains that the denomination began with a concern for the Great Commission. The original constitution describes their primary objective as "preaching the Gospel of Jesus Christ to all Nations of the world, throughout the world if possible." He notes that although the ABC is predominantly a Kamba church (the ethnic group living around Machakos), they have planted churches in Rwanda, Tanzania, and the Democratic Republic of the Congo; and wherever they go, they plant gardens like this one.

Thick Doctrines, Salvation, and Creation

To understand the connection between the Great Commission and the garden-like atmosphere, we need to explore how the ABC weaves together various doctrines into a thick tapestry. It is not just ascriptions of the divine that get pieced together. The ABC does the same with doctrines.

Preachers in the ABC accentuate the doctrine of creation. In mission-founded congregations, rarely does anyone mention creation—except perhaps when discussing the entrance of sin in the world. However, the ABC often mentions such creational aspects as work, responsibility, blessings, community, the importance of land, and the dignity of persons. They interpret creation through the twin lenses of Scripture and Akamba traditional values.

A focus on creational values enables the ABC to apply salvation to broader swaths of life. While mission-founded churches interpret the Great Commission exclusively for evangelism, the ABC gives it a broader scope of application. As the sister explained in her sermon, Christians should use salvation to bless people within all aspects of life, even to the point of "nation building." Hence, blessings are a form of public witness in the world.

What Salvation?

I should point out that the ABC does not lessen its emphasis on evangelism in order to expand its scope of witness. It regularly holds evangelistic campaigns, promotes overseas missions, and, at the end of every worship service, asks if anyone wants to receive Jesus Christ as Lord. As the earlier narrative highlighted, even a choir competition to the distant city of Taveta should result in people "getting saved." The ABC accentuates the person and work of Christ. A large crucifix hangs over the front of the church, and a cross lies at the center of their logo with the words, "Jesus said, Go ye into all the world." In such ways the ABC is faithful to the evangelical heritage it received from the early missionaries. Where it diverts from the mission-founded churches is *how* it relates salvation with the rest of creation.

Where Salvation?

The ABC is not unique in its focus on Christ. What is unique is *how* the church moves fluidly from salvation to all parts of creation. In a sermon, a preacher might begin anywhere—with the Garden of Eden, Abraham, Exodus, Nehemiah, Ezra, Proverbs (note the love for Old Testament texts!)—and move from these texts to the person of Christ, and then to public realities, such as creation, poverty, and nation building, to allow Christ's salvation a broader scope of application. For the ABC, it is less where the sermon starts and more how preacher uses movement. Movement across doctrines expands the scope of soteriological influence.

In another service, a lay leader begins with Nehemiah's rebuilding of the walls around Jerusalem. He likens the opposition Nehemiah experienced to spiritual warfare and says we need walls built on Christ's life to ensure they will last. In explicit terms, he tells parishioners that we need "to invite Jesus into our lives" and rebuke the devil in "the name of Jesus Christ." In other words, the preacher starts broadly with a focus on cosmological warfare and then quickly turns it to personal acceptance of Jesus Christ. From there he moves outward again into larger domains. He uses Nehemiah to talk about the ethnic discord Israel faced in Nehemiah's day and says we need reconciliation in the country of Kenya. He discusses economic hardships in Nehemiah's era and tells the story of a woman who has not worn any shoes for twenty years. He asks the congregation to consider political upheaval in Israel during the time of Nehemiah and discusses the upcoming elections. He says, "When will these [political] leaders ever save us?" After considering the social implications of Nehemiah for our day, he moves back to Christ to read Hebrews 12:1–3. The service ends with a call for people to receive Jesus as their Lord.

By moving from Nehemiah to Christ, the preacher starts with societal problems and moves to personal salvation. After focusing on Christ, he moves outward into domains of ethnicity, poverty, and political strife, before narrowing the focus to Christ, and then broadening it a final time by talking about Christ's lordship over the entire world (he "sat down at the right hand of the throne of God" [Heb. 12:2]). The sermon shows back-and-forth movement between large, societal affairs and individual confession of Jesus Christ.

Hence, no one in the ABC would find it incompatible to talk about evangelism *and* agricultural development, or to promote the Great Commission *while* enjoying the benefits of a lush garden. As seen above, the ABC began with the primary objective of "preaching the Gospel of Jesus Christ to all Nations of the world, throughout the world if possible," and uses that foundation to include other objectives such as "opening schools," along with the desire to "train some Christians to become leaders" and "help people by way of Medical Treatments, and to teach them the modern way of living."[23] Thus, even from the origins of the denomination in the 1940s, the ABC interpreted the Great Commission as mutually compatible with education and health.[24]

For the ABC, land, medicine, and education are all intrinsically interconnected with salvation. Movement of Christ across all the spaces of the cosmos expands the scope of the congregation's witness into the public realm.

After greeting parishioners after the service, we make our way into the bishop's residence that is located in the same compound. As we sit drinking *chai* (tea) and eating *mandazi* (fried donuts) and arrowroot, I ask the bishop various questions. He is personable, well educated, and articulate. He laughs easily and disarms any apprehensions. I inquire about

23. "Constitution and Rules of African Brotherhood Church," n.d.

24. This is in marked contrast with the Africa Inland Mission, which interpreted the Great Commission solely in terms of evangelism. See Gregg Okesson, "Africa Inland Church: Secularization and Rationalization," in *Re-imaging Modernity*, 79–114; Kevin Ward, "Evangelism or Education? Mission Priorities and Educational Policy in the Africa Inland Mission, 1900–1950," *Kenya Historical Review* 3, no. 2 (1975): 243–60.

the impressive ministries I hear about in the ABC. Then I ask him about the gardenlike atmosphere and why this is so important for the denomination.

Bishop Ndambuki explains to me that all pastors in the ABC do a three-month internship in an agricultural setting as a part of their theological training. They study chaplaincy, community development, primary health care, and agriculture—in addition to typical theological courses such as preaching, teaching, doctrine, and Bible study. He says, "[In the past] the Africa Inland Mission was concentrating on the gospel alone, but here they [the early ABC leaders] said, we want to go a step beyond the gospel and outreach the whole personality; that is why they looked at the holistic gospel. Wherever we have a church, we shall be planting a school, or a dispensary. . . . As they preach the gospel to convert people, they go another step and deal with the whole personality."

Bishop Ndambuki's language of the "whole personality" is much broader than individual, psychological needs but gives insight into how persons exist in relation to their communal, holistic environments. To accentuate this, he takes me back to the Garden of Eden and explains, "If you visited Eden, you will find it very beautiful, you will find fresh water, flowers, vegetation; all of these things were given to man so that he can emulate God. In the areas where we plant churches, where people meet with God, it needs to be beautiful, like God himself had shown Adam and Eve."

I ask the bishop if other ABC congregations also have lush gardens. He tells me one of the reasons pastors undertake agricultural training is to help them do the same wherever they go. The ABC wants church compounds to be places where people can see firsthand what the gospel looks like when it touches on all aspects of life. The focus is still on Christ, but movement between salvation and creation allows the gospel a broader expression. One of the roles of a pastor or sister is to visit people in their homes and help them evaluate basic needs. A pastor might recommend a parishioner plant fruit trees, harvest rainwater, or undertake other activities to help improve their lot. A sister might talk about ways to purify drinking water or what plants carry medicinal properties. They do this while they are sharing the gospel with them. Salvation and creation are intimately connected.

A few days later, I accompany Edward Nzinga to the ABC farm in Kibwezi, which lies three hours southeast of Machakos. We pass mile after mile of arid scrubland before arriving at the property, where Millicent Manesa, the program officer, greets us. She introduces us to the project as we tour the fifty-two-acre farm, which includes citrus trees intercropped with vegetables for export, an agroforestry plantation (emphasizing the introduction of medicinal, indigenous trees), livestock breeding, a community training center, an experimental plot where they demonstrate the latest hybrid seeds or drip-irrigation methods, water conservation, a health center, and a local congregation. I ask Manesa the reason for everything around me, and she says, "We want to change the place religiously"—which for the ABC means the gospel of Jesus Christ needs to influence all aspects of life.

She proceeds to explain that wherever the ABC plants a church, they call all the community leaders together and ask them what needs exist in the area. The local people might talk about the difficulties of getting crops to market or finding sufficient rainwater to irrigate their crops; they might ask for health-care clinics, or a place to store the upcoming harvest so that they can sell the produce when the market is conducive. The ABC will then organize the entire community toward these ends. In addition to planting a church, they open a clinic, introduce an agricultural test farm, and begin a primary school, along with strengthening the infrastructure of the community. They "want to change the place religiously."

"Change the Place Religiously"

When Millicent Manesa says that the ABC wants to "change the place religiously," she is not talking about electing a Christian president or about the wholesale adoption of Christian culture in Kenya. It is possible she would approve of both of these. I am not sure. What is clear, however, is that she interprets "religiously" to include agricultural and health development.

The ABC retains a robust Christology, but by emphasizing the power of the Holy Spirit, along with the supporting cast of creation, hard work, land, and blessings, it applies salvation to agriculture and other aspects of development. The church does not move away from Christ or personal evangelism in order to effect societal change but allows salvation to influence larger swaths of public life. The effect is palpable as evidenced by what ABC is doing not only in their compound but also in their region. I attended microenterprise meetings, where parishioners pool their collective savings to launch development projects throughout the entire region. Wherever they go, they plant gardens, start health clinics, and work closely with local communities to develop roads and infrastructure. They are sent as evangelists in and through land.

We might say: the ABC witnesses to land. The countryside in the region is largely arid. People struggle daily with drought and poverty. The land plays such an important role for the everyday lives of people within Ukambani that Christianity cannot just witness to people but must also witness to the publics that shape their lives, in this case agriculture and health.

Congregations and Thick Witness

The ABC weaves thickness into the congregation, which directly affects how they view the world around them. Their thickness relates to doxology, where praise poetry helps parishioners heap together ascriptions of God's nature and "pass through" such an identity. As they do, they bring things outside the church into the open weave of doxology. As land, earth, valleys, and mountains—or other public realities such as sickness or unemployment—get exposed to God's attributes, people think about the world differently. Praise poetry not only changes people but changes *people as they think about their public worlds*. When this happens, they engage the world through the changes wrought inside them.

For the ABC, everything begins with God. By saturating the entire worship service with ascriptions of God, doxology enables parishioners of the African Brotherhood Church to be sociological agents in the world. This does not mean they worship in order to undertake agency; rather, agency becomes a natural by-product of their doxology. Lamin Sanneh examines various cultures across Africa to understand how the names of God apply to larger domains of life, such as agricultural practices, festivals, and rites of passage. He says, "It is therefore hard to think of viable social systems without the name of God, but easy to envision societies that have become vulnerable because they lost the name or sense of the transcendent."[25] Praise poetry, I argue, provides parishioners with everything they need to become active agents in this world. One song in particular says, *Mambo sawa* (things are better), *Yesu akiwa enzini, mambo sawa sawa* (when Jesus is on the throne, things are getting better).

The ABC also weaves together thick doctrines. Preachers move back and forth between Christ and creational values. As they do so, salvation touches more aspects of life.

All of this is possible through the Holy Spirit. The dove features prominently on their logo. It is also embroidered on the tablecloth used for the Lord's Supper. They understand the Holy Spirit as the power behind the gospel. The early converts wrote Kiswahili hymns. One of these, as noted earlier, is always the first song in their liturgy and has a stanza that says, "God the Father, Son, and the Holy Spirit, let us see your power in this service." They frequently sing another hymn that reads, "God is here and that to bless us with the Spirit's quickening power." A pastor prays, "Let your Spirit guide us; be our power," or tells parishioners, "I believe by the power of the Holy Spirit we will not leave here the same." The Holy Spirit is the power of the gospel in and for human communities.

From God's nature, the ABC moves readily into the realm of creation. They move from doxology to agriculture and from salvation to development projects. They "emulate God" through how they relate to the land. They

25. Lamin Sanneh, *Whose Religion Is Christianity? The Gospel beyond the West* (Grand Rapids: Eerdmans), 31.

have an entire department devoted to health care. They begin microenterprise projects and start schools through the region. They are especially sensitive to marginalized segments of society, such as orphans, widows, the hearing impaired, and those trapped in poverty. Admittedly, some of these projects were strengthened because of the church's Memorandum of Understanding (MOU) with the Canadian Baptists. But the theology (and most of the practices) was already well in place before the Canadian Baptists came along. In all my years living in Africa, I never saw any church or denomination that was as active in agricultural development as what I observed with the ABC. They possess a robust soteriology through the ways they connect doxology with land, and salvation with creation.

Conclusion

The Africa Brotherhood Church offers an intriguing case study in public missiology. It is common for us in the West to judge a congregation's witness entirely by what they do outside the church. In the case of the ABC, what they do outside the church is considerable: they plant gardens, vigorously engage in health care, help communities improve their local infrastructure, begin microenterprise schemes, experiment in agricultural test plots, teach drip irrigation, and undertake development activities in multiple countries. But what they do on the outside is sourced by a robust doxology, with dynamic movements between doctrines. As this takes place, salvation comes in contact with broader aspects of life.

I offer the case study of the ABC as a great example of how movement cultivates a thickness, and how that thickness enters into the public realm, to witness to it from within.

8

Thick Place and Witness to Montreal— St. Jax Anglican Church, Montreal

> Place is a space which has historical meanings.
>
> —Walter Brueggemann, *The Land*

> And so, too, the Church of Jesus Christ is the place, in other words the space in the world, at which the reign of Jesus Christ over the whole world is evidenced and proclaimed.
>
> —Dietrich Bonhoeffer, *Ethics*

St. Jax Montreal is an Anglican church in the province of Quebec, Canada. The church is located in the heart of historic Montreal, which in these days is an odd place to find a vibrant congregation. Most of the historic churches are long gone, having sold their buildings to real estate developers and moved to suburban locations where property is more affordable. Not so with St. Jax. The church has witnessed dramatic growth over the past few years by reimagining its place within the urban center of the city. In this case study, I will narrate some seminal features of St. Jax's public missiology of place and argue that it uses a *thickness of place* to witness to the city of Montreal.

I disembark the subway at Rue Guy (Guy Street) and walk to the corner of Rue Sainte Catherine. It is everything one would expect in a downtown metropolitan context—although with a distinctly continental flair. Street signs are written in French. I hear a distinct French dialect spoken around me. Even the style of dress is more European than North American. It's like I have been teleported to Paris or Marseille, but with a distinctly Canadian twist.

I turn left on Rue Sainte Catherine and navigate the crowded urban thoroughfare. Pedestrians jostle past each other down the busy sidewalk. Vehicular traffic weaves in and out down the thoroughfare of Sainte Catherine. I pass Concordia University and several large multinational businesses such as McDonald's and Arc'teryx. Interspersed within these are smaller restaurants with names such as Jouney Mediterranean Cafe and Marché Ferdous. At one of these I stop and eat a shawarma. All the nations are here. Shops around me serve curry, tacos, Sichuan, and falafel, along with more authentic Montreal cuisine. Similar to urban centers throughout the world, Montreal is changing. There is an organic flow to the cultural identities I observe that seems to mirror the traffic weaving down Rue Sainte Catherine. Beneath all of the bustle lies an integrated way of life that makes sense to people living in the city.

I pass a number of homeless people leaning up against historic landmarks. Quite a few of these are First Nations (or Native Indian) people. One of them asks if I want to purchase an animal carving he made. A couple others request money for food. It's cold outside. Their bloodshot eyes and threadbare clothing narrate an agonizing tale. First Nations people have lived in Quebec for hundreds of years, dating back to when the land was heavily forested and they were masters of their own domain. Now they look for protection from the frigid winds behind buildings built by European hands. It is a painful irony set within a fiercely proud city.

Looking down Sainte Catherine, I see quite a few steeples in the distant horizon. The presence of so many historic churches in the city points to a long-standing Christian heritage. Even hospitals and public universities carry reminders of their Christian past, with plaques signifying when the buildings were consecrated or statues celebrating a former ecclesiastical leader. Christianity has long defined public life in Montreal. Today those symbols are neglected. Many of the historic churches are being sold to city developers. Plaques are faded. Statues of ecclesiastical nobility stand tall but lifeless, with elongated shadows stretching across the lawn like ghouls from a former day. Moss grows on them. A few show graffiti written across their sides. Most people walk past these Christian symbols without even noticing them.

Places and Memories

Places are filled with memories. Eric Jacobsen explains, "A sense of place is important in helping us connect not only with one another in our current time frame, but also temporally with those who have preceded us and those who will succeed us through holding memories."[1] For example, if you were to walk down the street you grew up on, a deluge of memories would hit you all at once: some good, others painful. Whether an open lot where you played soccer with friends, a tree at the neighbor's house, or where you fell off your bike, places carry memories, and memories stir up deep emotion. Or think about visiting a cemetery. Every time I visit my sister's gravesite, I weep unexpectedly. Seeing her name etched on a gravestone surrounded by a sea of other gravestones unlocks a hidden reservoir of emotion that spills out like water over a broken dam. Places such as a childhood home or a cemetery carry memories, and those memories release an outpouring of sentiment.

The same is true of cities. However, cities do not just carry personal memories but hold symbolic memories for millions of people. Consider locations such as Mecca, Jerusalem, or the Ganges River. These religious sites store meaning for adherents all around the world. Or reflect on the significance of the Statue of Liberty for immigrants who came to the United States in the early twentieth century, or the Cliffs of Dover for returning British World War I soldiers. Each of these places represents more than a monument or a majestic vista but symbolizes the hopes and dreams of an entire nation. People narrate national histories around places.

Memories associated with places are complex. They come to us with different layers, and each of the layers merges together with others over time. Furthermore, the layers of memories associated with a particular place can be told differently by different groups of people. They can even be contested memories, especially to the extent that they form the undergirding of national identity. It is for such reasons we can speak of memories attached to a place, such as a city, possessing a thickness. One of the reasons Jerusalem carries so much conflict and hope for billions of people around the world is that it lies at the heart of complex layers of memories. Let me show how this is true for the city of Montreal and how St. Jax navigates the thickness of memories to witness to the entire city.

The city of Montreal lies at the confluence of the St. Lawrence and Ottawa Rivers. It is located amid key navigational routes from the Atlantic Ocean into the interior of Canada. The city was built on an island and is the rightful home to the Iroquois and Mohawk,[2] First Nations peoples who have from time immemorial lived in the region. It would not be proper to narrate any

---

1. Eric O. Jacobsen, *The Space Between: A Christian Engagement with the Built Environment* (Grand Rapids: Baker Academic, 2012), 72–73.

2. Those from this region are called Mohawks, who are part of the six-nation Iroquois confederacy, but their indigenous name is Kahnawà:ke.

part of the story of Montreal without beginning with the sordid history of European settlers exploiting the Iroquois and Mohawk peoples along with the natural resources of the region. As European presence increased, the First Nations peoples were pushed out. Years later, when Canada became a nation, political leaders sought to "civilize" the indigenous people by placing their children in residential schools. It's estimated more than six thousand children died while in these homes, with many more exposed to sexual and emotional abuse. The entire nation of Canada is currently wrestling with this part of its collective past. The Truth and Reconciliation Commission, formed in 2008, found fault with the residential schools for their intentional acts of genocide against First Nations peoples. Memories of the abuses against First Nations people continue to haunt Montreal like specters of the past. This is the first layer of memories, and it is not one many people like to talk about.[3]

Montreal is an incredibly diverse city. Its history can be narrated through migratory waves, beginning with the French, then British, while presently told through recent immigrants (what some refer to as "new Canadians"). The first French settlement of Ville Marie began in 1642 as an outpost for French exploration into the interior of Canada. The region continued in French hands until 1760, when British troops defeated the French at the Battle of the Plains of Abraham. From this time onward, a deluge of immigrants from England, Scotland, and Ireland streamed into Montreal. Today, immigrants come from North Africa, Italy, Mexico, and Beirut. Montreal's ability to retain its French identity yet combine it with diverse nationalities may be one of the city's most notable achievements. However, this does not mean ethnic integration is easy or without conflicts. Francophone identities frequently clash with Anglophone identities, along with more recent conflicts with immigrants coming from all around the world. However, the city is finding a way. According to the national census of 2011, the most common languages in Montreal are French (63.3%), English (11.6%), Arabic (3.9%), Spanish (3.1%), and Italian (3.1%).[4] One might say that Montreal combines these uneasily.[5] Though priority is given to the Québécois (or French-speaking people of Quebec), the city is one of the world's leaders in forging a resilient intercultural identity.

3. To be fair, Canada has done a better job than the United States in acknowledging this layer of memories; however, few nations do well in remembering the violence meted out against indigenous people.

4. "Focus on Geography Series, 2011 Census: Census Metropolitan Area of Montréal, Quebec," Statistics Canada, modified September 21, 2016, http://www12.statcan.gc.ca/census-recensement/2011/as-sa/fogs-spg/Facts-cma-eng.cfm?LANG=Eng&GK=CMA&GC=462.

5. If you walk into a store, someone will likely greet you by saying, "Bonjour, hi," showing a unique integration of languages.

Yet another layer of Montreal's memories revolves around the historic presence of Christianity in the region. For hundreds of years the city was a mission station for Roman Catholic missionaries. After the British defeated the French in 1760, Montreal became a strategic outpost for British missions, leading to the growth of Anglicanism,[6] Presbyterianism, and Methodism throughout Quebec. For the next hundred years, Christianity played a leading role in all facets of public life, shaping key institutions of politics, health care, and education. Christianity's heritage with colonialism has become an enduring memory for the city—and perhaps the one memory Montrealers most want to erase from their collective heritage.

Christianity's grip on public life was openly challenged during the 1960s and 1970s with the Quiet Revolution. While the fires of change had long been smoldering in the city, those two decades represent a period of dramatic transformation of the public institutions and culture of Quebec. The Quiet Revolution was many things: economic growth, postwar development, and political change. But deep down it represented a reaction against three entities: the English, other colonial powers (including the United States, Canada's neighbors to the south), and the church—often with little distinction between the three. The Quiet Revolution ushered in a period of heavy secularization and radical independence. Though steeples continue to dot the horizon, reminding the city of its Christian heritage, the churches trigger deep disgust in the hearts of many Québécois. French curse words readily draw on ecclesiastical terms such as *sacrament* and *altar* to show the depth of repugnance to Christianity's historic presence within the city.

I have outlined a few of the memories of the city. To be the church of Jesus Christ in a context such as Montreal requires the negotiation and redemption of these layers. Unlike physical layers, memories do not sit on top of each other like a pile of pancakes but run together. People will invariably interpret Christianity, colonialism, and the oppression of First Nations peoples as a single narrative. Memories also depend on the person narrating the story. For the Iroquois and Mohawk peoples, the colonial heritage begins with the French; for the Québécois it revolves around the English; while for most it takes on a contemporary face through their US neighbors to the south.

This is the context in which St. Jax finds itself. Every congregation inhabits a certain place filled with layers of interconnected memories. Walter Brueggemann explains the importance of this reality when he says, "Place is a space which has historical meanings, where some things have happened which are now remembered and which provide continuity and identity across

---

6. The first Anglican church opened in 1814. Montreal officially became a diocese in 1850.

generations."[7] St. Jax occupies a strategic place within the heart of Montreal. The land and building hold historical meanings for the entire city. People remember getting married or having their first Communion in the church building. Others use the steeple as a landmark for traversing the city. For most people, however, the building is a symbol of Christianity's complicity in colonialism. St. Jax is aware of its place in the city and actively seeks to *re-place* itself in and for the city of Montreal.

I walk along Rue Sainte Catherine toward St. Jax. The church property occupies the majority of a city block. I pass a large garden with a walkway leading to a side door of the church. The nave extends almost to Rue Sainte Catherine, with a shorter walkway leading into the main building via the bell tower. Unlike suburban congregations, St. Jax flows organically with its environs. People access the church on three sides, with sidewalks leading into the building from three locations. The green space around St. Jax offers chairs and benches for people to sit in leisure. A small iron fence surrounds the garden, but nothing giving the impression of inhospitality. People wander in and out of the green space as they please, especially since the garden is adjacent to a busy sidewalk. St. Jax is currently working with Concordia University to convert the garden into a new city park. The church is likewise in the process of invigorating the garden with plants listed in the fifteenth-century colonizer Samuel de Champlain's manifest of flora for Nouvelle France.

As I stand looking at St. Jax from the sidewalk, it feels as if the nave comes out to greet people. Aromas from inside the church waft out into the city whenever anyone opens the doors. The garden extends all the way to the sidewalk. Passersby almost bump into the building as they walk down the street; and the entire city streams past St. Jax on a daily basis. Across the street is a police station. There is a Starbucks before that, another Starbucks beyond, and an Apple Store just a little farther down the street. Concordia University lies next door. McGill University is not far away. From St. Jax, it is just a short walk to banks, restaurants, shopping, hospitals, or a stroll through the Parc du Mont Royal (Royal Park). From the church's inception in 1864, the city of Montreal has grown around St. Jax, much like a garden grows around a stately oak tree. Thousands of people pass the church every day, whether heading to the subway, driving to work, or going out for a quick bite to eat. St. Jax occupies a critical place in the city.

I walk inside and pick up one of St. Jax's promotional booklets lying on a table. I read the following words: "Starting as a worship place for Anglo-Montrealers and holding the memories of city development, national history, warfare, boom and bust, we are excited for the future history of this space as a gathering place for all kinds of Montrealers,

---

7. Walter Brueggemann, *The Land: Place as Gift, Promise, and Challenge in Biblical Faith* (Minneapolis: Fortress, 1977), 5. He goes on to explain that "place is indeed a protest against the unpromising pursuit of space. It is a declaration that our humanness cannot be found in escape, detachment, absence or commitment, and undefined freedom."

especially those who are new to Quebec." I am immediately struck by the mention of "memories of the city." It shows a surprising awareness of St. Jax's social location in Montreal. Meanwhile, the inclusion of the words *warfare* and *bust* alongside more encouraging words of *development* and *boom* point to the recognition that memories are perceived as both negative and positive. Rather than being inhibited by this reality, St. Jax uses it to its advantage.

A Crisis of Place

We in the West are currently facing a crisis of place. Whereas in the past, places largely defined identity for people everywhere, we are now seeing a decisive shift from "place" to "space."[8] The development of cars, trains, and airplanes takes us past places with lightning-quick speed. We fly by places without even thinking of them.[9] "Motorways take us around historic places signifying them but avoiding them."[10] New construction is geared more toward quick-leveraged economic gains than any transcendent architectural statement. Not only do we experience a diminished sense of identity due to changes in travel and non-descript buildings, but our lives are defined by a hodgepodge of places. For example, we live in one location, work in another, shop elsewhere, and celebrate key events such as weddings and anniversaries in distant countries. Parishioners attend church in a suburb across the town, disassociating themselves from the immediate neighborhoods around the congregation. The average person feels unplaced—or at least placed in multiple ambiguous ways.

Globalization further robs places of any particular identity, trading local character for bland homogeneity. We build homes that all look alike, eat at restaurants with the same basic menu. Brands such as Apple, Coca-Cola, and Nike endeavor to make people all around the world feel connected by allegiance to a transnational identity.[11] We long for something original.[12]

Meanwhile, places shape a person's identity. When we meet someone, one of the first things we want to know about them is their "placement." We ask,

8. T. J. Gorringe, *The Common Good and the Global Emergency: God and the Built Environment* (Cambridge: Cambridge University Press, 2011), 71–72.

9. Craig G. Bartholomew says, "Place has become something that one moves through, preferably at great speed, and virtual reality is no replacement." *Where Mortals Dwell: A Christian View of Place for Today* (Grand Rapids: Baker Academic, 2011), 3.

10. Gorringe, *Common Good*, 75.

11. Gorringe explains that "standardisation and uniformity seem to be almost inevitable outcomes of a globalised economy dominated by massive globe-spanning corporations geared to mass production and marketing." *Common Good*, 72.

12. The desire for originality explains the recent rise of boutique stores, locally owned businesses that promote homegrown produce, and shops that sell the wares of local artisans.

"Where are you from?" And if they tell us they are from a specific country where we have lived, we want to know the precise location in that country. It's not enough to know they are Canadian; we want to know where in Canada. And if they say they are from Montreal and we happen to be from the same city, we ask for the specific neighborhood. Places help us make sense of others. They are identity markers we use to provide us with a place in the world.

In a globalized world defined by mass migration, placement poses a tremendous challenge. Migration confuses placement in the world, while thickening identity through multiple placements. A "transnational" person needs to tell their story thickly. For example, an Uber driver tells you he is of Berber descent from Libya but then lived in Paris for many years and now resides in Montreal. How do we understand such a person's placement in the world? Other migrants have been de-placed, such as First Nations persons living in their own country or a refugee forced to leave her homeland because of a civil war. Placement is much more challenging for these people, because they first need to be re-placed.[13]

As I shared in chapter 5, one the greatest assets any congregation possesses is their placement in the world. By emphasizing our placement in the world, we guard ourselves from trying to be God. Humans are not omnipresent, though modern transport makes us feel like we have grown wings. Our placement in the world is an important facet of our humanity. Any religion that ignores place can become dangerous; or, as Martyn Percy explains, "when un-earthed and de-coupled from social and cultural contexts, [religion] has a greater potential to become toxic and self-absorbed."[14] Place helps congregations become re-earthed into specific locations. However, it can also become a weapon to the extent that we use placement to interpret life for other people or restrict a given place to a specific ethnic group. All places possess boundaries, whether empirical (such as a national border) or imaginary (how we interpret who is a real Montrealer). In and of themselves, boundaries are important.[15] We can use boundaries to welcome others into who we are becoming and thus contribute to the *missio Dei*, or we can use boundaries to exclude others and be a source of anti-mission in the world.

---

13. One of my PhD students wrote a fascinating study on "re-placement" for internally displaced people in the Republic of Georgia; see Curtis Elliot, *Theologizing Place for Displacement: Reconciling, Remaking, and Reimagining Place in the Republic of Georgia* (Eugene, OR: Pickwick, 2018).

14. Martyn Percy, *Shaping the Church: The Promise of Implicit Theology* (Surrey, UK: Ashgate, 2010), 163.

15. M. V. McGinnis describes humans as "boundary creatures"; see "A Rehearsal to Bioregionalism," in *Bioregionalism*, ed. M. V. McGinnis (London: Routledge, 1999), 5, cited in Gorringe, *Common Good*, 78.

I walk inside St. Jax and meet the priest, Graham Singh. It's a weekday, and the building is completely open. Sun streams into the church through each of the thirty-one stained glass windows, casting a dazzling mosaic of light beams across the sanctuary. Singh takes me through the nave and into his office, which is partitioned off from the main meeting space. Singh is Indian and Scottish by ethnicity and, like many contemporary Montrealers, comes to the city with a complex identity. His father was born in British Guiana (now Guyana) and studied in Jamaica and England before immigrating to Canada. Graham's mother left the British Isles as a baby, as part of the postwar migration from the United Kingdom to Canada. Though Canadian by nationality, Singh retraced his family roots to reside in England for a season, and it was there he met his wife, Celine, a native of Paris, France. In many ways, Singh's complex, integrated identity makes him an ideal priest for a city like Montreal. His ethnic identity helps break down the long antagonism leveled against the Anglican Church, since he is neither European-looking nor white. Singh's identity is like the colors of light streaming into the building of St. Jax: brilliant, integrative, and complex.

We sit and talk. He moves the conversation toward the building—and it is hard to ignore everything around us. He explains that prior to his coming to Montreal, the congregation was in serious decline. The Anglican Church of Canada was trying to decide what to do with historic buildings throughout the country—and especially in urban locations such as Montreal. Singh had spent a number of years in London working at a church called Holy Trinity Brompton (home of Alpha), where he first caught the vision for reclaiming historic churches. With the decline of mainline congregations throughout the West, these historic churches were either sitting idle (and costing denominations enormous amounts of money) or being sold to developers and converted into high-priced condominiums. In 2013 the authorities in the Church of England commissioned Graham and Celine to return to Canada, where they were to re-mission congregations like St. Jax.

I ask Singh why we need historic churches. He explains that in the next ten years, denominations in Canada will be forced to close more than ten thousand of their twenty-eight thousand churches nationally. This is particularly true in Quebec, which experienced a 31 percent decline in church attendance from 1986 to 2001.[16] The Quiet Revolution lingers over the city like ominous clouds after a protracted storm. Historic buildings like St. Jax signify Christianity's complicity with colonialism. This does not seem to bother Singh. Though the city has a complex, multilayered past, it is one he feels the church of Jesus Christ needs to redeem. Singh wants to see churches re-missioned, which I interpret as another way of saying re-placed.

Singh talks about the memories haunting the city. He says that while Montreal has jettisoned its colonial past, these old churches "scream Anglophone authority" to all

16. "Canada's Changing Religious Landscape," Pew Research Center, June 27, 2013, https://www.pewforum.org/2013/06/27/canadas-changing-religious-landscape/.

who pass them by. On the one hand, re-missioning these historic buildings risks giving the impression that St. Jax is trying to resuscitate its colonial past; while on the other, Singh speaks of worse dangers in letting these churches fall into the hands of real estate developers. He asks me to consider how the closure of historic churches will affect the cities not only spiritually but also in regard to how these buildings contribute to public life. He says, "Folks in the neighborhood will tell you that this is their church, even if they have never been to the church, because it's their family church." I walk around the inside of St. Jax and see plaques with the names of people from the community killed during World Wars I and II. As more and more people migrate to urban areas, population growth will increase the pressure placed on transport systems and housing. Singh says, "Spaces that don't make financial value get squeezed out. Spaces to 'do life' get sold off."

We talk specifically about the location of St. Jax in the city. Four Starbucks stores opened within two hundred meters of the church. An Apple Store moved in three hundred meters away. Singh explains that the presence of retailers tells you a lot. They know the foot traffic and rent space only in locations where they are assured a certain number of people will pass their stores. With these stores so close to the church building, St. Jax occupies prime real estate. And the neighborhoods around the church are growing. City developers are currently building residential units for twenty thousand people within a half mile of St. Jax; space for another thirty thousand people will be added by the year 2030. St. Jax lies in the midst of it all. Graham says to me, "If cities need places to do life, can't church buildings be a great place to do that from?"

Cities and Third Places

Ray Oldenburg coined the term *third places* to describe locations where people gather. If a person's home is their first place and work is their second place, then third places are where people come together to play, rest, and relate with each other. These include cafés, coffee shops, bookstores, pubs, hair salons, and other such venues. In his book *The Great Good Place*, Oldenburg describes third places as those that capture "the core settings of informal public life."[17] He argues that the overall health of any location can be judged by the health of its third places. "We come dangerously close to the notion that one 'gets sick' in the world beyond one's domicile and one 'gets well' by retreating from it."[18] Oldenburg wants to flip that script to show how cities can heal through the use of third places.

17. Ray Oldenburg, *The Great Good Place: Cafes, Coffee Shops, Bookstores, Bars, Hair Salons and Other Hangouts at the Heart of a Community* (Philadelphia: Da Capo, 1989), 16.
18. Oldenburg, *Great Good Place*, 10.

Oldenburg defines a third place as "a generic designation for a great variety of public places that host the regular, voluntary, informal, and happily anticipated gatherings of individuals beyond the realms of home and work."[19] Since he released his book in 1989, many other scholars have written on the topic, highlighting a desire within Western societies to reclaim the importance of such venues for the health of entire communities. Oldenburg talks about the previous move from inner cities to suburban dwellings as a flight toward privacy, and how the current focus on third places shows a desire to reclaim our publicness.[20]

What benefits do third places provide? Oldenburg chronicles an impressive list, from offering neutral spaces outside home and work, to leveling the playing field across diverse ranks of life, to creating a medium where the primary activity is conversation and where people can dialogue across ideological differences in a safe place. The list goes on.[21] He describes third places as *inclusive* and *local*.[22]

As migration increases around the world, the *inclusive* nature of public places assumes heightened importance. I recall my dad telling me about the town in New York where he was raised. There were two ethnic groups living in the area, Italians and Swedes, and rarely did the two groups meet. Italians had their own neighborhoods, restaurants, and other meeting places, and the Swedes had theirs. In fact, my dad never ate pasta until he went away to college, since that was the food of "the other" ethnic group! As migration increases around the globe, third places increasingly bring diverse groups of people together into one location. Ideally, they are "neutral" sites with healthy power differentials (where no one group can dominate, such as at a public library, sports arena, or city park). Like the television show *Cheers*, they are places "where everyone knows your name." While all people yearn for such locations, those living in cities do so with greater urgency because of the increased mobility and diversity of people living in such contexts.

Third places are also *local*. Within inner-city locations, people walk to them, or people travel along public transport routes to a restaurant, arboretum, or playground. And third places take on the local character of the place: a pub serves local food and micro-brewed ale or will have memorabilia from the hometown sports team mounted on the walls. Once inside, everything about the place screams indigeneity. The local identity of a third place grounds people in the here and now and helps them feel like it is *their* place.

19. Oldenburg, *Great Good Place*, 16.
20. Oldenburg, *Great Good Place*, xiii–xiv.
21. Oldenburg, *Great Good Place*, 20–31.
22. Oldenburg, *Great Good Place*, xvii.

Third places also help us be human together. The desire for physical, corporate places of belonging is felt more acutely with changes in how people relate to each other. The internet, in particular, is currently redefining social templates for people all around the world. Changes in the speed of transportation and the rise of globalization leave people feeling unplaced (or at least placed in many different ways). All of this leaves people yearning for a place where they belong, where they can laugh, touch, and dialogue with each other outside work and home. Third places can humanize us.

As I explained previously, most of the problems we face in the world involve complex social ills. Meanwhile, the majority of the solutions Western societies leverage to these problems tend to be simple and individual.[23] Third places are an important part of the solution. They are complex in the sense of bringing diverse people together; they are social to the extent they encourage people to meet face-to-face in actual locations. Local congregations like St. Jax represent the ideal third places.

I enter St. Jax on a Sunday morning. The aroma of freshly brewed coffee wafts through the sanctuary. I move in the direction of the smell and find locally made bagels and cream cheese being served at a counter. The atmosphere is relaxed. People mingle. I hear parishioners talking about the Montreal Canadiens' hockey game as well as a local concert attended by many of the congregants that featured several youth from the church. People are friendly and warm. The congregation has only around 150 regular members, so visitors are conspicuous. Quite a few of them introduce themselves. I am immediately struck by the diversity of the parishioners. A German husband and wife tell me about how they arrived in Montreal. I meet a young Kenyan man who works for the church. I see several Asian women with their kids running freely around the sanctuary, and a few others who appear to be of African descent. I am introduced to a young Libyan man who is training to become a pilot. This is his first experience inside a church. Since I am also a first-time visitor, he asks me questions about the music and then inquires about the stained glass windows.

I look up. The stained glass windows above us reveal a picture of Christ seated on the throne. Saints appear on his right and left, and underneath Christ we see the eleven disciples reaching upward to the sky. Eight angels hover in the clouds over the exalted Christ, looking downward in a posture of subservience. Heaven and earth flow seamlessly together in this picture, which involves no less than twenty-five individual windowpanes. A person's hand stretches upward to touch the feet of Jesus. Everyone is looking at the face of Christ, with the following words from Revelation 3:21 inscribed underneath: "To him that overcometh will I grant to sit with me in my throne, even as I also overcame and am set down with my Father in his throne."[24]

23. Oldenburg, *Great Good Place*, 10.
24. This is written in the King James Version of the Bible.

We move into the main sanctuary where the pews have been removed and rows of closely packed chairs form a semicircle around a podium. I notice people hugging each other in warm welcome. A band is on stage with the words of songs projected onto large screens. The liturgy begins. St. Jax blends formal readings from the Book of Common Prayer with charismatic-style worship. We sing a particular song that invites the Holy Spirit to "Come flood this place and fill the atmosphere." Following this, a leader comes to the front and says, "Let everything that is happening around us be in us," and then he quotes from Psalm 122: "We said it is good to come into the house of the Lord." There is more singing. One song, "Come On and Dance," has lyrics that speak of dancing with a joyful heart before the Lord, where "feet start a tapping" and "hands start a clapping."

Once God is welcomed into the place, the entire service turns to a noticeable focus around the lordship of Jesus Christ. It is almost as if in welcoming God into the building, the stained glass windows are called to life. On one side of the sanctuary is the stained glass picture of Christ seated on the throne; on the other there is a single picture of Christ with the words *Salvator Mundi* (Savior of the World). In the middle behind the stage and podium is a picture of the resurrected Christ in all his glory. We sing contemporary songs such as "This Is Amazing Grace," in which we declare God is the "King of glory, the King above all kings" and the one "who breaks the power of sin and darkness."

Singh then comes to the front. He welcomes everyone and prays, "Be exalted in the places of our lives; recall those places to us, dear Lord [where you are at work]. Thank you for creation, this amazing world. We pray for those who work for peace, politics. The world has come to this city . . . call out those places around the world that need your help." He prays specifically for the Middle East, the East African drought, and a new leader in South Africa, and then continues, "We exalt you in this place."

After a sermon about the person of Christ from a visiting speaker, we sing the concluding song, "Turn Your Eyes upon Jesus."

God and Thickness of Place

St. Jax highlights vital linkages between God and place. The service actively welcomes God into the church building. As we will see later, the prominence of place within the service enables St. Jax to thereafter witness to the surrounding city of Montreal through its place in the city. They do this by means of worship, weaving the lordship of Christ into all spaces, and then mission, *re-placing* themselves within and for the city of Montreal. Worship and mission flow back and forth in regular cycles of movement.

There is strong theological rationale for connecting God with place. God is not a vaporous entity but a divine community of persons who creates and inhabits place. The Father brings order out of chaos; the Son holds everything together by his powerful word (and enters human place through the incarnation); the Holy Spirit fills the entire cosmos with God's presence. God inhabits place thickly through the different movements of the persons of the Trinity. God likewise desires for all humans to fill the earth thickly. God's blessings are for fruitfulness, and fruitfulness is for the flourishing of all things in specific locations. As the apostle Paul explains, "From one man he made all the nations, that they should inhabit the whole earth; and he marked out their appointed times in history and the boundaries of their lands. God did this so that they would seek him and perhaps reach out for him and find him, though he is not far from any one of us" (Acts 17:26–27). We might say that God inhabits place thickly and desires for humans to do likewise.

Humans "thin out" place by removing God from public life (such as in secularism) or elevating the material world as the greatest good (such as in materialism). A thicker understanding of place welcomes God into the created world as Lord of all. We are gardeners with God in creation and co-laborers in societal affairs. No independent place exists apart from God (Ps. 139:7–12), but God rules over all and in all. That is why Christ is so critical: he authenticates place through the incarnation. Or as Bonhoeffer explains, "There are not two realities but one reality, and that is the reality of God, which has become manifest in Christ in the reality of the world."[25] Christ then gifts the world back to humans, and specifically bequeaths it to his church, which means that local congregations fully occupy place in this world: the place *of* Christ *in* and *for* the world.

New Testament writers frequently draw on spatial images to understand the church, describing it as a building, a house, living stones, a body, or a temple. Bonhoeffer explains, "The Church does indeed occupy a definite space in the world, a space which is delimited by her public worship, her organization and her parish life."[26] Worship allows local congregations to inhabit space differently. Through the open weave of doxology and liturgy, God is welcomed into place in order to send parishioners into the world as the presence of Christ. Or as Bonhoeffer says, "And so, too, the Church of Jesus Christ is the place, in other words the space in the world, at which the reign of Jesus Christ over the whole world is evidenced and proclaimed."[27]

25. Dietrich Bonhoeffer, *Ethics*, trans. Eberhard Bethge (New York: Collier, 1986), 197.

26. Bonhoeffer, *Ethics*, 201. Craig Bartholomew explains how the church building's architecture bears witness to Christ: "When one thinks of all the church buildings in existence, the potential for a powerful public witness is staggering!" *Where Mortals Dwell*, 297.

27. Bonhoeffer, *Ethics*, 202.

Church buildings, as N.T. Wright explains, "*are not a retreat from the world but a bridgehead into the world*, a way of claiming part of God-given space for his glory."[28]

We see this in St. Jax. Parishioners welcome God into the building. Singh prays, "We exalt you in this place," even as worship songs invite the Holy Spirit to "come flood this place and fill the atmosphere." St. Jax opens itself to God's presence even as stained glass windows testify to the exalted Christ over the entire cosmos. All barriers between God and humans are broken down. By entering into place, Christ gives it back to the community as a means of blessing the nations. Even as Montrealers walk by St. Jax and shake their collective fists at religion, people inside are welcoming God into a specific human place to bless the entire city.

What does this mean for St. Jax's public witness? Initially, they cultivate a thickness of place *within* their worship. "Place" enters into the fabric of liturgy, and once there it gets opened to the lordship of Christ. This leads people to think about place differently. Public realities such as agriculture and politics are woven into the liturgy. People pray for the Middle East, a drought in East Africa, and a new political leader in South Africa.

The lordship of Christ holds everything together. God is welcomed into St. Jax, and by aligning Christ with multiple places in the world, through the person of the Holy Spirit, parishioners are sent out with a redeemed understanding of their *placement* in the world.

I ask Singh what role St. Jax should play within the city of Montreal. He explains that when missionaries travel to new locations, they begin by studying the third places in that setting. They go to libraries, outdoor fountains, coffee shops, gardens, markets, and local haunts. He describes third places as those sites where people do life together. Singh then says that in historic churches, such as St. Jax, you have all these places. Outside the building is a park. Inside the building are a wide variety of spaces that can be customized to serve a variety of needs, whether catering to large gatherings, such as a concert, or more intimate receptions, such as a wedding. Historic churches, he explains, are the ideal third places within any city.

As a third place, St. Jax wants to revitalize the entire city of Montreal. It's an audacious goal! In one of their publications, they explain their aim "to play our part in the

28. N. T. Wright, *Surprised by Hope: Rethinking Heaven, the Resurrection, and the Mission of the Church* (New York: HarperOne, 2008), 260 (italics original). Wright criticizes those who disparage old, historic churches. He says the reasons for doing so are often dualistic and/or materialistic. "We should reflect long and hard on a proper theology of place and space, thought through in terms of God's promise to renew the whole creation, before we abandon geography or territory" (260).

transformation of society," and elsewhere they talk about the "re-evangelization of the city." It's a bold vision, though not without difficulties. Singh readily acknowledges the building carries painful memories of the past, when Christianity was complicit with a myriad of colonial abuses. Hence, he says something needs to happen to the church building to release it from its past: to separate it from its memories.

The first thing they did in re-missioning St. Jax was to close the building for nine months. Shutting down the church served an important message in the city. It was like saying to the Quiet Revolution, "See, you won!" They boarded up the windows and placed a large "closed" sign across the doors. The entire property lay vacant. When they reopened the church, they changed the name from St. James the Apostle to St. Jax and did so as a community center with multiple expressions of church. Singh laughs about the state of the exterior after they reopened. He shows me broken tiles on the roof, along with cracks in the granite, but then explains that these blemishes fit exactly the narrative they want to communicate to the city of Montreal. He asks, "What if Christian ministry works better when we're the minority, or when it looks like we have failed?"

Despite being surrounded by aggressive forms of secularism throughout the city, St. Jax is a vibrant, confessing, Christocentric church. In order to re-place themselves in the city, they don't deviate from their theological heritage. Instead, they *add* to their identity: first, by becoming a community center, and second, by opening themselves to other congregations.

In order to be a community center, they regularly practice "partial, temporary de-consecration." During weekdays or on Saturdays, they open the church building and its surrounding green space as a third place to the city. They host events or welcome people to eat their lunch in their garden. To do so in a heavily secularized context, they need to temporarily deconsecrate the building. St. Jax cannot get rid of all spiritual influences. They take down the altar where the Eucharist is served and a few other sacred symbols but do not touch any of the permanent fixtures. The stained glass windows remain and speak loudly—even when there is no service. People know they are walking into a church. In deciding whom they will rent the facilities to, the church leadership has developed a simple, one-question matrix: "Does this in any way contribute to the narrative of our vision, to play our part in the re-evangelization of the nation and the transformation of society?" If it does, they will rent out the space to the users.

It is World Refugee Day. St. Jax's main sanctuary is filled with immigrants, sponsored in part by the United Nations High Commission for Refugees and a resident charity called Action Refuge Montreal. A group of Syrian men are performing a play chronicling their agonizing flight from the country during the civil war. Other refugee groups wait in the wings to perform their own dire drama. Singh explains to me that he walked into St. Jax on such a Saturday morning and was immediately met by a couple of Syrian men with long, flowing beards who welcomed him to the event and asked if he needed anything.

He chuckles as he recounts the encounter: "They feel like they are in the right place; they feel right at home, acting out their grief in a house dedicated to Jesus Christ." Such is the nature of "partial, temporary deconsecration."

St. Jax hosts Alcoholics Anonymous in the facility. They also worked out an agreement with the city of Montreal to run twenty-two public concerts every year. In an effort to reconcile the presence of Alcoholics Anonymous with the concert series, they do not allow alcohol to be served at any of the concerts out of concern for those who struggle with addiction. They have also opened their doors to a group of former Cirque du Soleil performers to produce a small evening circus show for families. With over ten thousand employees, Cirque du Soleil represents one of Quebec's most important cultural exports. The new group, called La Monastere (The Monastery), likewise represents a particular expression of post–Quiet Revolution secular spirituality. By opening their doors to La Monastere, church leaders are regularly invited to make public announcements welcoming people from the event to their church activities.

Graham explains the incredible "social capital" St. Jax receives from its relationship with the city. In one of St. Jax's publications, the mayor of Montreal writes a glowing commendation: "By uniting our efforts [with St. Jax], we improve access to community and culture activities and make them available to more and more Montrealers." This is a far cry from the anti-church sentiment of the Quiet Revolution. By welcoming the city into St. Jax, people are exposed to architectural elements that publicly witness to the lordship of Christ (such as with the stained glass windows or other artwork). St. Jax also strengthens "social capital" ties with the city, allowing the church to witness more broadly throughout all of Montreal and into greater swaths of life.

For example, Singh talks about a local fitness center. He started going there to improve his overall health and struck up a friendship with the owner. He ended up losing twenty pounds, and the owner came to an Alpha course at St. Jax and became a believer. Both parties benefited from the relationship! Unfortunately, the fitness center came under hard financial times, and St. Jax ended up purchasing the equipment at a local bankruptcy auction. They are currently in the process of converting the basement of the church building into a community fitness center, desirous of being a place of holistic health for the entire city of Montreal.

However, St. Jax is more than just a third place; it is also a church (or, more accurately, a place with multiple expressions of church). They currently have five congregations meeting on their property. These include two smaller Sunday congregations, one large church that uses St. Jax for a monthly prayer meeting, one Chinese church, and a student ministry. Each of these congregations feels like St. Jax is their place. One finds decorations and symbols of the other churches interspersed among the Anglican furnishings. St. Jax does not subtract from its identity by opening its doors to other churches but adds to it. There is a warm generosity to the church's use of place. They are unflinching in their doctrinal beliefs but open and hospitable to the entire city.

Re-placing Place

St. Jax does not only want to be a third place; they desire to *re-place* place for the purposes of "re-evangelizing the city of Montreal." In order to do so, they begin by re-placing the memories attached to places. People living around St. Jax view the church in a complex assortment of positive and negative ways. They remember getting married in the building and seeing their children baptized there. Even those who have never set foot inside the church assume ownership of the garden, the view of the steeple across the Montreal skyline, and even the sound of the bells echoing across the distant hills. They might even go so far as to embrace the spiritual nature of the church (though in a secular, pluralistic way). St. Jax occupies strategic, symbolic presence in the city. Nevertheless, it screams colonialism to all who pass by. In order to navigate its complex place in Montreal, St. Jax intentionally keeps the building in a state of disrepair. They want people to think, "Look, the Quiet Revolution won!" In this way, the building is much like the incarnation of Jesus Christ in the world, imaging God to the city through broken shingles and cracks in its granite walls.

"Partial, temporary deconsecration" is an attempt at re-placing the memories of the past. It started with closing the building completely for nine months. Then they changed the name. The change of name acknowledges that names carry meaning. As Martyn Percy explains, "Naming a place is a power statement, and one that inevitably raises questions of ownership, and therefore fans out into the wider social and political arena."[29] By renaming the church St. Jax, they are telling the city they are different. The old is gone. The new has come and is rebirthed *within* and *for* the entire city of Montreal.

In a city that bristles at anything restrictive, St. Jax weaves a confessing congregation within a larger community center. Some might interpret this as a loss of identity: giving up everything that makes a congregation truly Christian. Yet by becoming a community center they do not lose any of their confessing identity. The Anglican community of St. Jax still meets in the facility, and, as the previous narrative demonstrates, they accentuate the lordship of Jesus Christ. Different movements are happening all the time. First, place enters into the open weave of liturgy. Having become converted to Christ, people leave the church to bless the entire city through a sanctified understanding of place. Second, they are constantly moving back and forth between being a confessing church and being a community center. Consecration and

---

29. Percy, *Shaping the Church*, 164. He later says, "Places and churches exist on many levels, and their boundaries, though real, even perhaps geographical and firmly fixed in culture, are nevertheless subjective and porous" (165).

deconsecration are regular rhythms within the church. Third, by opening their doors to multiple congregations and welcoming diverse Montrealers into their presence, St. Jax weaves ethnicities together into a thicker identity. As these movements happen, they thicken their understanding of place.

How then does a thickness of place enable them to witness to the city?

St. Jax regularly offers Alpha courses, where people in the community searching for spiritual truth can come in a nonthreatening atmosphere to ask questions and learn about Jesus Christ. They hold these Alpha courses regularly in the church sanctuary. It's an example of confessing church and third place coming together as one. Let me briefly highlight three other examples to show their public witness.

The first involves a young woman from the Middle East. She came to Montreal after the Arab Spring. Her father was a mosque builder. From her earliest recollection of childhood, she had been taught to appreciate the architecture associated with religious places. It is not surprising that the sacred beauty of St. Jax grabbed her attention. Despite being a cultural Muslim, she attended various events held at St. Jax. The church leadership developed a relationship with her and asked her to attend an Alpha course. She resisted. But then she unexpectedly attended a leadership event where people were praying for the Alpha courses. She then attended another prayer event, this time for a prison ministry. To this day, she keeps coming to various church activities. In a way, St. Jax has become a religious third place for her while living in a distant land. She might come because of the architectural beauty, or perhaps the warm welcome she receives from the community. It might be a hundred other reasons. But still she comes.

The second story involves a group of project managers. They developed a business plan for revitalizing the area surrounding St. Jax and pitched it to the city. But the plan was rejected. They were discouraged and showed up one day unexpectedly at St. Jax looking for pastoral support. None of them came from a Christian heritage, and perhaps not a single one of them had ever entered into a church building before. But there they were, meeting with the church leadership and asking for prayer. The next day they wrote an urgent message, explaining that, miraculously, the plan had been reconsidered and accepted by the city council. They could only explain this as divine intervention. The social capital that St. Jax holds in the community opened the door for a group of businesspeople to come to the church looking for prayer, and there they encountered God through the miraculous.

The final story involves the mayor of the city. As I explained earlier, the mayor had gotten to know St. Jax by hosting a citywide concert series on the premises. One day, there was a press conference for a refugee ministry.

They were using St. Jax because all the refugee ministries in the city respect the church. There were four TV stations in attendance, along with various dignitaries, including the mayor. While everyone was sitting around the room during the pre-conference meeting, the mayor unexpectedly turned to Singh and asked him to pray for the event. Everyone in the room was shocked. Such a request was astonishing in a city that had experienced the Quiet Revolution.

Witnessing through Place

Each of these stories intimates public witness. The first involves a young woman; the next, several community leaders; and the third, the mayor of the city. But each of these stories is larger than the individuals involved. In the first, we see the influence St. Jax is having across religious boundaries (which I experienced personally when I met two Muslim men from the Arab world who were attending a church for the first time). The second highlights the social capital the church has developed within the business sector and how it affords them regular opportunities to speak spiritually into commercial matters. The final story moves broadly into political dimensions of life. Together the stories show that St. Jax has become an important agent in the life of the city.

St. Jax witnesses to larger publics in the way they welcome God into place. By welcoming the persons of the Trinity into place, they thicken place. And in thickening place, they equip congregants to be agents of God's mission in and for the city of Montreal.

Parishioners thus think about place differently, and they think about their place in the world through Christ. When congregants leave the church, they do so as evangelists to the exalted Christ precisely through their "placement" in the world. For example, a bivocational leader teaches English as a second language to Arabic-speaking trainee airline pilots. Through relationships he has cultivated at work, several of the pilots came to St. Jax for different community events and even attended a church service (I met two of these when I attended the church). Another parishioner is involved in one of the political parties. She explains that what St. Jax is doing in the community opens up "political space" for the church to speak more boldly into city politics. For example, St. Jax was invited to speak to the city council and used that to invite the entire city to their carol sing one Christmas. Meanwhile, St. Jax has a parishioner who serves on a local school board. She has used that "social space" to develop stronger linkages between St. Jax and the local educational system, advocating for change.

Placement requires intimacy with the physical environment. In the same way that someone who builds a storefront carefully considers the pedestrian traffic, the nearby housing, and the vehicular flow around the storefront, so a church must likewise think carefully about how it relates to its surroundings. Eric Jacobsen describes two contrasting types of churches: embedded and insular. An insular church is set off from its surrounding community. Usually, the first thing someone encounters when visiting an insular church is a large parking lot set back from the main road.[30] An embedded church, meanwhile, would be your classic parish congregation. It is defined by how the church "facilitate[s] direct connections between the interior space of the church building and the public space of the wider society outside."[31] St. Jax is a perfect example of an embedded congregation. The city flows around St. Jax like a garden surrounds a majestic oak tree. One can reach out and touch it, smell the leaves, sit in its shade, and play in its branches.

St. Jax uses its proximity to the surroundings to witness to the entire city of Montreal. The dividing lines between the church and community are crossed and recrossed many times every day. The church consecrates, deconsecrates, and reconsecrates in regular cycles of movement. St. Jax desires to be a place of holistic health for the entire city. They open their garden to anyone who wants to eat lunch or enjoy outdoor concerts. They are developing a fitness center in the basement of the church to cater to the physical health of people (and when they talk about fitness, they integrate spiritual, physical, emotional, and mental components). They envision the fitness center being a place where people give brief talks that integrate spiritual insights into physical exercise.

With a strong focus on immigrants, St. Jax desires also to be a place of ethnic healing. As an integrated person himself, Singh embodies this kind of reconciliation within his person. They have a Kenyan on their staff. The church adopted a Syrian refugee family. They rent out space to refugee ministries and host other events on their premises. St. Jax wants everything to communicate: "This is a place where you belong!"

In the past, Anglican churches in Montreal privileged people from an Anglo background. By welcoming diverse migrant communities, St. Jax is not only broadening its constituency but sending a message to the entire city that the days of colonialism are past, and the future of Montreal is

---

30. Jacobsen explains, "The insular church is not set up to attract (or even communicate with) the pedestrian on the street, because the layout of the property doesn't encourage pedestrian traffic. The church is oriented toward people driving cars. The church visually relates to the neighborhood through its large sign(s) directed toward the street. The architecture of the building is most likely to be utilitarian." *Space Between*, 190.

31. Jacobsen, *Space Between*, 190.

with the migrant. This does not mean St. Jax welcomes everyone equally. I was not aware of seeing any First Nations people attending the church, and the challenges of managing child safety regulations alongside welcoming those living with homelessness is as difficult as it is in any urban context. However, St. Jax's welcome of immigrants points to a deeper, thicker understanding of what it means to be Montrealers. They extend their arms outward like the nave of the building, welcoming diverse others into who they are becoming.

St. Jax witnesses to the city of Montreal through the complex ways they relate God with place, and then God's place with the surrounding city. The complexity of movements corresponds to a thickness of public witness.

Conclusion

A congregation is always embodied in a community, and hence every church occupies place in the world, and that is a good thing—and essential to its witness. One danger I see in contemporary discussions on missional ecclesiology is that in reaction to the abuses of a previous era, we jettison any focus on a church building and neglect how it can be used as a means of witness to its surroundings. The case study of St. Jax shows how a congregation can witness to an entire city *through its placement*. In a city heavily beset by a colonial heritage, St. Jax occupies place differently. Rather than using place territorially,[32] St. Jax weaves God with place, and God's place *in* and *for* the entire city of Montreal. Let me give a final illustration of what this looks like.

Every congregation exists in intimate relationship with its surroundings. I have been describing this through different analogies, but perhaps the best would be a *terroir*. This is a term used in the wine industry to describe the local identity of a region. Alister McGrath explains, "The characteristics of the wine produced in a given *terroir* are shaped by the soil, the climate, the grape types, and the methods of production—all of which are specific to that given locale."[33] A *terroir* involves the microclimate, trees, and surrounding vegetation growing in the region, along with more subjective factors such as

32. Bonhoeffer explains, "The Church has neither the wish nor the obligation to extend her space to cover the space of the world. She asks for no more space than she needs for the purpose of serving the world by bearing witness to Jesus Christ and to the reconciliation of the world with God through Him." *Ethics*, 202.

33. Alister E. McGrath, "The Cultivation of Theological Vision: Theological Attentiveness and the Practice of Ministry," in *Perspectives on Ecclesiology and Ethnography*, ed. Pete Ward (Grand Rapids: Eerdmans, 2012), 107–23, here 119. He uses the analogy of a *terroir* for understanding local congregations.

the "spirit" of the workers of the vineyard. In the telling words of two wine aficionados, a *terroir* is "a sense of place. Terroir can be a complex, layered, and misunderstood topic in the wine industry, but basically, it means that a wine smells and tastes of the place it was created."[34]

Embedded congregations such as St. Jax function as a *terroir* in and for their community. They are, as the wine aficionados write, "complex, layered, and misunderstood," with "smells and tastes of the place [they were] created." Every congregation receives from its surroundings, while imparting nutrients back into the soil to influence the smells and tastes of the entire city. Movement happens back and forth. That is what I have been describing in this chapter. St. Jax is like an oak tree planted in a garden that influences the bouquet of the entire city of Montreal. Nutrients work their way through the different movements. As parishioners become converted through the movements of the Trinity, they are released as a *terroir* to the entire city.

St. Jax is producing a marvelous bouquet, filled with robust flavors and textures; and the entire city of Montreal receives this as a blessing, as a great example of public witness.

34. Thomas Pastuszak and Jessica Brown, "The Pair: The Best Examples of Terroir," Saveur, May 25, 2015, https://www.saveur.com/pair-understanding-terroir-wine.

9

Thick Identity and Witness to All Nations—Bethel World Outreach Church, Nashville

My house shall be a house of prayer for all the nations.

—Mark 11:17

We practice the discipline of intentional inconvenience.

—Pastor James Lowe

Bethel World Outreach Church[1] is an ethnically and racially diverse congregation located in the affluent suburb of Brentwood, outside Nashville, Tennessee.[2] From its modest origins as a Bible study for white business professionals, Bethel has grown to become a robust multicultural congregation of approximately two thousand parishioners, with satellite campuses throughout Nashville, daughter churches in cities of Knoxville, Memphis,

1. In subsequent references I will refer to the church as Bethel.
2. In this chapter I will be using *race* and *ethnicity* synonymously. I am aware there are differences in the meanings given to these terms, but I will use them interchangeably in the context of this case study.

Dallas, and Cincinnati, and sister congregations in India, China, Poland, and Iran. Bethel uses a thickness of identity to witness to the nations.

Driving down Interstate 65 south of Nashville, I pass a statue of Nathan Bedford Forrest, the former Confederate general and Ku Klux Klan leader. It is located on private property near the interstate. I proceed a little farther and notice a large billboard advertising Bethel World Outreach Church.[3] There is nothing particularly surprising about this. I see signs for churches everywhere. After all, this is the Bible Belt. What is surprising is the image on the sign. There are two hands: one white and the other black, with palms pressed together as if in a posture of prayer. Inscribed over the hands are the words DEVOTION, DIVERSITY, and DISCIPLESHIP. I'm curious. The proximity of Bethel's sign to Nathan Bedford Forrest's statue is striking. Racial tensions are high across the country. The United States is currently embroiled in its latest iteration of civic religion, where large numbers of people calling themselves Christians appear more interested in building walls than tearing down racial divides.

I get off the interstate and find myself in Brentwood, a wealthy bedroom community just south of Nashville. The median household income is $141,000. By all appearances, it is not the kind of place where I would expect to see blacks and whites worship together. Out of a total population of forty thousand people, Brentwood is 83.7 percent white, 7.7 percent Asian, 3.56 percent black, and 3.3 percent Hispanic.[4]

The main church building lies at the corner of Granny White Pike and Old Hickory Boulevard. From the outside, the church building appears like many other large American churches. The architecture is bland, trading any historic statement for the sake of convenience, comfort, and size. They have recently completed an $8 million building campaign to increase the occupancy of the sanctuary to seat fifteen hundred people. From the outside, the church fits its surroundings: it is wealthy and monochromatic, almost giving the appearance of a large warehouse, except for a large metal cross in front.

I park my car and am immediately welcomed by a team of people wearing T-shirts with the words "Glad you are here!" The greeters are diverse: a couple blacks, one white, a Latino, and an Asian. One of them asks if I am new to the church, and when I say yes, she immediately takes me by the arm and treats me like I am her long-lost relative. I have been to thousands of churches in my life. I am cautious of taking the role of greeters too seriously, knowing they are strategically placed there for the purpose of increasing church membership. But this time it feels different. Maybe it's because I am in the South,

3. I am indebted to David Houston, Delvin Pikes, and Steve Murrell for some of the material in this chapter, which I borrow from their ethnographic research papers submitted for a course requirement in their doctor of ministry program at Asbury Theological Seminary. I use their material with permission.

4. "Brentwood, TN: Heritage," Data USA, https://datausa.io/profile/geo/brentwood-tn/#category_heritage.

where hospitality is a prominent cultural value. Or perhaps it's because there is something different here: a genuineness that arises deep within the bowels of the congregation. They whisk me away into the church.

Race Relations and "Complicated Wickedness"

How we treat the "other" is an age-old challenge. In the United States, the problem of the other began with the treatment of indigenous peoples during the settling of the American colonies, and then took on new manifestations with the slave trade, the Civil War, and Jim Crow laws in the South, leading to the civil rights struggle during the 1950s and 1960s. More recently, we have seen tensions reappear through the senseless shootings of young black men, compounded by sharp differences in how we treat immigration. Racial problems are like magma underneath the ground, rising to the surface whenever cracks appear in the earth. These challenges are a prime example of "complicated wickedness."

Like all complex problems, racial tensions comprise a single story told differently by different groups of people. I will not attempt to rehearse the United States' history of race here; to be honest, it lies beyond my scope of analysis. And even if I were to attempt such a task, I would inevitably interpret the history through my own lenses. As one who has drunk deeply from the cisterns of African Christianity, and as the father of two biracial children, I view race through my own life experiences. We all do.

Not only do we interpret life through our own lenses, but publics in the world reinforce our existing beliefs. Social media such as Facebook and Twitter use sophisticated algorithms to show people only those posts or tweets that reinforce their own beliefs, creating ideological echo chambers. Even when we encounter contrasting positions, social media is not exactly a healthy place for creating discussion across racial divides, but inevitably stokes fear or elicits anger. These deep-seated emotions are further bolstered by ideologies regarding what it means to be an American, sometimes fueled by religious sentiment.[5] Hence, the United States' experience with race possesses a multifaceted thickness, formed from multiple layers.

If this is the context of public life in the Unites States, it is every bit a problem for congregations. Martin Luther King Jr. famously quipped that 11:00 a.m. on a Sunday morning represents the most segregated hour in American

---

5. As R. Scott Appleby explains, "Ethnicity thus serves not only to differentiate and classify peoples but also to evaluate them comparatively, lifting one's group above others, frequently by invoking a 'sacred' warrant." *The Ambivalence of the Sacred: Religion, Violence, and Reconciliation* (Lanham, MD: Rowman & Littlefield, 2000), 60.

life. In this case study, I will show how one church in the South cultivates a thickness of identity to witness to complex publics associated with race.

It is notable that this case study arises in Nashville. At the end of the Civil War, black communities in the region slowly began to rebuild their existence. For the first time since arriving in the Americas as slaves, blacks in the post-bellum South experienced the slightest whispers of hope. These hopes were quickly dashed, however, by a series of setbacks in the form of the Jim Crow laws, which were state and local laws codifying segregationist practices. Though the Thirteenth Amendment had officially abolished slavery in 1865, Jim Crow laws sought to restrict blacks' access to public life. They regulated black access to public domains such as employment, voting, housing, and transport and were often enforced by former Confederate soldiers who held key governmental positions in the judicial system or police force.[6] Jim Crow laws amounted to a different kind of slavery, one enforced not by whips and chains but by laws and regulations.

Despite these debilitating restrictions, black churches grew rapidly during the postbellum period. Even as Jim Crow laws restricted blacks in public life, the black church arose as a counterpublic in the world. Unlike in white churches, the liturgy, songs, and preaching found in black churches were always focused on public life. Inside the churches, blacks made ready connection between the "good news" of the gospel and public issues such as freedom, rights, and poverty. Hence, it should not come as any surprise that the black church contributed significantly to the civil rights movement. In Nashville, for example, the Nashville Christian Leadership Council was created in 1958 and initiated a series of nonviolent protests throughout the city. In 1960 the now famous Nashville sit-ins began, which played a prominent role in desegregation, culminating nationally in the establishment of the Civil Rights Act of 1964.

Despite these advances, deep divisions continue to exist. Today the percentage of whites living in poverty in Nashville is 10.4 percent, while for blacks it is more than double that, at 25.3 percent. We also see broad educational differences across the city, depending on where one lives. And churches throughout Nashville largely reflect the sociocultural divide.

The story of Bethel World Outreach Church turns all of this on its head. It began as a white church focused on private, spiritual realities and has turned

---

6. Richard Alba and Nancy Foner write, "Abolition was followed by a harsh regime of insti-tutionalized racial oppression, entailing a century of legal segregation in the South and new era of white supremacy that defined African Americans in Southern states as second-class citizens, confining them to separate schools, public places, and public transportation and depriving most of the right to vote." *Strangers No More: Immigration and the Challenges of Integration in North America and Western Europe* (Princeton: Princeton University Press, 2015), 100–101.

into a multicultural congregation positioned for public witness. Let me narrate how and why this occurred.

Bethel began in 1984 when Ray McCollum hosted a Bible study in his house. The study eventually grew so large it became a congregation. They ended up needing to rent space to meet at a local bank. At that time, the church was called Bethel Chapel, and the demographics largely reflected those of the surrounding Brentwood estates. Most of the congregants were middle- to upper-class whites. Bethel grew steadily during that period, and in 1987 they purchased the property at the corner of Granny White Pike and Old Hickory Boulevard, where the church currently sits. Neither the neighborhood around Bethel nor the demographic of the parishioners attending the church in the late 1980s gave any indication it would grow into a vibrant, multicultural congregation.

In 1993 Rice Broocks moved to Nashville. He had been planting churches around the world. In 1994 Broocks and Steve Murrell, through the assistance of Bethel, helped launch a global church planting / campus ministry movement called Morning Star International, which eventually became Every Nation, a missions organization that exists "to honor God by establishing Christ-centered, Spirit-empowered, socially responsible churches and campus ministries in every nation."[7] Hence, from the early days Bethel was deeply involved in global missions, but the congregation itself was still predominantly white.

In 1997 they changed the name to Bethel World Outreach Church to signify the greater influence they desired across the globe. In 2000 Bethel named Broocks as senior pastor and adopted the vision "Reaching a city to touch the world," with three primary values: devotion, diversity, and discipleship. Broocks had previously planted a church in Cape Town, South Africa, where he first saw the image of the two hands. When he became senior pastor, he borrowed that image for Bethel. He then hired two assistant pastors, Tim Johnson, a black pastor from Washington, DC, and Burt Thompson, a white pastor from Calgary, Alberta.

One of the first things Broocks did after being appointed senior pastor of Bethel was to stand up on a Sunday morning and announce, "I don't want to pastor a white church!" Church attendance experienced a sharp decline after this announcement.[8] However, Broocks had seen firsthand the

---

7. "Who We Are," Every Nation, October 9, 2017, http://www.everynation.org/about/.

8. People told me 250 parishioners left the congregation after Broocks made that announcement. I asked Broocks about this and he laughed, calling it "urban legend." But he did say that Bethel saw a significant exodus of white people from the congregation during that time, though some of it he attributes to their love of the previous pastor rather than direct opposition to becoming a multicultural church.

horrors of apartheid in South Africa and was burdened by more than one hundred nations living in the city of Nashville. He wanted Bethel to be different. He explained to me, "We weren't willing to do church without [the nations]."

From that time onward, Broocks always welcomed Pastor Tim Johnson on stage with him. After the 2001 terrorist attacks in New York City, Broocks and Johnson flew every week to New York City to help plant a church there, which has subsequently planted three other congregations, with attendees from sixty-eight ethnic groups. Sharing the stage with Johnson was always more than show. For Broocks, it was an intentional act of demonstrating that a black pastor and a white pastor could serve together. After Johnson's departure, Broocks did the same with Pastor James Lowe, who came from inner-city Detroit. In 2012 Broocks transitioned to an oversight role as bishop of the Bethel churches. He handed sole pastoral responsibility of Bethel in Brentwood over to Pastor Lowe. During the commissioning service, Broocks symbolically took off his coat and laid it over Pastor Lowe's shoulders. Since then, the two have worked closely together. Their relationship has been a visual representation of the two praying hands, and Bethel has blossomed as a multicultural congregation through their relationship.

Today, Bethel boasts more than two thousand members. They have planted daughter churches throughout Tennessee as well as in Phoenix, Cincinnati, and Dallas. Their demographics have also changed. From their origins as a predominantly white congregation, Bethel has grown to a church that is approximately 60 percent black and 20 percent white, with the remainder being Asian and Latino/a. They have parishioners representing fifty-two nations.

Multicultural Congregations in the United States

Is 11:00 a.m. on Sunday morning the most segregated hour in American life? The data tells a mixed story. In 1998 a study on multiracial congregations was commissioned, called the National Congregations Study (NCS). It revealed that only 7.4 percent of US congregations were multiracial (defined as no racial or ethnic group being more than 80 percent of the population of the congregation).[9] From 1998 to 2013 the percentage of multicultural

9. Kevin D. Dougherty and Michael O. Emerson, "The Changing Complexion of American Congregations," *Journal for the Scientific Study of Religion* 57, no. 1 (March 2018): 24–38. The reason for using 80 percent in the definition is that once other groups reach a critical mass of 20 percent, they have greater power for influencing the whole (25).

congregations nearly doubled.[10] Using data from the NCS, Kevin Dougherty and Michael Emerson estimate, "In 1998, 12.7 percent of all US congregants were affiliated with a multiracial congregation. The percentage climbed to 15.1 percent in 2006 and 18.3 percent in 2012. Hence, about one in five Americans now attend a place of worship where 20 percent or more of fellow congregants are of a different race or ethnicity."[11] According to these statistics, the United States is becoming more congregationally diverse. To get a better grasp of why and how it is happening, we need to drill deeper into the underlying reasons.

Dougherty and Emerson analyze various factors contributing to the rise of multiracial congregations. They cite the following elements as conducive to the growth of culturally diverse churches: (1) moving toward diversity out of a sense of mission rather than necessity, (2) possessing charismatic worship, (3) lying in proximity to urban centers, (4) being located in the western United States rather than in the South, (5) being associated with larger congregations, (6) having younger demographics, (7) using small groups, and (8) possessing a more recent history.[12] All these factors increase the likelihood that a church will be multiracial. But two other factors play an even greater role: (9) having key leaders from racial populations[13] and (10) the relative diversity of the neighborhood around the church. With regard to the latter, when the surrounding community is diverse, there is a greater chance the church will be diverse. As Dougherty and Emerson explain, "Racial diversity in congregations is more difficult in a racially homogeneous community."[14]

The good news is that the United States is becoming more diverse. As of 2016, whites were still the majority at 76.9 percent, Hispanic or Latino/a were next at 17.8 percent, then African Americans at 13.3 percent, and Asians at 5.7 percent.[15] But these categories only tell part of the story. According to a

10. Korie L. Edwards, Brad Christerson, and Michael O. Emerson, "Race, Religious Organization, and Integration," *Annual Review of Sociology* 39, no. 1 (2013): 211–28; see also Dougherty and Emerson, "Changing Complexion," 29.

11. Dougherty and Emerson, "Changing Complexion," 29.

12. Dougherty and Emerson, "Changing Complexion," 26–27; see also Michael O. Emerson and Karen Chai Kim, "Multiracial Congregations: An Analysis of Their Development and Typology," *Journal for the Scientific Study of Religion* 42, no. 2 (2003): 217–27.

13. Dougherty and Emerson, "Changing Complexion," 26–27. The authors go on to explain, "Racially diverse leaders are a visual representation of the importance of diversity, and this representation matters significantly as the leaders provide 'conspicuous diversity' (Marti 2012)" (27).

14. Dougherty and Emerson, "Changing Complexion," 26.

15. "Quick Facts: United States," United States Census Bureau, https://www.census.gov/quickfacts/fact/table/US/PST045216.

Pew Research Center study, by the year 2055 there will be no single ethnic majority.[16] Other scholars estimate that by 2035 "minorities will outnumber whites among the population under the age of forty."[17] Most of this diversity is happening through the migration of peoples. According to the same Pew study, "Nearly 59 million immigrants have arrived in the US in the past 50 years, mostly from Latin America and Asia. Today, a near-record 14% of the country's population is foreign born compared with just 5% in 1965."[18] For example, in the New York City borough of Queens, people speak more than 150 languages.[19] As these statistics imply, the United States is becoming more ethnically diverse, and this bodes well for the future of multicultural congregations like Bethel World Outreach Church.

Furthermore, according to the National Congregation Study, the data shows that increased diversity of a neighborhood (meaning the greater the number of ethnic populations living in an area) accelerates the likelihood of multicultural congregations. Dougherty and Emerson refer to this as the Entropy Index, which they use to analyze the number of ethnic groups (and their size) within a congregation.[20] Not only are US congregations becoming more diverse, but the *degree of diversity* within congregations is also increasing. Using the Entropy Index, Dougherty and Emerson conclude that in 1998 congregations were eight times less diverse than their surrounding neighborhoods, while in 2012 they were only four times less diverse.[21] This shows that congregations are slowly coming to reflect the demographics of their immediate communities.[22]

The data is not all positive. When a neighborhood is largely composed of two racial groups, it is less likely they will see a successful multicultural congregation.[23] This is likely due to power struggles between the groups, along with historic patterns of black-white tension in the United States (and it is

16. D'Vera Cohn and Andrea Caumont, "10 Demographic Trends That Are Shaping the U.S. and the World," Pew Research Center, March 31, 2016, http://www.pewresearch.org/fact-tank /2016/03/31/10-demographic-trends-that-are-shaping-the-u-s-and-the-world/.

17. Alba and Foner, *Strangers No More*, 42.

18. Cohn and Caumont, "10 Demographic Trends."

19. Alba and Foner, *Strangers No More*, 39–40.

20. Dougherty and Emerson, "Changing Complexion," 28–29.

21. Dougherty and Emerson, "Changing Complexion," 31–32.

22. Dougherty and Emerson, "Changing Complexion," 34–35.

23. Dougherty and Emerson, "Changing Complexion," 26. There is also evidence that Latinos are less likely to participate in multiracial congregations than they did in the past, perhaps because of shifting templates where more Latinos are moving away from Catholicism in favor of Protestantism, along with a rise of Latino congregations across the country. Dougherty and Emerson report that "Latino participants in multiracial congregations dropped from 22 percent in 1998 to 13 percent in 2012" (34).

more likely to be true in places in the South than in other parts of the country). However, the greater the number of ethnic groups living in a neighborhood, the more likely we will see fruitful congregational integration.[24]

Comparing this data with Bethel, it would appear that in many ways Bethel supports the research done by the National Congregation Study: they have charismatic-style worship, younger demographics, small groups, close proximity to a large city, and a diverse leadership team, plus the church is of more recent origins. However, in other ways Bethel represents something of an enigma. They are located in the South, and the diversity inside the congregation stands in stark contrast to the demographics found in the surrounding neighborhood of Brentwood. At times, it seems they are swimming upstream.

Inside the church, I approach a "Connection Desk." I am greeted by more warm smiles. They hand me various gifts. All have "3D" on them—which stands for DEVOTION, DIVERSITY, and DISCIPLESHIP. I look around the foyer and notice 3D printed everywhere: on banners, T-shirts, and name tags, as well as on pens, posters, and other ephemera. The only things rivaling the 3Ds are signs with the black and white hands in a posture of prayer.

I enter the original sanctuary. It has a global feel to it. There are world maps on the walls. I count at least fifty country flags hanging from wires and see the words "My house shall be a house of prayer for all the nations" inscribed in large letters on the sides of the sanctuary walls. Moving back into the foyer, I observe parishioners dressed in African clothes and am introduced to a young Nigerian man (who is baptized later during the service). Bethel feels more like a missions mobilization center than a church. But then I enter into the new sanctuary.

Three enormous video screens hang over the stage, offering a dazzling show of high-quality graphics. It's like I have walked into a concert hall, something one would expect in Music City. The seating is arranged amphitheater-style. The worship has already started. I enter a row, inconspicuous to those around me. A diverse team of musicians leads worship in a blend of music styles that include contemporary worship songs, gospel music, and traditional hymns. At one moment we are singing to an acoustic guitar, and the next moment alongside a piano. The worship team features seven singers: two white, three

24. I will be using the word *integration* as opposed to the more common word *assimilation*. In the past, America operated on a model of assimilation, as implied by the idea of being a "melting pot." Today, integration is a better word. Alba and Foner explain that integration "refers to the processes that increase the opportunities of immigrants and their descendants to obtain the valued 'stuff' of a society, as well as social acceptance, through participation in major institutions such as the educational and political system and the labor and housing markets." *Strangers No More*, 5.

black, one Asian, and one Latino. The ethnic composition of Bethel feels as integrated as the music itself.

I look around. Most parishioners are young, likely in their twenties and thirties. I see quite a number of multiracial families: black men with white wives; white women with black husbands; blacks and whites with Asian or Latino/a spouses; along with parents with children who appear to be adopted from different countries. I estimate that 60 percent of the congregants are black, 20 percent are white, and the rest are Asian and Latino/a. However, even these percentages fail to account for interracial marriages, biracial people, and parishioners from fifty-two countries. Bethel is like a beautiful tapestry filled with different shades and flecks of color.

Not surprisingly, the diversity found in the pews is reflective of the diversity within the church leadership. I pick up a bulletin. It has pictures of the white bishop, Dr. Rice Broocks, and the black senior pastor, James Lowe. I ask about others on the leadership team and am told that Bethel's music director, Will Smith, is black; the primary singers, Kristin Hill and Robert Torrez, are white and Latino, respectively. The chief administrator and finance manager, Vinay Dawwani, is an Indian married to a Filipina woman. Pastor Carol Fidler, who leads the discipleship program, is white; while Pastor Delvin Pikes, who champions Bethel's outreach to the surrounding colleges, is black.[25] Diversity is embedded in every aspect of the church leadership. It is in their DNA.

As one of the flagship churches for Every Nation,[26] Bethel possesses intimate connections in every part of the world. Every Nation began as a campus ministry initiative, which soon morphed into a church planting movement, then turned into a missions organization, and subsequently has become a denomination. Association with Every Nation has influenced this congregation in every possible way.[27] On its website, Bethel highlights missionaries serving in Poland, Mexico, Canada, South Africa, India, Ireland, Peru, New Zealand, Ukraine, Fiji, and "restricted access countries," with many others serving in the United States. Whether global diversity influences Bethel's congregational diversity, or whether hiring black pastors inspired a global movement, is hard to say. Movement happens back and forth, cultivating a thickness of identity.

I sit with Pastor Lowe between the two church services. He asks me, "Do you know why we're effective as a multicultural congregation?" I can tell he is about to disclose to me some great secret and lean forward awaiting his response. He says, "We practice the discipline of intentional inconvenience. No two services are the same. We never let people feel comfortable."

25. I was invited to attend a leadership retreat for the church staff. I would estimate there were twenty-five to thirty people in attendance. The ethnic/racial diversity in the room was indicative of the ethnic/racial diversity of the congregation.
26. The other flagship churches are located in the Philippines.
27. Every Nation's international headquarters is located down the street in Brentwood. Many of Every Nation's leadership team members regularly attend Bethel.

Thin and Thick Identities

Why is it so hard to cultivate diversity? That is one of the hardest questions and requires something of a philosophical answer. Jürgen Moltmann says it is because we only know through community and we only congregate with people similar to us.[28] He calls this the "principle of correspondence." We know this to be true. We can walk into a room and instinctively "read" those around us, looking for likeness. When we see it, we gradually move in that direction. And don't just attend to physical likeness but are sensitized to a variety of things, such as the lilt in a voice, facial expressions, body posture, and even subtleties of dress. We crave similarity.

While the principle of correspondence is a powerful force of social identity, it does not provide us with very comprehensive knowledge. It is accurate for the people in our particular group but is not expansive of others from the outside. Moltmann explains that if we only know through likeness, then we only know ourselves. He says, "I do not perceive what is different in kind and alien in other people. I filter it out."[29] Hence, our knowledge is reinforced rather than challenged. We reify "our group" instead of growing through difference. Thus our knowledge takes on certain tribal characteristics.[30]

The principle of correspondence therefore leads to *thin* identities. And anything thin feels instinctively insecure. It is for such reasons that scholars talk about "white fragility" to describe the feelings of anxiety white people experience when their social norms are challenged by people different from themselves.[31] When this happens, people self-protect. Sometimes self-protection is as simple as avoiding those different from us: we worship with people from our own race or live around those from a similar socioeconomic status. Deep down we feel guilty about the principle of correspondence, and so we attribute positive characteristics to our own group while ascribing negative characteristics to others, doing so through the language of "purity" and "danger."[32] For example, we speak of ourselves as "law-abiding citizens," "hardworking," and "patriotic," while calling others "illegals," "lazy," and "un-American."

28. Jürgen Moltmann, *God for a Secular Society: The Public Relevance of Theology* (Minneapolis: Fortress, 1999), 135–52, here 135–38.

29. Moltmann, *God for a Secular Society*, 138.

30. Moltmann says, "The principle of correspondence does not lead to any increase in knowledge, but only to the continually reiterated self-endorsement of what is already known. The principle of likeness leads to caste and class societies, and destroys interest in the livingness of life, which consists of polarities and contrasts." *God for a Secular Society*, 139.

31. See Robin DiAngelo, "White Fragility," *International Journal of Critical Pedagogy* 3, no. 3 (2011): 54–70.

32. I am referring to Mary Douglas's work *Purity and Danger: An Analysis of Concepts of Pollution and Taboo* (New York: Routledge, 1966).

The language of purity and danger lends sacred warrant to the principle of correspondence. It deepens our exclusion of others, sometimes through religious warrant.

Moltmann argues that all of this stems from how we view God. "Applied to God, the 'likeness' principle leads either to the divinization of human beings or to the humanization of God."[33] In the ancient world, *knowing* took place primarily through perception: people were constantly trying to discover God through self-knowledge. But since God is wholly other, it follows that no one can know God other than God. In the modern world, we are not just content to perceive the world but want to control everything around us. When applied to God, we want to make God in our own image. Or as Moltmann says, "Like the beautiful youth Narcissus, modern human beings, wherever they may turn—whether it be to other people, to other 'nature,' or to the Wholly Other of the divine—always see everywhere only their own reflection."[34]

Fortunately, we have other options. We inhabit a world of difference, and that difference begins with God's triune nature, which is subsequently shared with humans (and the rest of creation). Thus Moltmann explains that not only do we know through similarity, but we also can know through dissimilarity— which leads to a better way of knowing. He says that when we know through similarity, "we somehow feel endorsed," and the feeling is pleasant. But when we know through difference, "the initial effect is pain." He goes on to explain, "We feel the resistance of the alien. We feel the contradiction of the other. We sense the claim of the new. The pain shows us that we must open ourselves, in order to take in the other."[35] The principle of correspondence does not add anything to our knowledge but continually reinforces what is already there. The principle of dissimilarity forces us to constantly take in the other, and through the pain of contradiction, we are compelled to make room for the other within ourselves.[36]

I would suggest that the principle of dissimilarity lies behind Pastor Lowe's secret of "intentional inconvenience." When most parishioners in a congregation share the same ethnic background, a worship service can be easily constructed around the needs of the majority group. However, in a church as diverse as Bethel, with parishioners from numerous countries, the worship

---

33. Moltmann, *God for a Secular Society*, 140.
34. Moltmann, *God for a Secular Society*, 142.
35. Moltmann, *God for a Secular Society*, 144.
36. Moltmann, *God for a Secular Society*, 145. Moltmann explains that this is only possible if built on the foundational principle of "loving our enemies" (146), and particularly the kind of suffering found within the cross (148).

constantly needs to change to allow for different worship styles and cultural expressions. As Pastor Lowe said, "No two services are the same. We never let people feel comfortable." Intentional inconvenience, as practiced by Bethel, promotes knowledge through dissimilarity. It thickens identities through the context of worship.

Of course, diversity itself is not the same as integration. We need something strong enough to hold diverse elements together. Diversity for the sake of diversity amounts to nothing other than a bunch of marbles rattling around in a tin can: they bang against each other and make a lot of noise—and there is already too much of that happening in the world! Diversity needs a center, a center powerful enough to hold all the elements together without destroying the integrity of the parts. This is what we have in Jesus Christ, through the Holy Spirit (Eph. 2:15–18).

If the principle of correspondence seeks to craft God after the image of humans, the principle of dissimilarity argues that God can only be known as a divine community. We are called to image God through the *diversity in unity* found in the Trinity. Hence, *what* we believe about God directly influences *who* we are and *how* we undertake God's mission in the world.

Inside the church service, we sing songs that declare God as "King," Christ as "Lord," and Holy Spirit as "power"—where the persons of the Trinity relate to one another through diversity in unity. And people worship God through their bodies. They lift hands in the air or dance around in their pews. We sing, "We give everything to find you," "Rise and sing, elevate the King," "Lift you higher," "How great you are!" and "I will bless the Lord." Praise reverberates throughout the building as worship reflects on the Trinity. As Pastor Lowe later tells parishioners, "Sometimes praise goes deep; it goes into your hands, comes out of your mouth, and sometimes gets into your feet. Give him the glory!"

The middle school pastor, Brycen, comes on stage. After welcoming everyone to Bethel, he prays, "We thank you," "You see a breakthrough," "We confess Jesus is Lord." He immediately brings public issues into the context of worship, praying for the victims of a shooting that had just occurred in Nashville, along with those suffering from poverty in the community. He tells people, "We're a praying church. Things change because of prayer." Coming on stage after him is an Egyptian pastor and his Bolivian wife, who share about what the church is doing around the world. They showcase various ministries in the Philippines, along with what Bethel's missionaries are doing in Latin America. Video testimonies transport the congregation around the globe. There is a video that deals with societal injustices. It names one of these problems as racial violence and says, "There's a cure for all of it [injustice], and his name is Jesus. He is a fact. If we don't make that public, somebody is going to be denied the cure."

Worship continues. We sing songs that emphasize Christ's lordship and God's king-ship and sovereignty over the entire world. Appeal is made to the Holy Spirit's power in the world. Other lyrics proclaim the persons of the Trinity as majestic, powerful, able, and glorious. Worship is repetitive but integrated. Images of different countries lie on the background of slides behind the lyrics of the songs. As we sing about Christ's power, parishioners see maps of the Philippines and Eastern Europe. During the of-fering, a white police officer who attends the church walks up and down the aisles giving people hugs.

Pastor Lowe then comes on stage and preaches in a manner that makes it feel like we are still singing. Word, song, and dance flow together into one synchronized movement. At one moment he is preaching, and at the next he breaks into song. The sermon is titled "Authority in Truth," taken from Hebrews 1:1–4. On the background of the slides we see a picture of Washington, DC. Pastor Lowe says, "Let's hear from the Spirit." He focuses on Christ's authority over the entire world. "The Potter has power; the Potter doesn't get input from the clay. He's not concerned with the clay's opinion." He cites John 10:17, where Jesus says, "The reason my Father loves me is that I lay down my life—only to take it up again." Interspersed within these statements, he mentions politics, education, and the current state of morality in the nation. He refer-ences the shooting that happened in Nashville and then talks about the ways people interpret life through the lenses of politics or education, and says, "But he [Jesus] is the only authority." Pastor Lowe tells the people, "When the enemy tells you what God cannot do, you just ask him who holds everything together by his powerful word" (referencing Heb. 1:3).

Christ's Power and the Nations

Bethel saturates the entire service with Christ's power, through the power of the Holy Spirit and for God the King. From song to prayer to sermon to every-thing else occurring in the service, they orient everything around "him who holds everything together by his powerful word." Before and after the weeks I attended, Pastor Lowe preached sermons titled "Gospel Is Public Truth," "Truth Is a Person," and "Truth Is Reconciliation," as a part of a sermon series dealing with Broocks's latest book, *The Human Right*.[37] However, all of the messages accentuate Jesus's nature through the other persons of the Trinity. It is as if Bethel knows they need something powerful enough to hold all their diversity together. That power is only found in the person of Jesus, through the *diversity in unity* of the persons of the Trinity.

---

37. Rice Broocks, *The Human Right: To Know Jesus Christ and to Make Him Known* (Nashville: Thomas Nelson, 2018).

Christ's power accomplishes two things for Bethel. First, it brings all their incredible diversity together into a new whole. As diversity increases, a congregation needs something powerful enough to integrate the different elements. Or as Vinoth Ramachandra explains, "The greater the diversity in a society, the greater the cohesion it requires to hold itself together and nurture its diversity."[38]

Second, internal *diversity in unity* leads to public witness. It is not just that Bethel focuses on Christ. Even homogeneous churches do that. It is how they use that power to move outward into public "spaces." They start with what happens inside the congregation. They sing songs with lyrics such as "rise and sing, elevate the King," and then proceed to discuss various ministries around the globe, and then back to Christ, and then to the shooting in Nashville. By moving back and forth across global spaces, Bethel thickens its witness. At one moment we are singing about Christ, and at the next we are hearing about a fledgling congregation in Lima, Peru. At one moment we are praising the Spirit's power, and at the next we are shaking hands with someone different from us. Sometimes it happens explicitly, such as with Pastor Lowe's statements about national politics and how Jesus is the sole authority. Other times it happens implicitly, such as when a diverse team of musicians sings about Christ, while the sides of the sanctuary display the words "My house shall be a house of prayer for all the nations."

Pastor Lowe preaches while a picture of the Washington Monument lies in the background slide. In a different service, he speaks about the civil rights movement and says that one of its greatest faults was that it did not "make Jesus more prominent." In keeping with the robust heritage of black churches addressing public issues, Bethel speaks matter-of-factly about problems of race and poverty. On a different week, as Pastor Lowe preaches on "The Gospel Is Public Truth," we see slides of people in Washington, DC, holding placards protesting different societal injustices. He speaks openly about his own upbringing as a young black man in inner-city Detroit, but then brings everything back to Jesus. As the video explains, "There's a cure for all of it [injustice], and his name is Jesus. If we don't make that public, somebody is going to be denied the cure."

For some churches, mentioning Christ in the context of public issues might suggest a retreat from public life—as if using a simple spiritual answer to address a complex social dilemma. Not so with Bethel. They frame Christ's power through the persons of the Trinity. This accomplishes two things

38. Vinoth Ramachandra, *Subverting Global Myths: Theology and the Public Issues Shaping Our World* (Downers Grove, IL: IVP Academic, 2008), 149.

simultaneously: holding together their diversity into a thicker form of unity and propelling themselves outward as witnesses into the public realm. We see the connection between integration and witness in the songs themselves (such as "Jesus at the Center," with the lyrics "We will follow Him in going to the lost and the nations of the world") and in the church's theme verse, "But you will receive power when the Holy Spirit comes on you," which continues, "and you will be my witnesses in Jerusalem, and in all Judea and Samaria, and to the ends of the earth" (Acts 1:8). Inward thickening leads to outward witness.

In some other American churches, a christological emphasis aids believers therapeutically; Christ is seen primarily as a friend, lover, comforter, brother, or helper. In Bethel there is less of this.[39] For them, the primary focus is on Christ as King and Lord; he is holy, majestic, powerful, able, and glorious. They boast a high Christology, which subsequently propels parishioners outward into the world through the power of the Holy Spirit.

As the service comes to a close, Pastor Lowe opens the altar to anyone who wants prayer. Music plays quietly in the background. The leadership team comes to the front, stretching out lengthwise across the front of the stage. I count twelve leaders in all from side to side. The diversity of those who stand in front reflects the diversity of the entire congregation. I am up in the balcony sitting next to a Latina woman, who is sitting next to what appears to be an Ethiopian young woman. Several people in front of me are wearing African-style clothing.

I am curious about the power dynamics. They sing about Christ's power, but does it influence the ways people treat each other? They are ethnically diverse, but do people associate only with their own kind? I watch as people approach the altar. Will white congregants receive prayer from white leaders? Will black parishioners go to black leaders? After all, the principle of correspondence is strong, and its vigor only increases in the context of something as intimate as prayer. As people approach the front, goose bumps appear on my skin. A young white woman walks to the front, pauses, and, though several white leaders are available, approaches a black woman. I almost become undone when a white man embraces a black man. They grip each other tightly and pray with tears streaming down their faces.

I am told that during the height of tensions in the United States between police officers and the black community a couple years back, the white police officer I saw earlier walking up and down the aisles asked if she could pray publicly for the black community. Of course, this does not mean Bethel does not struggle with tensions.

39. I did notice an emphasis on healing in their services, but this was sourced through the power of the Holy Spirit.

People tell me Pastor Lowe is very concerned with the diminishing number of white families attending the church. One informant even suggested he does not talk about politics as much as he used to for fear of losing more white families. The principle of dissimilarity causes pain, and when pain bumps up against political or economic ideologies, it produces an inevitable reaction. Despite the ongoing tensions, my observations from Bethel show that their incredible diversity is held together by a powerful force, which then propels them outward, as witnesses of a new counterpublic within the world.

Thick Identity and Public Witness

What kind of public witness does Bethel possess? Let me suggest that Bethel witnesses to its surrounding publics in three interconnected ways.

Witness through Transnational Networks

First, let me explain Bethel's public witness through the language of transnationalism. Mike Rynkiewich describes transnationalism as "the constant flow back and forth of goods, ideas, and persons that occurs in some diaspora communities."[40] Meanwhile, Ted Lewellen defines a transnational migrant as "[a person] who maintains active, ongoing interconnections in both the home and host countries and perhaps with communities in other countries as well."[41] Lewellen further explains that transnational migrants force us to think of identity in different kinds of ways. Rather than viewing identity through the lens of a specific location, we become aware that transnationals occupy what Lewellen calls "social space," defined by movement across networks.[42]

If we think of Bethel as a transnational community, it follows that its witness transcends the immediate surroundings of the church building to include far-reaching social space. Although it is easier to study the public witness of a parish congregation (as we did with the first two case studies), transnationalism expands the scope of Bethel's witness around the world. With parishioners from fifty-two countries, Bethel is well positioned to witness to the nations through an enlarged transnational identity. The entire congregation lives between two places. Movement is constantly taking place between their present location in Nashville and their home countries of Mexico, Ethiopia,

40. Michael Rynkiewich, *Soul, Self, and Society: A Postmodern Anthropology for Mission in a Postcolonial World* (Eugene, OR: Cascade, 2011), 212.

41. Ted Lewellen, *The Anthropology of Globalization: Cultural Anthropology Enters the 21st Century* (Westport, CT: Bergin and Garvey, 2002), 151.

42. Lewellen, *Anthropology of Globalization*, 151.

Philippines, or England. Bethel uses that transnational identity to support missionaries around the world, send short-term mission teams, and receive visitors from those locations. They use transnational identities to transmit financial remittances around the world and even plant churches in distant places. Admittedly, it is harder for me to gauge what kind of witness they are having through transnational identities, since much of it happens far away from the church. It is easier for me to see public witness in the first two case studies, since this was readily apparent in the communities surrounding the church building. The case study of Bethel is much broader and thus harder to evaluate.

As I shared earlier, Bethel constantly welcomes global publics into the context of worship. Bethel continually reminds parishioners that Christ holds the nations together through the divine community. Ethnic identity is not a separate category from worship or holiness but something carefully integrated into the inner life of the community.

It is not surprising to see that Bethel has planted so many daughter churches in the region around Nashville and in New York City, along with having sister congregations in India, China, Poland, and Iran. The entire congregation is constantly on the move. Groups go on short-term mission trips. Individual parishioners visit their homes during the holidays. Their proximity to the international headquarters of Every Nation further strengthens any movement.

Part of this movement is that parishioners are constantly encountering difference. They experience it in the different worship styles, or in the food served at community events. They are confronted by the pain of the other in the lives of parishioners who have experienced bigotry or violence. Global disasters take on a new level of meaning for them since it is likely that some parishioners will be directly affected by a drought in East Africa, a tsunami in Southeast Asia, or a shooting in Nashville. The differences they face in the context of worship do not just pertain to highly sanitized, spiritual points of reference but include "complicated wickedness" as it is experienced around the world. Transnationalism usually pertains to a person who lives in between two worlds, but the entire Bethel community offers us insight into an enlarged transnational community deeply engaged in global publics.

Witness through Apologetics

Not only does Bethel witness through an expanded view of transnationalism, but they also approach witness with a decidedly apologetic posture. Because of their relationships with Every Nation and its focus on reaching college students around the world, Bethel naturally gravitates toward an apologetic form of evangelism, and they regularly teach parishioners to share their faith with others *in the context of rival beliefs*. They do not witness only to people, but their passion for apologetics also naturally includes the publics surrounding people.

To understand what this looks like, we need to return to Rice Broocks, who currently serves as bishop of the Bethel churches.[43] Broocks is the author of the book (and later well-known movie) *God's Not Dead*. For years, he has been sharing Christ with agnostics, skeptics, atheists, and people from other religions all around the world. Since Broocks lives in Nashville, he uses Bethel to field-test his methods for apologetics; and because of the transnational identities found in Bethel and the church's relationship with Every Nation, these apologetic approaches inevitably make their way around the world.

For example, they have initiated SALT: Start a conversation. Ask questions. Listen to their responses. Tell the story of Jesus. They have trained the entire congregation to build relationships with people—at home, work, or around the community—in which they ask, listen, and share with others about Jesus Christ. In a similar manner, Broocks developed what he calls "The God Test," which started in paper form and has since morphed into a downloadable smartphone app. "The God Test" has a series of ten questions. Depending on how one answers a question, the app raises additional questions. "The God Test" has been downloaded over 100,000 times, with more than two million responses from people around the world. Bethel encourages parishioners to do it with friends and coworkers. And they share these resources with churches in the Philippines, Poland, and Fiji, where such resources are contextualized for specific audiences.

Bethel is very involved in witnessing to individuals. Of all the churches highlighted in this book, they are the most assertive in evangelism and discipleship. Furthermore, by focusing on apologetics, Bethel witnesses *to people as they relate to their publics*. The very nature of apologetics involves connecting God with complex public realities. By asking people questions about God, church members inevitably bump up against topics such as evolution, corruption, racism, pluralism, and secularism. The goal of apologetic methods as taught by Bethel is to build healthy relationships with diverse people and share the gospel of Jesus Christ to people *in the context of the things they care most about in the world*. This inevitably takes them deeper into the public realm, and when they encounter complex social problems, they witness to people (and public realities) by being a different kind of complex social entity in the world.

43. Broocks explained to me that blacks refer to him as "Bishop," while whites call him "Overseer."

Witness through Racial Reconciliation

Finally, Bethel witnesses to racial reconciliation throughout the city of Nashville. They use the thickness of their identity to show the surrounding community that there is another way of being human in the world. Whenever racial tension arises (and it is a common occurrence), Broocks and Pastor Lowe receive phone calls. The mayor of Nashville has called them; so too have the police. They have been asked to speak in inner-city schools. And other congregations throughout the area have likewise reached out to them. Bethel has become a leader in racial reconciliation throughout the entire region.

For example, fifteen years ago Broocks received a phone call from the pastor of a large white congregation on the other side of the city. The pastor wanted to know how Bethel navigates racial boundaries so effectively. Broocks and this pastor have spoken almost every single day for the last fifteen years! Broocks and Pastor Lowe have become mentors to numerous pastors in the city. However, the influence does not stop there. Bethel has planted diverse, thriving multicultural congregations in Cincinnati, in Dallas, and in towns throughout Tennessee. But even this does not tell the entire story. In the days following the 9/11 terrorist attacks, Broocks decided that Bethel needed to respond to the crisis. He called a friend of his, Ron Lewis, from North Carolina, and the two, along with Tim Johnson, traveled every week to New York City for several years. They planted a church in Times Square, which has subsequently planted three other congregations, including ones in Philadelphia and New Jersey. And wherever Bethel plants churches, they sow seeds of racial reconciliation. The image of the two hands lies at the very center of their ecclesiology. The congregation in Times Square currently has parishioners from sixty-eight nations. They are in the process of planting Spanish-, Russian-, and Arabic-speaking congregations. Bethel witnesses by planting churches, cultivating diverse communities around the world.

Rice Broocks and Pastor Lowe would be the first to tell you that they encounter many problems along the way. It is hard to hold together such incredible diversity, and more difficult still to witness through that diversity. One of the keys to Bethel's effectiveness is that they locate diversity between devotion and discipleship. Diversity is not a goal independent of worship or holiness. Ethnic difference gets inserted into song and prayer. Parishioners are constantly challenged by the pain of the other. Global issues are constantly woven into the inner life of the divine community. And they use movement between devotion, diversity, and discipleship to weave a thickness of identity into the community, and then witness to the nations about the reconciliation of Jesus Christ in and for the world.

One sees many examples of this in the congregation. They host community events to showcase their love for the nations. Parishioners build relationships with diverse others in the public realm, whether at work, in neighborhoods, or in their communities. When people ask them why they promote such beautiful, living examples of racial reconciliation, they use that opening to tell people about the gospel of Jesus Christ. And they welcome such people into the inner life of the divine community. They invite diverse people into who they are becoming

Conclusion

Bethel World Outreach Church presents an intriguing case study for a public missiology. What began as a Bible study with white business professionals in the affluent suburb of Brentwood has grown into a flourishing multicultural congregation that sows seeds of racial reconciliation and public witness throughout Nashville and around the world. At the very core of their public witness is the kingship of Christ, through the power of the Holy Spirit, which I have explained as the only thing powerful enough to hold such incredible diversity together. The way they bring these ethnicities (and the publics surrounding them) into contact with the divine community allows them to be converted, so that Bethel functions as a public church, or as collective agents of a new eschatological identity inserted into the world.

Admittedly, it is more difficult to evaluate Bethel's effectiveness than to evaluate the effectiveness of our other two case studies since much of Bethel's witness takes place around the world. Transnational identities are like a two-way highway moving back-and-forth to distant countries. However, it is in Bethel's church planting that we see best how they witness to public realities. They are constantly forming new diverse communities. Bethel is thus a good example of what Lesslie Newbigin calls the "hermeneutic of the gospel" and "the basic unit of [a] new society."[44]

44. Lesslie Newbigin's words; see this book's introduction.

Conclusion

How Local Churches Witness in a Complex World

I began this book with Lesslie Newbigin's claim that "the basic unit of [a] new society is the local congregation." I explained what this looks like through the movements occurring in and around the congregation and how those movements result in a thickness of witness.

The theological basis for thick witness arises from the persons of the Trinity. Who God is directly leads to what God is accomplishing in this world. In and through God's nature (flowing through creation), thickness results in fruitfulness and flourishing. It is a witness from within. I have sought to show that Christian communities accomplish this by being "the hermeneutic of the gospel" and the "the basic unit of [a] new society."

All congregations possess some kind of thickness. Admittedly, not all use their thickness for witness. The three case studies I presented at the end of the book demonstrate what thick witness looks like in local congregations. I intentionally highlighted case studies from three different countries to show various resources that congregations utilize to thicken witness. The case study in Machakos, Kenya, uses a *thickness of doxology* to witness to land and poverty; the one in Montreal utilizes a *thickness of place* to witness to an entire city; and the case study from Nashville draws on a *thickness of identity* to witness to ethnicity. In each of these case studies, the persons of the Trinity are involved in the worship, liturgy, and sermons, laying the theological basis for what the church does out in the public realm. God is re-weaving communities of witness into all parts of his created world.

Let me conclude this book by offering some suggestions for how local congregations can thicken their witness within and for the public realm.

Do Not Fear Thickness

If I could say one thing to evangelical leaders these days, it would be that the world is becoming more and more complex (thick) through the interpenetration of domains and the migration of people all around the world, and rather than fearing this reality and attempting to return to a simpler time (it never was!), we need to embrace complexity (thickness).

Of course, I do not mean Christians should embrace all kinds of thickness in the world. We see too many examples of what Wesley called "complicated wickedness" to believe that all forms of thickness are good. Sin "burrows into the bowels" to distort the cohesion of God's created world.[1] Political systems privilege certain people. Publics of this world become idolatrous, offering themselves as visions of eternity. Local congregations can easily become co-opted by publics. Meanwhile, people use their God-given power to dominate, oppress, and exploit others. We see all of this in the world today. It is easy, therefore, and all too convenient, to label all forms of thickness evil, since that is what we know. The world as we know it is thickening. God is calling the church to enter into that thickness, to witness to it from within—through the in-breaking of the kingdom of God within human communities. And to do so through movement.

By speaking of complexity, I do not want to limit the discussion to academic elites. Complexity is not a puzzle to be solved by the right specialists or a topic restricted to highbrow intellectuals. One of the reasons I describe public missiology in this book using the qualifier "of the local congregation" is to accentuate how God accomplishes his mission *through* local communities. We might think of the local congregation in simple terms, but I seriously doubt that there is a single simple church. Churches are filled with people who relate to their surrounding publics in highly complex ways: we have farmers, stay-at-home moms and dads, business owners, schoolteachers, scientists, construction workers, engineers, medical professionals, and the list goes on. What is more, each of these people does not just relate to the public realm through one primary domain, such as land, home, economics, education, science, or medicine, but each parishioner is also a consumer, a political agent, and a person who relates intimately with their environment.

---

1. Cornelius Plantinga, *Not the Way It's Supposed to Be: A Breviary of Sin* (Grand Rapids: Eerdmans, 1995), 75.

The congregation's intimacy with swirling, interpenetrating public realities is one of the greatest strengths any local congregation possesses. It is *out of our publics* that we witness to God's mission in the world, and it is *for the flourishing of the public realm* that we witness.

As I said at the outset of this book, thin forms of faith will struggle to interpenetrate the thickness of contemporary publics. Fortunately, we have local congregations who witness to the public realm out of their thickness. Complexity or thickness thus is not the enemy of the Christian faith and might just be our greatest ally.

Study Local Congregations

We need to devote more time to the study of local congregations. Ever since I decided to use ethnography for the study of African Christianity, I have never looked back. It has opened my eyes to the amazing gifts arising out of local congregations wherever I have traveled. It is one thing to read a book on theology but quite another to enter into churches where people sing, dance, and respond to the movements of the divine community in their midst. It is one matter to write about the missional nature of the church and another to actually study how local congregations witness in and through their publics.

You do not need to be a sociologist or anthropologist to do so. I am not. But I have learned to appreciate and use their methods for understanding the theology emergent within the churches. You can as well. I kept chapter 6 fairly simple for the purpose of making the study of local congregations accessible to anybody.

I would encourage churches to follow the steps I offer in chapter 6 for the study of their own local congregation. After you have done it a couple of times, you might pick up a book like *Studying Congregations* to go deeper into ethnography.[2] The study of congregations will likely reveal themes you have never noticed before. These themes offer critical insight into the church's habitus, which then becomes the primary means of its witness in and for the public realm.

Thicken God's Nature within Congregations

The church is the image of the Trinity in and for the world. If this is true, then every congregation needs to examine in what ways they are faithful to the image of the divine community and in what ways they are not.

2. Nancy T. Ammerman et al., eds., *Studying Congregations: A New Handbook* (Nashville: Abingdon, 1998).

We need more of the Trinity, and specifically more movement between the divine persons to strengthen the thickness of the congregation, for the purpose of imaging the Trinity for the publics of this world. A study of the *missio Dei* shows this to be the case, and it would be good for us as congregations to mirror (or image) the movements of the persons of the Trinity in and for the flourishing of the public realm.

Leaders who coordinate church services, or those who preach from the pulpit, need to be theologically equipped to introduce the persons of the Trinity in ways that reflect the mutuality, self-giving, and thickening of divine community. However, the Trinity is not something merely for what we do inside a church building, but it spills out of the service into the streets, neighborhoods, and third places of the community. As we saw in the case studies, the African Brotherhood Church weaves together a thickness of the persons of the Trinity within its doxology to equip parishioners to witness to land and poverty. Bethel does something similar to fashion diverse communities who live in unity and witness to a new way of being human in the world. The Trinity matters for public life! It matters for economics[3] and politics.[4] And if it matters for these domains, then it matters for the swirling complexity of contemporary publics.

In the West, our current diet of worship songs is one-dimensional and thin. Our leadership structures too readily mirror a hierarchical Trinity, instead of a community expressed through love, mutuality, and active sending. We are also so eager to get outside the gathered body into public spaces that we neglect who it is we image (with the inevitable result that we image only ourselves). God's nature needs to be sung, prayed, danced, and liturgized by the corporate body. The church is a public in the way that it gathers *and* scatters, and greater efforts need to be made to hold these together as movements like breathing or weaving or dance or dialogue or ecology.

Thicken the Scope of Salvation

Similarly, we need to thicken our understanding of salvation. How can we presume to witness to nationalism, ethnocentrism, or political and economic ideologies with an understanding of salvation that focuses on only one aspect of Jesus's life (such as the cross)? If salvation is ultimately the reconciliation

---

3. See M. Douglas Meeks, *God the Economist: The Doctrine of God and Political Economy* (Minneapolis: Fortress, 1989).
4. See Theodore Weber, *Politics in the Order of Salvation: Transforming Wesleyan Political Ethics* (Nashville: Kingswood, 2001); Gregory Coates, *Politics Strangely Warmed: Political Theology in the Wesleyan Spirit* (Eugene, OR: Wipf & Stock, 2015).

of all things to the person of Christ (Eph. 1:10), and if it is accomplished through the entirety of Christ (Rom. 5:10) and through the presence and power of the Holy Spirit (Rom. 8:9–11), then we need more of Christ, and more of the Holy Spirit, in order to thicken God's salvation within and for the fullness of life.

I hope by now the rationale for this is apparent. We might try to witness to individuals with a thin form of salvation that just focuses on Christ's death, but that salvation will invariably pertain to only one aspect of that person's life (their sins or future eternity) but leave the rest of their humanity alone. To broaden what salvation means for a person's entire life, we need to thicken it with more of Christ through more of the Holy Spirit. If this is true for an individual, it is also true for the publics surrounding our congregation.

A congregation that skips past the incarnation in order to get to the cross will undoubtedly possess a robust understanding of Christ's death but will struggle to apply it to our humanity as well as the publics emerging from humanity. Another congregation that focuses entirely on Christ's humanity, and only deals with the cross as it relates to structures in society, will be active in justice-related activity but will struggle to apply salvation for holiness, and thus the sanctification of publics. We need all of Christ (and especially how his incarnation, teachings, sufferings, death, resurrection, and ascension move together) in order to thicken salvation into all spaces of life.[5]

I am constantly telling my students that we need *more of* the gospel of Jesus Christ for *more of* our humanity for *more aspects* of this world. This is not just a theological exercise for budding pastors but something that needs to be lived out (or dramatized) within local congregations. And this "more of the gospel" for "more of our humanity" has to be shared with the world, which means the whole of the public realm, for the flourishing of all of life.

Thicken the Ethnic Composition of Our Churches

God's mission is taking us on a journey from particularity to universality, but without ever leaving particularity behind. God is thickening human identity in this world. I strongly believe that multiethnic congregations are the best witnesses of that new social reality in the world.

As we saw in the last chapter, the world is becoming more diverse through the migration of people. Scholars estimate that there are more than sixty-five

---

5. Some Anabaptists, drawing on the work of Walter Brueggemann, bemoan how the Apostles' Creed moves from "born of the Virgin Mary" to "suffered under Pontius Pilate" with only a comma separating the two and thus neglects the entire life of Christ between his birth and death.

million people in the world who have been forcibly displaced from their homes. Some estimate that upwards of one billion people could be displaced by the year 2050.[6] Many others are on the move looking for better lives for their families. Congregations such as Bethel are slowly becoming more common and represent well the thickening of witness within American life.

One of the strengths of a multiethnic, multiracial congregation (yet admittedly one of its greatest challenges) is that it must constantly wrestle with multiple, contesting publics. A homogeneous congregation will likely comprise parishioners from a single way of seeing the world and surrounded by neighborhoods, shops, and businesses that endorse the same way of seeing the world. Not so with a multiethnic church. They are usually located in diverse areas (as we saw in the last chapter) and filled with congregants from diverse backgrounds. Thus they are constantly confronted by difference in their gathering. Worship needs to weave through a greater number of threads. Congregants are continually exposed to the viewpoints of the other. Their gathering is thicker and thus (when done well) more representative of the divine community.

When such congregations scatter, they witness into broader swaths of human life. Parishioners function as evangelists through their transnational identities. They disperse into wider areas of life and show the world there is another way of being human.

Preach and Liturgize for Monday Morning

As I have explained throughout, we actually want publics to enter into the church, where they can be exposed to the gospel of Jesus Christ and the divine community. Of course, by welcoming them into the church we need to be extremely careful not to inadvertently endorse them without any gospel critique or baptize their ideologies with sacred energy. Instead, we need to preach and liturgize *for* the surrounding publics. Or as I heard one speaker say: preach for Monday morning.

How then do we preach or liturgize for Monday morning? We need to become master weavers. First of all, with great dexterity and sensitivity, we need to welcome publics (in the form of invisible ideologies or social imaginaries) into the fabric of a liturgy, sermon, or prayer. We need to be delicate with these actions lest by pulling the strings too tightly we overpower the publics

6. Baher Kamal, "Climate Migrants Might Reach One Billion by 2050," Inter Press Service. August 21, 2017, http://www.ipsnews.net/2017/08/climate-migrants-might-reach-one-billion-by -2050/.

and cause them to retreat underground, or by weaving too softly we fail to expose publics to the full resources of the Trinity.

This acknowledges that publics are not just physical locations, such as with a coffee shop, but are sites for the contestation of power. Contemporary publics clamor for attention. They want everyone to look at them. They desire to be a center. They are totalizing for the people who embrace them. By preaching for Monday morning, we are not rejecting the public realm. Publics are good and arise from creation and our human imaging in the world. But in preaching with publics in mind, we are allowing everything to come under the lordship of Jesus Christ. All publics possess an "open weave," which means they can be interpenetrated by the kingdom of God.

Inside our churches we find political ideologies along with secular eschatologies such as materialism. We discover other invisibilities, such as ethnic privilege or nationalism. And we inevitably discern allegiances to sports teams and transnational companies with pseudo-religious meanings such as Manchester United or Apple. One of the primary reasons leaders hesitate to speak of public realities inside the church is they fear losing parishioners (along with their tithes!). The invisible powers attached to public realities such as nationalism are too influential in the lives of our parishioners, so we hesitate to bring them out into the open. However, in failing to do so, we either allow these publics to shape the internal life of the congregation (giving them our silent nod of approval) or we do not think of publics as capable of being redeemed and thus leave them untouched. We thin out our witness.

How then do you preach or liturgize for Monday morning?

The first thing you need to do is to coax the invisible ideologies out into the open. This might be as vague as referencing "work," "home," or "play" in prayers, or as specific as mentioning political and economic ideologies, commercialism, ethnicity, or nationalism in sermons. If this strikes you as foolhardy, it most likely means you think of these publics as inextricably dirty (and by that I mean unredeemable), or else you fear too greatly what it will mean for attendance or tithing. An ideology, as Alistair Kee explains, "is a shy creature: it does not want to be seen, to be identified, to be named. It would rather that its view of reality were simply taken for granted, without further thought. Its rests content if its values and prejudices are simply assumed as too obvious to be contested."[7] By naming the ideologies, we bring them out into the open. Of course, we need to be wise in how we expose them to the gospel. Direct, open attacks against powerful ideologies are not always the

---

7. Alistair Kee, "Blessed Are the Excluded," in *Public Theology for the 21st Century*, ed. William F. Storrar and Andrew R. Morton (New York: T&T Clark, 2004), 352.

best choice. Many churches need to be discipled to allow more and more of the world to be confronted by the gospel.

We need to weave! Weaving places threads alongside other fibers and then connects them together, such as with a knot. What if, for example, we set the kingship of God alongside political ideologies? Or if the cross of Jesus Christ stood next to nationalism? Or if business practices were invited to gaze deeply into the life-giving power of the Holy Spirit? And this is just the beginning. What if we were to keep telling the story of the Gospels in a way that challenges invisible metanarratives, such as progress, freedom, or ethnic privilege? Richard Bauckham says, "When Christians find their metanarrative in confrontation with an alternative, aggressive metanarrative—whether that of globalization or Islam or something else—nothing is more important than telling the biblical stories, especially that of Jesus, again and again."[8] By telling these stories over and over again, we thicken our witness.

Jesus weaved while he was on earth. At times he spoke in direct, open terms, railing against the "yeast of the Pharisees," but more often he spoke in an indirect manner, which I liken to weaving. The best example is Jesus's use of parables, which make up nearly one-third of his teachings in the Synoptic Gospels. Parables reveal and hide. They draw on everyday language (even doing so through the "publics" of first-century Palestine such as farming or ethnicity), speaking to common people in their public life. Parables disclose to the world a new reality of God's kingdom in the world, which requires embodied actions. Christopher Marshall explains what this looks like in the Gospels:

> [The parables] usually begin by portraying familiar circumstances, drawing hearers into the story and lulling them into a false sense of security about the way the world operates. But then something baffling occurs, something surprising and shocking, something that reverses expectations or confounds calculations. A rupture rents the realism. Impossibly huge harvests are reaped; debts of astronomical size are forgiven; wedding invitations are declined with unimaginably rude excuses, in breach of every rule of village hospitality; latecomers to the workplace are paid the same wages as early starters; true virtue is exhibited by hated apostates and compromised tax collectors. Things are obviously not as they seem. Something peculiar is happening.[9]

By telling such parables, Jesus weaves difference into public life. In a world of economic reciprocity, Jesus tells stories of lavish generosity without any

---

8. Richard Bauckham, *Bible and Mission: Christian Witness in a Postmodern World* (Grand Rapids: Baker Academic, 2003), 101.

9. Christopher D. Marshall, "Parables as Paradigms for Public Theology," in *The Bible, Justice, and Public Theology*, ed. David J. Neville (Eugene, OR: Wipf & Stock, 2014), 41.

expectation of return. In an age where elite Jewish religious leaders defined public behavior, Jesus introduces the heroic acts of the Samaritan. The parable, as Marshall later explains, "is about *God* and what God is now doing behind the scenes to change the world by bringing his royal justice to earth and what this means practically for those who embrace it."[10]

We also need to weave. The resources for our weaving can be stories such as Jesus told (and I personally believe we need to preach more from Jesus's parables), but as the three case studies in the second half of this book showed, weaving can involve doxology, place, and ethnicity. We can weave by highlighting a Scripture verse on a PowerPoint slide that shows a public crisis (as we saw with Bethel in chap. 9) or by doing something as simple as praying for what occurred in the headlines that week. A general rule is that if anything contributes too strongly to the identity of the people, then it needs to enter into the open weave of liturgy, sacrament, or preaching.

Be a Public Church in and for Your Communities

Who the church is when gathered together directly relates to who we are when scattered. We take a habitus with us wherever we go. I have sought throughout this book to integrate gathering and scattering through the imagery of movements. Back-and-forth movement thickens the witness of the church in and for its surrounding neighborhoods.

We are the church collectively, which means that when we scatter into the surrounding publics, we do so as a collective image of the Trinity—in and for our communities. This is often easier to see in parish congregations, such as with the case studies of the Africa Brotherhood Church (chap. 7) and St. Jax (chap. 8). However, I would say that it can also be true for a commuter congregation or a multiethnic church, but we need to look at the collective witness across a broader geographical field, such as Bethel's influence (chap. 9) throughout neighboring states and even around the world.

When we hear the words "public church," it is easy to think solely in terms of its political influence, or the voice of its leaders in larger societal affairs. Both Martin Marty and James Davison Hunter chronicle some of the dangers with this way of looking at the church's publicness (as well as providing some hope).[11] I have sought to argue for the church's publicness through the ways it reconfigures publics within its collective identity, and how it uses that

10. Marshall, "Parables," 41.
11. Martin E. Marty, *The Public Church: Mainline, Evangelical, Catholic* (1981; repr., Eugene, OR: Wipf & Stock, 2012); James Davison Hunter, *To Change the World: The Irony,*

new social order to show the world there is another way of being human. Of course, this does not discount the public voice of key church leaders. But we do not change the world through individuals. We change it through complex, overlapping communities of witness—or, as I am arguing, through congregations who embody the Trinity in their corporate dispersive nature.

Location matters. Many churches around the world are moving away from traditional buildings in favor of meeting in coffee shops, pubs, theaters, malls, and schools. There is much to like in this trend. Meeting in public places can strengthen public witness. A congregation that worships together in a school will be constantly reminded of education and the need to weave God's truth into all aspects of life. The same is true of a church that meets in a pub. Gathering together in these locations strengthens the dispersive nature of the congregation. It reminds Christians of the public realm and facilitates greater contact between worship and public realities. But there are dangers. A church that meets in a business can be co-opted by an economic ideology. A community that gathers in a city center can become so much a part of that location that they offer it no gospel difference and instead simply reinforce the status quo. It is imperative to constantly evaluate the strengths and weaknesses of any location and how the church functions "as a hermeneutic of the gospel" witness within and for those places.

Send Parishioners as Evangelists in and through Their Publics

Let me conclude with an evangelistic call. Unlike other evangelistic entreaties, this one does not involve going to the front of the church while the piano gently plays "Just as I Am" in the background, nor does it involve equipping people with simplistic strategies, such as the Four Spiritual Laws or the Romans Road. If we are going to equip parishioners to witness to their surrounding publics, then we need to think about the training of congregants differently. What I am proposing here is in keeping with the apostolic nature of the church. We are a sent community for the salvation of the entire world. If we are going to be faithful to that "sentness," we cannot just save individuals but must save *people in and for their publics*.

How do we equip parishioners for such a task? If we are conducting evangelistic training (which we must do), then we need to encourage parishioners to locate the gospel in relation to the aspects of life people most care about. In Tanzania, that would involve poverty, evil spirits, agriculture, patron-client

---

Tragedy, and Possibility of Christianity in the Late Modern World (New York: Oxford University Press, 2010), esp. 99–193.

relationships, health, and religion, with discussions taking place in the coffeehouse, around the water tap, in fields, or in the open meeting space of the village. In Montreal, it would be the colonial heritage, secularity, religiosity, Canada's neighbors to the south, the justice of First Nations people, economics, and immigration. In the United States, we have to talk about ethnicity, race, freedom, and what it means to be an American. We cannot witness to the reign of Christ over the entire world without reference to these publics. People carry their publics with them wherever they go. My neighbors in Tanzania could not jettison poverty, no matter how hard they tried. A First Nations person living in Quebec cannot step out of the long-standing heritage of colonialism, nor should we expect that of them. And you? Can you take your political ideologies, or your views of what it means to be American, British, Kenyan, or Indian, and simply lay those aside, as if stepping culturally naked into the Christian faith? It is not possible. Our evangelism and discipleship can never be separate from the public issues that define reality for people all around the world.

This cannot merely be a matter of discussion but must change how we live. We cannot speak out against bigotry while abusing people within our churches or neighborhoods. We cannot decry injustices while hoarding resources for ourselves. Witness must take seriously what it means to embody the kingdom of God within the confessing community, and then what it means to live out that reality openly within and for the public realm.

Some of the apologetics training done by Bethel World Outreach Church might help us witness more broadly. However, there is no single strategy for equipping people to witness to persons and their publics, except to constantly weave threads throughout the entire cosmos. Weaving relates to connections, and Christians need to be master weavers in helping people see how Christ relates to *this* life, *here*, *now*, and to *creation*, along with pointing everything toward the future eschaton and the reconciliation of all things. Witness connects everything into a new, thicker whole—with Christ as the center.

And then we need to send our parishioners into their homes, places of work, and third places in the community. Send them into politics and into economics, media, and education. Send them into coffee shops and sports venues. And especially send them into locations where "complicated wickedness" rears its ugly face. Send them with a big enough gospel that relates to all of life. For example, when parishioners witness to a sick friend in the hospital, they are witnessing not just to that person's salvation but also to the broader meanings of health in God's kingdom. When teachers witness in their jobs at schools, they are witnessing not just to their coworkers but also to what it means to be agents of God's wisdom within and for the world.

Witness is always *to* persons and their publics, *through* the habitus of the entire local congregation, and *for* the flourishing of all things *under* the reign of Christ! The public problems of this world are so great, and humans around the world feel them so thickly, we cannot do anything but thicken our witness. For that, I propose, we need congregations that function as the "hermeneutic of the gospel" and "the basic unit of [a] new society."

Appendix

Public Missiology: A Brief Introduction

THE PUBLIC MISSIOLOGY WORKING GROUP

Public missiology proposes a new paradigm to reinterpret and to reformulate contemporary concepts of Christian mission at a time of nearly stupefying cultural, social, technological, and environmental change. A new historical era is taking shape around us, one that no longer can be explained adequately in modern and postmodern language, an era without a name other than *post*-postmodern.

Taken as a whole, our present missiological paradigms, formed in modernity and postmodernity, are failing to arrest the loss of Christian witness, its public coherence, its generative public voice, and its integrity and credibility, especially in North America. Nor do present paradigms adequately address the reality that long-established, modern, and durable modes of public order

---

The Public Missiology Working Group includes the following individuals:
Gregory Leffel, One Horizon Institute
Charles Fensham, Knox College, Toronto School of Theology, University of Toronto
George Hunsberger, Western Theological Seminary (emeritus)
Robert Hunt, Perkins School of Theology, Southern Methodist University
William Kenney, One Horizon Institute
Gregg Okesson, dean, E. Stanley Jones School of World Mission, Asbury Theological Seminary
Hendrik Pieterse, Garrett-Evangelical Theological Seminary

are themselves fracturing, creating new, unarticulated, and unstable forms of social and cultural life.

New and untested modes of public order emerge in the shadow of a looming and unprecedented ecological and technological crisis threatening the future of the environment and humanity itself. Managing this crisis stretches human ingenuity to the limit—exacerbated by other trends, among them the crisis of liberal democracy; surging economic inequality; mass migration; identity conflict; and fading community life, human solidarity, and belonging. To this compounding crisis, mission must speak in a new language yet to be conceived and respond with new practices yet to be invented.

What's at Stake?

Creating healthy and inclusive modes of public order is the primary human task—a biblical task begun by tending a Garden—and one in which mission operates as redemptive leaven as the dough (healthy public life) expands. Indeed, cultivating flourishing modes of public life—including the uplift and healing of individuals, publics, and the earth—lies at the very center of the missionary enterprise.

At stake is the health of every public's mode of life. Mission's full soteriological influence begins within a public's social imaginary—that is, within its collective consciousness, spirituality, and the logics that define the mode of life upon which its public order is built. A social imaginary is created and recreated through routine, daily public interactions, and collectively organizes our thoughts, ethics, politics, economies, social structures, power structures, laws, sensibilities, and our faith and reaches into our everyday life decisions.

Poor social imaginaries blind us. Well-constructed ones liberate the vision and creativity we need to imagine and develop new habits, social relationships, civic practices, and diaconal ministries. And new energies must be liberated as we encounter a new and difficult era, a post-postmodern, post-Christian life-world that none of us has ever seen—a life-world that deeply challenges mission's redemptive possibilities.

Why "Public"?

The term "public" is proposed to frame a new paradigm to grasp the dynamics of our emerging life-world. Why "public"? Commonly available concepts—such as society, culture, politics, economy, or ecology and their analogue fields of sociology, anthropology, political science, economics, or earth science—fail to provide a fully integrated, or *synoptic*, vision of the whole of public life, nor do they fully explain the complex sources of social change and the operation and manipulation of socioeconomic and sociopolitical power. Hence, the general academic trend toward interdisciplinary cooperation as well as the need for a new framing term to concentrate such work. "Public" is proposed as a framing concept to analyze our complex modes of human life as such (including Christian interaction with them) as well as to orchestrate multiple interdisciplinary projects to understand them and to promote their health and vigor.

"Public" is defined as the site of, and the entire space of, human-to-human and human-to-nonhuman interaction, whether conceived of as local or universal spaces. Public is thus a complex, contested semiotic space—i.e., symbolic and interactive—through which humans continuously give rise to new forms of social structures, cultural consciousness, and relations to the natural world. Grasping this complexity or interwoven "thickness" requires myriad, networked philosophical, phenomenological, hermeneutical, empirical, and pragmatic approaches. And what is grasped by these approaches must range through the human experience from the level of social, cultural, diaconal, and routine daily practices both personal and collective, secular and religious through to the meta-level of human metaphysical and ontological consciousness.

At its core, public life is defined as the space where humans collectively build their life-worlds by searching for and by creating imagined orders—"assemblages" of nature and culture—and then drawing meaning from these, including their sense of the meaning of life, their faith, and their awareness of God. This generative process is a quintessentially human quest, repeated in every society and now also globally, to find and to perfect an all-embracing public order—in classical terms a "cosmo-public" or "cosmopolis." These terms more accurately reflect the biblical language of *oikoumene* and *kosmos* than the more general English "world" and enrich the understanding and world-orientation of the ongoing Christian movement.

Public Missiology

Missiology works with the advantage that it, too, creates a synoptic vision to articulate the entire Christian movement in its engagement of the whole gospel with the whole of public life as the public weaves together and builds its world. As such, it possesses the conceptual capacity to grasp the public whole at the point of its intersection with the whole of Christian engagement.

Public missiology warns that such advantage is lost when missiology is overly preoccupied with the church itself and its survival in public life. A public missiology requires that the public be addressed in the foreground as the space of emerging public orders, while the church remains vitally involved—especially through local congregations—to discern, serve, influence, witness to, and share in what emerges.

Thus, public missiology joins together two holistic, synoptic discourses— "public" and "mission"—in a single frame and within a comprehensive thematic to examine their interaction and to guide (to the limit of its resources) a healthy interaction. This task includes reassessing (1) the aims and world-orientation of mission to the present crisis of public life, (2) the *church's* role as sign and agent of God's mission, (3) the *"world,"* or *"public,"* that mission engages, and (4) their *intersection* and *interpenetration*.

Public missiology proposes a "public turn" (a turn *toward* and *for* the public's well-being) in the Christian understanding of the world and the place of Christians within it. It recognizes that the church participates in and is enclosed within public life such that the health of the public, good or ill, is reflected in the health of the church, and thus the church has a deep stake in the public's flourishing. By moving "public" to the center of missiological reflection and reconsidering the reciprocal interaction between "public" and mission, public missiology encourages new directions of inquiry, fresh research programs, and innovative forms of practice related to mission within our emerging modes of public life. This brief introduction summarizes substantial work already accomplished to reframe contemporary missiology and is a first and necessary step to prepare the ground for new initiatives.

Affirming Our Tradition

Significant shifts in historical eras naturally require new priorities and paradigms of thought and action. Missiology has been here before. Public missiology stands in a line of similar historical paradigm shifts in mission. Examples include the post-war ecumenical paradigm, which renewed normative, trinitarian concepts such as *missio Dei* and the reign of God; the 1960's cultural and social "revolution," which produced a "cultural turn" and renewed emphasis on contextualization, inculturation, and "people groups"—a new ethics emphasizing peace, justice, the integrity of creation, and theologies of liberation; David Bosch's 1991 proposals for a paradigm shift in postmodern mission; the missional church "conversation," guided by the Gospel and Our Culture Network; and public and political theologies. Public missiology assumes, embraces, includes, and extends these recent paradigms, celebrating their robustly trinitarian, ecumenical, missional, soteriological, and cruciform normative emphases on witness in word and deed to faith in Christ, the reconciling reign of God, life in the Holy Spirit, and repair of the world.

Public missiology extends our tradition, endeavoring to make the gracious liberality and the generative, cooperative, redemptive sensibilities of Christian witness intelligible to the public as public life itself reshapes the public order and the church's operating context in a rapidly changing, post-postmodern era. A missiological understanding of *public* and a publicly informed understanding of *mission* will co-evolve to the benefit of each as each mutually influences the other. At heart, then, public missiology is an invitation to renew Christian initiative to engage our emerging public order in fresh ways and with intelligence, love, faith, and hope for the flourishing of all in the presence of God and together with one another.

Bibliography

"African Brotherhood Church." *Ecumenical Review* 24, no. 2 (January 1972): 145–59.

Alba, Richard, and Nancy Foner. *Strangers No More: Immigration and the Challenges of Integration in North America and Western Europe*. Princeton: Princeton University Press, 2015.

Ammerman, Nancy T., Jackson W. Carroll, Carl S. Dudley, and William McKinney, eds. *Studying Congregations: A New Handbook*. Nashville: Abingdon, 1998.

Anderson, Benedict. *Imagined Communities: Reflections on the Origin and Spread of Nationalism*. London: Verso, 1983.

Appadurai, Arjun. *Modernity at Large: Cultural Dimensions of Globalization*. Minneapolis: University of Minnesota Press, 1996.

Appiah, Kwame Anthony. *Cosmopolitanism: Ethics in a World of Strangers*. New York: Norton, 2006.

———. "Is the Post- in Postmodernism the Post- in Postcolonialism?" In *Contemporary Postcolonial Theory: A Reader*, edited by Padmini Mongia, 62–63. London: Arnold, 1996.

Appleby, R. Scott. *The Ambivalence of the Sacred: Religion, Violence, and Reconciliation*. Lanham, MD: Rowman & Littlefield, 2000.

Arendt, Hannah. *The Human Condition*. Chicago: University of Chicago Press, 1958.

Barber, Karin. *The Anthropology of Texts, Persons and Publics: Oral and Written Culture in Africa and Beyond*. New York: Cambridge University Press, 2007.

Bartholomew, Craig G. *Where Mortals Dwell: A Christian View of Place for Today*. Grand Rapids: Baker Academic, 2011.

Barz, Gregory. *Performing Religion: Negotiating Past and Present in Kwaya Music of Tanzania*. Amsterdam: Rodopoi, 2003.

Bass, Dorothy C., ed., *Practicing Our Faith: A Guide for Conversation*. San Francisco: Jossey-Bass, 1997.

Bauckham, Richard. *Bible and Mission: Christian Witness in a Postmodern World.* Grand Rapids: Baker Academic, 2003.

Bediako, Kwame. *Christianity in Africa: The Renewal of a Non-Western Religion.* Maryknoll, NY: Orbis, 1996.

Berkhof, Hendrikus. *Christ and the Powers.* Translated by John Howard Yoder. Scottdale, PA: Herald, 1977.

Bevans, Steve. "A Prophetic Dialogue Approach." In Ott, *Mission of the Church*, 3–20.

Bevans, Steve, and Roger Schroeder. *Prophetic Dialogue: Reflections on Christian Mission Today.* Maryknoll, NY: Orbis, 2011.

Blackburn, Jonathan. "The Role of Black Churches in Response to African-American Well-Being in the Rust Belt Region: A Single Location Case Study of East Side Churches of Buffalo, NY." PhD diss., Asbury Theological Seminary, 2015.

Bonhoeffer, Dietrich. *Ethics.* Translated by Eberhard Bethge. New York: Collier, 1986.

Bosch, David. *Transforming Mission: Paradigm Shifts in Theology of Mission.* Maryknoll, NY: Orbis, 1991.

Bourdieu, Pierre. *The Logic of Practice.* Translated by Richard Nice. Stanford, CA: Stanford University Press, 2000.

Breitenberg Jr., H. Harold. "What Is Public Theology?" In Hainsworth and Paeth, *Public Theology for a Global Society*, 3–17.

Broocks, Rice. *The Human Right: To Know Jesus Christ and to Make Him Known.* Nashville: Thomas Nelson, 2018.

Brueggemann, Walter. *Genesis.* Interpretation. Louisville: Westminster John Knox, 1986.

———. *The Land: Place as Gift, Promise, and Challenge in Biblical Faith.* Minneapolis: Fortress, 1977.

———. *Theology of the Old Testament: Testimony, Dispute, Advocacy.* Minneapolis: Fortress, 1997.

Chabal, Patrick. *Africa: The Politics of Suffering and Smiling.* London: Zed, 2009.

Chung, Paul. *Public Theology in an Age of World Christianity.* New York: Palgrave Macmillan, 2010.

Clements, Keith. *Learning to Speak: The Church's Voice in Public Affairs.* Eugene, OR: Wipf & Stock, 2000.

Clifford, N. K. "His Dominion: A Vision in Crisis." *Studies in Religion* 2, no. 4 (1973): 316–26.

Clines, D. J. A. "Image of God." In *Dictionary of Paul and His Letters*, edited by Gerald F. Hawthorne, Ralph P. Martin, and Daniel G. Reid, 426–28. Downers Grove, IL: InterVarsity, 1993.

Comaroff, Jean, and John Comaroff. *Of Revelation and Revolution.* Vol. 1. Chicago: University of Chicago Press, 1991.

"Constitution and Rules of African Brotherhood Church," n.d.

Corbett, Steve, and Brian Fikkert, *When Helping Hurts: How to Alleviate Poverty without Hurting the Poor . . . and Yourself*. Chicago: Moody, 2014.

Crouch, Andy. *Playing God: Redeeming the Gift of Power*. Downers Grove, IL: IVP Books, 2013.

Cunningham, David S. *These Three Are One: The Practice of Trinitarian Theology*. Malden, MA: Blackwell, 1998.

DeBorst, Ruth Padilla. "An Integral Transformational Approach." In Ott, *Mission of the Church*, 41–67.

de Gruchy, John W. "From Political to Public Theologies: The Role of Theology in Public Life in South Africa." In Storrar and Morton, *Public Theology for the 21st Century*, 45–62.

DiAngelo, Robin. "White Fragility." *International Journal of Critical Pedagogy* 3, no. 3 (2011): 54–70.

Dougherty, Kevin D., and Michael O. Emerson. "The Changing Complexion of American Congregations." *Journal for the Scientific Study of Religion* 57, no. 1 (March 2018): 24–38.

Douglas, Mary. *Purity and Danger: An Analysis of Concepts of Pollution and Taboo*. New York: Routledge, 1966.

Dulles, Avery. *Models of the Church*. New York: Doubleday, 1978.

Edwards, Korie L., Brad Christerson, and Michael O. Emerson. "Race, Religious Organization, and Integration." *Annual Review of Sociology* 39, no. 1 (2013): 211–28.

Eiesland, Nancy L., and R. Stephen Warner. "Ecology: Seeing the Congregation in Context." In Ammerman, Carroll, Dudley, and McKinney, *Studying Congregations*, 40–77.

Elliot, Alison. "Doing Theology: Engaging the Public." *International Journal of Public Theology* 1, no. 3 (2007): 290–305.

Elliot, Curtis. *Theologizing Place for Displacement: Reconciling, Remaking, and Reimagining Place in the Republic of Georgia*. Eugene, OR: Pickwick, 2018.

Ellul, Jacques. *Money and Power*. Eugene, OR: Wipf & Stock, 1984.

Emerson, Michael O., and Karen Chai Kim. "Multiracial Congregations: An Analysis of Their Development and Typology." *Journal for the Scientific Study of Religion* 42, no. 2 (2003): 217–27.

Englund, Harri, ed. *Christianity and Public Culture in Africa*. Athens: Ohio University Press, 2011.

Fiddes, Paul S., and Pete Ward. "Affirming Faith at a Service of Baptism in St. Aldates Church, Oxford." In Scharen, *Explorations in Ecclesiology and Ethnography*, 51–70.

Ford, David. "Theology." In *The Routledge Companion to the Study of Religion*, edited by John R. Hinnells, 61–79. New York: Routledge, 2010.

Forrester, Duncan B. *Truthful Action*. Edinburgh: T&T Clark, 2000.

Geertz, Clifford. *Available Light: Anthropological Reflections on Philosophical Topics*. Princeton: Princeton University Press, 2000.

———. *The Interpretation of Cultures: Selected Essays*. New York: Basic Books, 1973.

Gifford, Paul. *Christianity, Development and Modernity in Africa*. London: Hurst, 2015.

———. *Christianity, Politics and Public Life in Kenya*. London: Hurst, 2009.

Gill, Robin. "Three Sociological Approaches to Theology." In *The Social Context of Theology*, edited by Robin Gill, 3–14. London: Mowbrays, 1975.

Gorringe, T. J. *The Common Good and the Global Emergency: God and the Built Environment*. Cambridge: Cambridge University Press, 2011.

Graham, Elaine. *Between a Rock and a Hard Place: Public Theology in a Post-secular Age*. London: SCM, 2013.

———. "Power, Knowledge, and Authority in Public Theology." *International Journal of Public Theology* 1, no. 1 (2007): 42–62.

Guder, Darrell L. *Be My Witnesses: The Church's Mission, Message, and Messengers*. Grand Rapids: Eerdmans, 1985.

———. *Called to Witness: Doing Missional Theology*. Grand Rapids: Eerdmans, 2015.

———, ed. *Missional Church: A Vision for the Sending of the Church in North America*. Grand Rapids: Eerdmans, 1998.

———. "A Multicultural and Translational Approach." In Ott, *Mission of the Church*, 21–39.

Habermas, Jürgen. *The Structural Transformation of the Public Sphere: An Inquiry into a Category of Bourgeois Society*. Translated by Thomas Burger with the assistance of Frederick Lawrence. Cambridge, MA: MIT Press, 1991.

Hainsworth, Deirdre King, and Scott R. Paeth, eds. *Public Theology for a Global Society: Essays in Honor of Max L. Stackhouse*. Grand Rapids: Eerdmans, 2010.

Hauerwas, Stanley, and William H. Willimon. *Resident Aliens: Life in the Christian Colony*. Nashville: Abingdon, 1989.

Hawthorne, Gerald. *The Presence and the Power: The Significance of the Holy Spirit in the Life and Ministry of Jesus*. Eugene, OR: Wipf & Stock, 2003.

Hoekendijk, Johannes. *The Church Inside Out*. London: SCM, 1967.

Hooker, Morna, and Frances Young. *Holiness and Mission: Learning from the Early Church about Mission in the City*. London: SCM, 2010.

Hopewell, James. *Congregations: Stories and Structures*. London: SCM, 1987.

Howell, Brian. "Contextualizing Context." In *Power and Identity in the Global Church: Six Contemporary Cases*, edited by Brian M. Howell and Edwin Zehner, 1–25. Pasadena, CA: William Carey Library, 2009.

Hunsberger, George. "The Missional Voice and Posture of Public Theologizing." *Missiology* 34, no. 1 (2006): 15–28.

———. "Sizing Up the Shape of the Church." *Reformed Review* 47, no. 2 (Winter 1994): 133–44.

―――. *The Story That Chooses Us: A Tapestry of Missional Vision*. Grand Rapids: Eerdmans, 2015.

Hunt, Robert. "Public Missiology and Anxious Tribalism." *Missiology* 44, no. 2 (2016): 129–41.

Hunter, James Davison. *To Change the World: The Irony, Tragedy, and Possibility of Christianity in the Late Modern World*. New York: Oxford University Press, 2010.

Jackson, Michael, and Ivan Karp, eds. *Personhood and Agency: The Experience of Self and Other in African Cultures*. Stockholm: Almqvist & Wiksell, 1990.

Jacobsen, Eric O. *The Space Between: A Christian Engagement with the Built Environment*. Grand Rapids: Baker Academic, 2012.

James, Christopher B. *Church Planting in Post-Christian Soil: Theology and Practice*. New York: Oxford University Press, 2018.

Katongole, Emmanuel. "Field Hospital: HEAL Africa and the Politics of Compassion in Eastern Congo." *Missiology* 45, no. 2 (January 2017): 25–37.

―――. *The Sacrifice of Africa: A Political Theology for Africa*. Grand Rapids: Eerdmans, 2010.

Kee, Alistair. "Blessed Are the Excluded." In Storrar and Morton, *Public Theology for the 21st Century*, 351–64.

Kidula, Jean Ngoya. "Music Culture." In *Music in the Life of the African Church*, edited by Roberta King, 37–56. Waco: Baylor University Press, 2008.

Kim, Sebastian. *Theology in the Public Sphere: Public Theology as a Catalyst for Open Debate*. London: SCM, 2011.

Kinnaman, David, with Aly Hawkins. *You Lost Me: Why Young Christians Are Leaving Church . . . and Rethinking Faith*. Grand Rapids: Baker Books, 2011.

Kreider, Alan. *The Patient Ferment of the Early Church: The Improbable Rise of Christianity in the Roman Empire*. Grand Rapids: Baker Academic, 2016.

Kreider, Alan, and Eleanor Kreider. *Worship and Mission after Christendom*. Harrisburg, VA: Herald, 2011.

Kuyper, Abraham. *Lectures on Calvinism: Six Lectures from the Stone Foundation Lectures Delivered at Princeton University*. Peabody, MA: Hendrickson, 2008.

Lewellen, Ted. *The Anthropology of Globalization: Cultural Anthropology Enters the 21st Century*. Westport, CT: Bergin and Garvey, 2002.

Lewis, C. S. "The Founding of the Oxford Socratic Club." In *God in the Dock: Essays on Theology and Ethics*, edited by Walter Hooper, 126–28. Grand Rapids: Eerdmans, 1970.

―――. *Mere Christianity*. New York: Collier, 1943.

Lindsey, William. "Telling It Slant: American Catholic Public Theology and Prophetic Discourse." *Horizons* 22, no. 1 (1995): 89–103.

Lonsdale, Jon. "Compromised Critics: Religion in Kenya's Politics." In *Religion and Politics in Kenya: Essays in Honor of a Meddlesome Priest*, edited by Ben Knighton, 55–94. New York: Palgrave Macmillan, 2009.

————. "Kikuyu Christianities: A History of Intimate Diversity." In Maxwell with Lawrie, *Christianity and the African Imagination*, 157–98.

MacIntyre, Alasdair C. *After Virtue: A Study in Moral Theory*. Notre Dame, IN: University of Notre Dame Press, 1984.

Malesic, Jonathan. *Secret Faith in the Public Square: An Argument for the Concealment of Christian Identity*. Grand Rapids: Brazos, 2009.

Marshall, Christopher D. "Parables as Paradigms for Public Theology." In *The Bible, Justice, and Public Theology*, edited by David J. Neville, 23–44. Eugene, OR: Wipf & Stock, 2014.

Marty, Martin E. *The Public Church: Mainline, Evangelical, Catholic*. 1981. Reprint, Eugene, OR: Wipf & Stock, 2012.

Mathewes, Charles. *A Theology of Public Life*. Cambridge: Cambridge University Press, 2007.

Maxwell, David. "Introduction: Christianity and the African Imagination." In Maxwell with Lawrie, *Christianity and the African Imagination*, 1–25.

Maxwell, David, with Ingrid Lawrie, eds. *Christianity and the African Imagination: Essays in Honour of Adrian Hastings*. Leiden: Brill, 2002.

Mbiti, John. "When the Bull Is in a Strange Land, It Does Not Bellow." In *Christ and the Dominions of Civilization*, edited by Max L. Stackhouse and Diane B. Obenchain, 145–70. Vol. 3 of *God and Globalization*, edited by Max L. Stackhouse. Harrisburg, PA: Trinity Press International, 2002.

McGrath, Alister E. "The Cultivation of Theological Vision: Theological Attentiveness and the Practice of Ministry." In Ward, *Perspectives on Ecclesiology and Ethnography*, 107–23.

McKnight, Scot, ed. *Jesus Is Lord, Caesar Is Not: Evaluating Empire in New Testament Studies*. Downers Grove, IL: IVP Academic, 2013.

————. *Kingdom Conspiracy: Returning to the Radical Mission of the Local Church*. Grand Rapids: Brazos, 2014.

Meeks, M. Douglas. *God the Economist: The Doctrine of God and Political Economy*. Minneapolis: Fortress, 1989.

Meneses, Eloise, et al. "Engaging the Religiously Committed Other: Anthropologists and Theologians in Dialogue." In *On Knowing Humanity: Insights from Theology for Anthropology*, edited by Eloise Meneses and David Bronkema, 10–30. New York: Routledge, 2017.

Meyer, Birgit. "Going and Making Public: Pentecostalism as Public Religion in Ghana." In Englund, *Christianity and Public Culture in Africa*, 149–66.

Moltmann, Jürgen. *The Church in the Power of the Spirit: A Contribution to Messianic Ecclesiology*. London: SCM, 1977.

————. "The Destruction and Healing of the Earth." In *The Spirit and the Modern Authorities*, edited by Max L. Stackhouse and Don S. Browning, 166–90. Vol. 2 of *God and Globalization*, edited by Max L. Stackhouse. New York: T&T Clark, 2001.

————. *God for a Secular Age: The Public Relevance of Theology*. Minneapolis: Fortress, 1999.

————. "Political Theology in Germany." In Storrar and Morton, *Public Theology for the 21st Century*, 37–43.

————. *The Trinity and the Kingdom: The Doctrine of God*. Minneapolis: Fortress, 1993.

Morton, Andrew R. "Duncan Forrester: A Public Theologian." In Storrar and Morton, *Public Theology for the 21st Century*, 25–36.

Moschella, Mary Clark. *Ethnography as a Pastoral Practice: An Introduction*. Cleveland: Pilgrim, 2008.

Mouw, Richard. *Political Evangelism*. Grand Rapids: Eerdmans, 1973.

Muck, Terry C. *Why Study Religion? Understanding Humanity's Pursuit of the Divine*. Grand Rapids: Baker Academic, 2016.

Murray, Stuart. *Post-Christendom: Church and Mission in a Strange New World*. Eugene, OR: Cascade, 2018.

Myers, Bryant. *Engaging Globalization: The Poor, Christian Mission, and Our Hyperconnected World*. Grand Rapids: Baker Academic, 2017.

Newbigin, Lesslie. *Foolishness to the Greeks*. Grand Rapids: Eerdmans, 1986.

————. *The Gospel in a Pluralist Society*. Grand Rapids: Eerdmans, 1989.

————. *The Household of God: Lectures on the Nature of the Church*. 1953. Reprint, Eugene, OR: Wipf & Stock, 2008.

————. *The Open Secret: An Introduction to the Theology of Mission*. Rev. ed. Grand Rapids: Eerdmans, 1995.

————. "Stewardship, Mission, and Development." Address, Annual Stewardship Conference of the British Council of Churches, Stanwick, UK, 1970.

————. "The Trinity as Public Truth." In *The Trinity in a Pluralistic Age: Theological Essays on Culture and Religion*, edited by Kevin J. Vanhoozer, 1–8. Grand Rapids: Eerdmans, 1997.

————. *Truth to Tell: The Gospel as Public Truth*. Grand Rapids: Eerdmans, 1991.

Noll, Mark. *The Scandal of the Evangelical Mind*. Grand Rapids: Eerdmans, 1994.

Offutt, Stephen, F. David Bronkema, Krisanne Vaillancourt Murphy, Robb Davis, and Gregg Okesson. *Advocating for Justice: An Evangelical Vision for Transforming Systems and Structures*. Grand Rapids: Baker Academic, 2016.

Okesson, Gregg A. "Christian Witness to Institutions: Public Missiology and Power." *Missiology* 44, no. 2 (2016): 142–54.

————. "Public Theology for Global Development: A Case Study Dealing with 'Health' in Africa." *The Asbury Journal* 67, no. 1 (2012): 56–76.

————. *Re-imaging Modernity: A Contextualized Theological Study of Power and Humanity within Akamba Christianity in Kenya*. Eugene, OR: Pickwick, 2012.

Oldenburg, Ray. *The Great Good Place: Cafes, Coffee Shops, Bookstores, Bars, Hair Salons and Other Hangouts at the Heart of a Community*. Philadelphia: Da Capo Press, 1989.

Orobator, Agbonkhianmeghe. "Ecclesiology in Crisis: A Contextualised Theological Study of the Church of Africa in the Situation of HIV/AIDS, Refugees and Poverty." PhD diss., University of Leeds, 2004.

———. *Theology Brewed in an African Pot*. Maryknoll, NY: Orbis, 2008.

Ott, Craig. *The Mission of the Church: Five Views in Conversation*. Grand Rapids: Baker Academic, 2016.

Ott, Craig, and Harold A. Netland, eds. *Globalizing Theology: Belief and Practice in an Era of World Christianity*. Grand Rapids: Baker Academic, 2006.

Parsons, Talcott. *The Evolution of Societies*. New York: Prentice Hall, 1977.

Percy, Martyn. *Shaping the Church: The Promise of Implicit Theology*. Surrey, UK: Ashgate, 2010.

Plantinga, Cornelius. *Not the Way It's Supposed to Be: A Breviary of Sin*. Grand Rapids: Eerdmans, 1995.

Pohl, Christine. *Making Room: Recovering Hospitality as a Christian Tradition*. Grand Rapids: Eerdmans, 1999.

———. "Practicing Hospitality in the Face of 'Complicated Wickedness.'" *Wesleyan Theological Journal* 42, no 1. (Spring 2007): 7–31.

Radner, Ephraim. *A Brutal Unity: The Spiritual Politics of the Christian Church*. Waco: Baylor University Press, 2012.

Ramachandra, Vinoth. *Subverting Global Myths: Theology and the Public Issues Shaping Our World*. Downers Grove, IL: IVP Academic, 2008.

Richter, Sandra L. *The Epic of Eden: A Christian Entry into the Old Testament*. Downers Grove, IL: IVP Academic, 2008.

Robertson, Roland. "Globalization and the Future of 'Traditional Religion.'" In Stackhouse and Paris, *Religion and the Powers of the Common Life*, 53–68.

———. *Globalization: Social Theory and Global Culture*. Newbury Park, CA: Sage, 1992.

Rynkiewich, Michael. *Soul, Self, and Society: A Postmodern Anthropology for Mission in a Postcolonial World*. Eugene, OR: Cascade, 2011.

Sanneh, Lamin. *Whose Religion Is Christianity? The Gospel beyond the West*. Grand Rapids: Eerdmans, 2003.

Scharen, Christian, ed. *Explorations in Ecclesiology and Ethnography*. Grand Rapids: Eerdmans, 2012.

———. *Fieldwork in Theology: Exploring the Social Context of God's Work in the World*. Grand Rapids: Baker Academic, 2015.

Schreiter, Robert. *Constructing Local Theologies*. Maryknoll, NY: Orbis, 1985.

———. "Theology in the Congregation: Discovering and Doing." In Ammerman, Carroll, Dudley, and McKinney, *Studying Congregations*, 23–39.

Seamands, Steve. *Ministry in the Image of God: The Trinitarian Shape of Christian Service*. Downers Grove, IL: InterVarsity, 2005.

Smit, Dirkie. "Notions of the Public and Doing Theology." *International Journal of Public Theology* 1, no. 1 (2007): 431–54.

Smith, Christian. *American Evangelicalism: Embattled and Thriving*. Chicago: University of Chicago Press, 1998.

Smith, Christian, and Melina Lundquist Denton. *Soul Searching: The Religious and Spiritual Lives of American Teenagers*. New York: Oxford University Press, 2005.

Smith, James K. A. *Awaiting the King: Reforming Public Theology*. Grand Rapids: Baker Academic, 2017.

———. *Desiring the Kingdom: Worship, Worldview, and Cultural Formation*. Grand Rapids: Baker Academic, 2009.

———. *Imagining the Kingdom: How Worship Works*. Grand Rapids: Baker Academic, 2013.

———. Series editor's foreword to *Fieldwork in Theology: Exploring the Social Context of God's Work in the World*, by Christian Scharen, xi–xiii. Grand Rapids: Baker Academic, 2015.

Snyder, Howard A., with Joel Scandrett. *Salvation Means Creation Healed: The Ecology of Sin and Grace*. Eugene, OR: Cascade, 2011.

Stackhouse, John G., Jr. *Making the Best of It: Following Christ in the Real World*. New York: Oxford University Press, 2008.

Stackhouse, Max L. *Apologia: Contextualization, Globalization, and Mission in Theological Education*. Grand Rapids: Eerdmans, 1988.

———. "General Introduction." In Stackhouse and Paris, *Religion and the Powers of the Common Life*, 1–52.

———. *Globalization and Grace*. Vol. 4 of *God and Globalization*, edited by Max L. Stackhouse. New York: Continuum, 2007.

———. "Reflections on How and Why We Go Public." *International Journal of Public Theology* 1, no. 3 (2007): 421–30.

Stackhouse, Max L., and Peter J. Paris, eds. *Religion and the Powers of the Common Life*. Vol. 1 of *God and Globalization*, edited by Max L. Stackhouse. New York: T&T Clark, 2000.

Stanley, Brian. "Conversion to Christianity: Colonization of the Mind?" *International Review of Mission* 92, no. 366 (2003): 315–31.

Stark, Rodney. *The Rise of Christianity: How the Obscure, Marginal Jesus Movement Became the Dominant Religious Force in the Western World in a Few Centuries*. San Francisco: HarperSanFrancisco, 1997.

Storrar, William F., and Andrew R. Morton, eds. *Public Theology for the 21st Century*. New York: T&T Clark, 2004.

Taylor, Charles. *A Secular Age*. Cambridge, MA: Belknap, 2007.

Tennent, Timothy C. *Invitation to World Mission: A Trinitarian Missiology for the Twenty-First Century*. Grand Rapids: Kregel, 2010.

Thumma, Scott L. "Methods for Congregational Study." In Ammerman, Carroll, Dudley, and McKinney, *Studying Congregations*, 196–239.

Tizon, Al. *Whole and Reconciled: Gospel, Church, and Mission in a Fractured World*. Grand Rapids: Baker Academic, 2018.

Tracy, David. *The Analogical Imagination: Christian Theology and the Culture of Pluralism*. New York: Crossroad, 1981.

Treier, Daniel J. *Virtue and the Voice of God: Toward Theology as Wisdom*. Grand Rapids: Eerdmans, 2006.

Van Gelder, Craig and Dwight J. Zscheile. *The Missional Church in Perspective: Mapping Trends and Shaping the Conversation*. Grand Rapids: Baker Academic, 2011.

Vanhoozer, Kevin J. *The Drama of Doctrine: A Canonical-Linguistic Approach to Christian Doctrine*. Louisville: Westminster John Knox, 2005.

———. "One Rule to Rule Them All: Theological Method in an Era of World Christianity." In Ott and Netland, *Globalizing Theology*, 85–126.

———. "What Is Everyday Theology?" In *Everyday Theology: How to Read Cultural Texts and Interpret Trends*, edited by Kevin J. Vanhoozer, Charles A. Anderson, and Michael J. Sleasman, 15–62. Grand Rapids: Baker Academic, 2007.

Volf, Miroslav. *After Our Likeness: The Church as the Image of the Trinity*. Grand Rapids: Eerdmans, 1998.

———. *Exclusion and Embrace: A Theological Exploration of Identity, Otherness, and Reconciliation*. Nashville: Abingdon, 1996.

———. *Flourishing: Why We Need Religion in a Globalized World*. New Haven: Yale University Press, 2015.

———. *A Public Faith: How Followers of Christ Should Serve the Common Good*. Grand Rapids: Brazos, 2011.

———. "Soft Difference: Theological Reflections on the Relation between Church and Culture in 1 Peter." *Ex Auditu* 10 (1994): 1–29.

Volf, Miroslav, and Dorothy C. Bass, eds. *Practicing Theology: Beliefs and Practices in Christian Life*. San Francisco: Jossey-Bass, 2001.

von Rad, Gerhard. *Genesis*. Philadelphia: Westminster, 1961.

Walls, Andrew. "Christian Scholarship in Africa in the Twenty-First Century." *Transformation* 19, no. 9 (October 2002): 217–28.

———. *The Cross-Cultural Process in Christian History*. Maryknoll, NY: Orbis, 2002.

———. "Globalization and the Study of Christian History." In Ott and Netland, *Globalizing Theology*, 70–82.

———. *The Missionary Movement in Christian History: Studies in the Transmission of Faith*. Maryknoll, NY: Orbis, 1996.

Ward, Kevin. "Evangelism or Education? Mission Priorities and Educational Policy in the Africa Inland Mission, 1900–1950." *Kenya Historical Review* 3, no. 2 (1975): 243–60.

Ward, Pete, ed. *Perspectives on Ecclesiology and Ethnography*. Grand Rapids: Eerdmans, 2012.

Warner, Michael. *Publics and Counterpublics*. New York: Zone, 2005.

Weber, Theodore. *Politics in the Order of Salvation: Transforming Wesleyan Political Ethics*. Nashville: Kingswood, 2001.

Wilfred, Felix. *Asian Public Theology: Critical Concerns in Challenging Times*. Delhi: India Society for Promoting Christian Knowledge, 2010.

Wink, Walter. *Naming the Powers: The Language of Power in the New Testament*. Minneapolis: Fortress, 1986.

Wright, Christopher J. H. *The Mission of God: Unlocking the Bible's Grand Narrative*. Downers Grove, IL: IVP Academic, 2006.

———. *Old Testament Ethics for the People of God*. Downers Grove, IL: InterVarsity, 2004.

Wright, N. T. *The Day the Revolution Began: Reconsidering the Meaning of the Jesus's Crucifixion*. New York: HarperOne, 2016.

———. *How God Became King: The Forgotten Story of the Gospels*. New York: HarperOne, 2012.

———. *The New Testament and the People of God*. Minneapolis: Fortress, 1992.

———. *Surprised by Hope: Rethinking Heaven, the Resurrection, and the Mission of the Church*. New York: HarperOne, 2008.

Yoder, John Howard. *The Christian Witness to the State*. Scottdale, PA: Herald, 2002.

Zeigler, Philip. "God and Some Recent Public Theologies." *International Journal of Public Theology* 4, no. 2 (2002): 137–55.

Zscheile, Dwight. "Forming and Restoring Community in a Nomadic World: A Next Generation Perspective on the Future of the Discipline of Missiology." *Missiology* 42, no. 1 (January 2015): 26–38.

Index